The Mechanical Baby

From Metlinger's *A Regimen for Young Children,* a middle-class family of the fifteenth century: The father, at the table, is doing his accounts; a child reads a book. The mother and eldest daughter (unmarried, as shown by her braids) are spinning while the mother rocks the cradle with her foot. A dog lies asleep on the floor.

The Mechanical Baby

A Popular History of the
Theory and Practice of Child Raising

DANIEL BEEKMAN

LAWRENCE HILL & COMPANY

Westport, Connecticut

Library of Congress Cataloging in Publication Data

Beekman, Daniel.
The mechanical baby.
Biography: P.
Includes index.
1. children – Management – history.   2. children – care and
hygiene – History. I. Title.
HQ769.B3538   649'.1'09   76-18055
ISBN 0-88208-073-3

Jacket Illustration: Unknown American Artist. Emma Van Name. c. 1795.
Oil on canvas. 29 x 23 inches. Collection of Whitney Museum of American
Art. Gift of Edgar William and Bernice Chrysler Garbisch.

Acknowledgments: See Pages VII & VIII

First Edition: August, 1977

1 2 3 4 5 6 7 8 9 10

Lawrence Hill & Company, Publishers, Inc.

Manufactured in the United States of America
by Ray Freiman & Comapny

to the memory of
my father, the physician,
and to
my mother, the historian

Acknowledgments

Work on this book would have been seriously impeded and, in some cases, made impossible except for the assistance of some individuals: the staff of the New York Academy of Medicine Library, particularly Mrs. Cheryl Silver, and of the Rare Book & History Room there, Mrs. Alice Weaver and Mr. Elliott Zak. Special thanks go to Mrs. Sali Morgenstern who translated Old German and Latin texts for me. Miss Jean Miller of the Medical Library Center of New York for allowing me free access to the Center's collection of old magazines on child care is hereby thanked. The staff of the New York Public Library Rare Book Room was also patient and helpful in my research. Special thanks go to Miss Ruth Price for her editorial assistance on this complicated project. Special thanks also to Mrs. Louise Bates Ames, co-director of the Gesell Institute of Child Development, for permission to quote from the early works of Dr. Arnold Gesell: *Mental Growth of the Pre-School Child* (1925), *Infancy and Human Growth* (1928), *The Guidance of Mental Growth in Infant and Child* (1930) and *The Atlas of Infant Behavior* (1934).

Excerpts reprinted with permission of Macmillan Publishing Co., Inc. from BABIES ARE HUMAN BEINGS by C. Anderson Aldrich and Mary M. Aldrich. Copyright 1938, 1954 Macmillan Publishing Co., Inc.

Excerpts reprinted with permission of Holt, Rinehart and Winston, Publishers, from INFANTS AND CHILDREN by Frederic H. Bartlett. Copyright 1933, 1942, 1944 by Frederic H. Bartlett. Copyright 1961, 1970, 1972 by Phillis Bartlett Pollard and Frederic Pearson Bartlett.

Excerpts reprinted with permission of Bertha Klausner International Literary Agency, Inc. from YOU, YOUR CHILDREN, AND WAR by Dorothy Baruch (Prentice-Hall). Copyright 1942 by Dorothy W. Baruch, renewed 1970 by Hyman Miller.

Excerpts reprinted with permission of The Bobbs-Merrill Company, Inc. from STOP ANNOYING YOUR CHILDREN by W. W. Bauer. Copyright 1947, 1975 The Bobbs-Merrill Company, Inc.

Excerpts reprinted by permission of Association Press from DEMOCRACY IN THE HOME by Christine Beasley. Copyright © 1954 by the National Board of Young Men's Christian Associations.

Acknowledgments

Excerpts reprinted with permission of Alfred A. Knopf, Inc. from THE DAY CARE BOOK: *The Why, and How of Community Day Care* by Vicki Breitbart. Copyright © 1974 by Vicki Breitbart.

Excerpts reprinted with permission granted by Russell Sage Foundation from Urie Bronfenbrenner's TWO WORLDS OF CHILDHOOD: U.S. AND U.S.S.R. (New York: Russell Sage Foundation, 1970) p. 7, 8, 17, 18, 21, 63, 64, 78, 80, 81. Copyright © 1970 Russell Sage Foundation.

Excerpts reprinted with permission granted by International Universities Press, Inc. from YOUR CHILD MAKES SENSE by Edith Buxbaum. Copyright © 1949, 1975 by International Universities Press.

Excerpts reprinted with permission granted by Doubleday and Co. from YOUR CHILD'S SELF ESTEEM by Dorothy Briggs. Copyright © 1970 by Dorothy Briggs.

Excerpts reprinted with permission of Harper and Row, Publishers, Inc. from INFANT AND CHILD IN THE CULTURE OF TODAY by Arnold Gesell and Frances L. Ilg. Copyright 1943 by Arnold Gesell and Frances L. Ilg, renewed 1971 by Frances L. Ilg, Gehard Gesell and Katherine Gesell Walden.

Exerpts reprinted with permission of Dr. Alice Ginott from BETWEEN PARENT AND CHILD by Haim Ginott. Published by Macmillan Publishing Co., Inc. Copyright © 1965 by Haim Ginott.

Excerpts reprinted from PARENT EFFECTIVENESS TRAINING by Thomas Gordon. Copyright © 1970 by Thomas Gordon. Published by Peter H. Wyden, Inc., a division of David McKay Co., Inc. Reprinted by permission of publishers.

Excerpts reprinted with permission of Nash Publishing Corporation from HOW TO PARENT by Fitzhugh Dodson. Copyright © 1970 by Fitzhugh Dodson.

Excerpts reprinted with permission of W. H. Freeman and Co., Publishers, for "Checks on Population Growth 1750-1850" by William L. Langer. Copyright © 1972 by Scientific American, Inc.

Excerpts reprinted with permission of the Viking Press, Inc. from CHILDREN ARE THE REVOLUTION by Marvin Leiner. Copyright © 1974 by Marvin Leiner.

Excerpts from THE COMPLETE BOOK OF ABSOLUTELY PERFECT BABY AND CHILD CARE by Elinor Goulding Smith, Copyright © 1957 by Elinor Goulding Smith. Reprinted by permission of author.

Excerpts reprinted by permission of Simon and Schuster, Inc, Pocket Books division, from BABY AND CHILD CARE by Benjamin Spock. Copyright © 1945, 1946, 1957 by Benjamin Spock, M.D.

Excerpt reprinted by permission of Simon and Schuster, Inc, from THE MAN IN THE GREY FLANNEL SUIT by Sloan Wilson. Copyright © 1955 by Sloan Wilson.

Excerpts reprinted by permission of W. W. Norton, Inc. from PSYCHOLOGICAL CARE OF INFANT AND CHILD by John B. Watson. Copyright 1928 by W. W. Norton. Copyright renewed 1956 by John B. Watson.

Excerpts from OUR AMERICAN BABIES by Dorothy V. Whipple, Copyright 1944, 1972. Reprinted by kind permission of Dorothy V. Whipple

The Mechanical Baby

Contents

Epigraph

"For a childe naturally neither laments nor cries so long as he doth abide in his mothers wombe.

"And I have often observed that a childe neither cries, nor makes any noise, neither sighs, though he be halfe come forth, what paine or anguish soever he suffers in the passing. But as soon as he is born and sees the light (besides the alteration in the ayer which he finds) even very necessity and his owne feeling doe force and as it were wring from him cries and moanes, thereby to show in what he need be stands of helpe."

— Jacques Guillemeau, 1609

Introduction

"The normal child is healthy in every way. His manners need no correcting. Instead, what is important is to prevent corruption . . . We must take care with each of the things which offer the chance of corruption: children's manners may be corrupted by bad habits in eating and drinking, in the patterns of exercise and shows, in all the things they see or hear, and in all other areas of culture."

This advice from the Greek physician Galen (c. 175 A.D.) will not sound entirely foreign to many parents today. Over the centuries, parents have tried to adapt children to society's demands while protecting them from society's ills. This has not necessarily been an easy task. In compiling and interpreting the material for this book, I discovered that while many older child-raising practices were strange (even dangerous, horrifying in retrospect), parents and children depicted in the literature were types familiar to us today. It is worth remembering that no matter how child-care advice changes, children themselves have changed little throughout history.

The Mechanical Baby began as an historical detective story, an attempt to trace a popular idea of the 1960s: the belief that certain social phenomena — the counterculture with hippies, drugs and sex; the peace movement — were the result of Dr. Spock's "permissive" methods of child care that became popular in the years after World War II. I realized early in my research that Spock, while certainly the most popular writer on child care, is only one of a series of figures whose advice has reflected the nature of society and morality in a given historical period.

The earliest books on child care contain a body of knowledge passed orally through generations of parents. It is a mixture of simple and superstitious methods, some helpful and some dangerous. Soon after books appeared, however, professionals entered the child-raising scene, people who claimed to know better than mothers how children should be raised. The picture of mother and child became one of mother, expert and child, and mothers were often made to feel less competent than authors, no matter how bizarre the writers' ideas were. Poets, midwives, physicians, priests, philosophers, even novelists had ideas on how best to bring up the baby. One image that repeatedly struck me as I researched was a picture of a mother who, hearing her child cry, rushes for the book rather than the baby.

The close relationship between the history of child care and the history of society as a whole emerged for me. I found that it was necessary to relate the changes in styles of child care to social developments. After the industrial revolution, for example, efforts were made not only to raise good children but also to raise children different from and by implication better than their parents. Each generation seemed to sense, as we do today, that the world is changing and that children must be raised for the new world in which they will have to live.

In many books child care takes on the character of social indoctrination. Some authors even assert that it is possible through upbringing and eugenics to breed certain ideas and kinds of behavior into or out of society. A few of these revolutionaries *manques*, having failed to rock the world, tried to rule the cradle.

I have included in this book primarily comments on the nature and theory of child care, practical advice, generally omitting parallel medical (pediatric) developments and the evolution of education. The book's pattern is chronological, concentrating on the years from birth to adolescence. I have selected from each historical period not only the most popular material but also, when many sources were available, those excerpts which touched me personally across the centuries.

The research for this project involved reading more than eight hundred books and at least one hundred pamphlets and magazines. *The Mechanical Baby* is not intended, however, to be a scholarly reference work; rather, it is an historical essay and anthology. My intent is to share with the reader the experience I had in discovering much of this material, an experience not unlike archaeology, of digging into a cave to uncover a forgotten world. In child-care books, the past comes alive in a personal way through down-to-earth (and sometimes not-so-down-to-earth) advice on how to treat the new members of society. Sometimes the advice is cruel, misguided or superstitious but also, sometimes, it is funny, tender and warm. These are the books by which our ancestors raised their children; they almost bring the past back as flesh and blood. In fact, it is remarkable that Galen's advice on child care can reach across seventeen centuries, offering not only sound ideas but simultaneously a community with our past:

"When handling small children who are healthy, it is important to avoid excessive disturbance. So, when they cry or scream or are upset, we should understand that it means something is disturbing them, and we must try to discover what they need and give it to them before their minds and bodies become more overly excited. When they are teething or hurt somewhere from outside cause, or when they want to move their bowels or urinate or are hungry or thirsty, they show their needs by a continuous restlessness as if distressed. They suffer because they are cold and want to be warm, or are too hot and want to be cool, or are uncomfortable in their swaddling bands, for swaddling bands can be uncomfortable when children want to move from side to side or move their arms or legs. And even quiet itself can be a burden to them . . . .

"When they cry or are unhappy, not the least of solutions is to place the child at the breast. From experience, nurses have noted three remedies for children's distress: one, that already mentioned, and the other two are gentle movement [rocking] and singing which quiets the child and induces sleep."

PART ONE

Beginnings
(1450-1750)

"If the hands are kept clean because their work is about silk, fine linen, laces of gold or silver, is not man more precious and worthier to be kept clean than all of these?"

FELIX WURTZ (1563)

CHAPTER 1

The Child of the Poets

"I will bathe my baby frequently
From illness and disease to keep it free. . . .

"Now note carefully the things I say:
You have to bathe your baby every day.
Be sure the water is lukewarm and mild
And promptly after bathing take the child,
With rose oil rub its body, stroke each limb
Up and down — it helps to strengthen them,
And while they are still tender bend them so
That they well-formed and straight and fine will grow.
The baby's ears and little head you may
Also form and shape the nicest way.
And finally stroke its belly. Then and there,
Still offering the child the wisest care,
Stretch the baby's arms and legs well out
And with clean cloths now bind them firm and straight.
Cover its head lightly, neatly around,
Then in the cradle gently put it down,
Making no noise, a quiet cool dark place
Covering the child's eyes to keep its face
From sun, so it will strengthen without fright.
When afterwards it wakens from its sleep
Then turn its eyes towards daylight."

Dated 1429, almost twenty years before the advent of printing, Heinrich von Louffenburg's *Regimen of Health for Young Children* is a link to the child-care practices of the late Middle Ages. Some of the methods he recommends are still more ancient. The use of swaddling, binding the child's body and limbs with bands of cloth, and the salting of newborn infants — "Soon as the child is born, you must combine/Rose oil and salt, and rub them on his skin" — are mentioned in the Bible. The statement (Ezek 16:4) that "Thou wast not salted at all, nor swaddled at all" is an accusation of barbaric upbringing.

While von Louffenburg was a priest rather than a doctor, his poem nevertheless contains medical recipes that dated back more than a thousand years and continued to be used for as many as three centuries after him:

> "Should teething hurt the child and give him pains,
> Rub his gums with chicken fat and hare's brains. . . .
>
> "Take honey and incense, salt and liquorice,
> Mix them well together, rub his tongue with this,
> So that he will learn to speak the sooner
> And more easily."

Other prescriptions may have had a more pragmatic base, typified by the diet von Louffenburg suggests for pregnant women:

> "From barley and raw fruit they must abstain
> And from all kinds of fish they should refrain.
> Soft-boiled eggs are good for them, 'tis clear,
> As are veal, wild fowl, young lambs, stags and deer
> And chicken suits them well. . . . "

While the prejudice against fish and fruit seems capricious, the prohibition against barley may come from the fact that grain was sometimes contaminated by ergot, a fungus that when eaten could induce miscarriage.

When von Louffenburg's poem was printed in 1491, a series of woodcuts were added showing the child in the bath, being fed and asleep in his cradle. One of these portrays the child learning to walk with a pusher.

More than four hundred years later, the United States Children's Bureau pamphlet *Infant Care* (1924) by Dr. Martha Eliot describes essentially the same device:

> "A small weighted platform. . . mounted on four casters: A handle

like that of a baby carriage is attached to the end of the platform, slanting backwards so as to come within reach of the baby. He should be able to grasp it easily as he stands. This contrivance will give him some support in learning to walk."

Infant Care also argued against "baby walkers. . . Babies should not be encouraged to walk until they are quite ready for it. Too early walking may cause bowlegs; also the baby is held for too long a time in a confined space and in a more or less rigid position and is easily overtired." An illustration of an early baby walker appears in the next chapter (page 24).

Poetry may seem an unsuitable form for books on child care, yet for more than three hundred years, these poems were among the most popular works on the subject. There is both a logical and an esthetic reason for this. In a world where literacy was limited, poetry functioned as a mnemonic device, assisting in transmitting child-raising advice from person to person. Esthetically, at a time when printed material was scarce, the child-care poem might have been read as much for its poetic value as for its contents.

It is, in fact, a poem rather than a prose work that holds the record for longevity among child-care books. Schevole de St. Marthe's *Paedotrophia, or The Art of Bringing Up Children*, written in Latin in 1584, was considered valuable enough to be reissued by Dr. Henry Tytler in 1797, 213 years later. Even after two centuries, Tytler comments: "Notwithstanding the changes which must have taken place in medical practice since the time of St. Marthe, the regimen he prescribes is always excellent and many of his remedies [are] still in use."

Paedotrophia is a far more important work than von Louffenburg's early effort. Its author, a lawyer and an excellent poet, became interested in the problems of child care when one of his own children became ill. After consulting the best available physicians without success, he decided to treat his son himself. A biography of St. Marthe, written by Gabriel Michel, is included as part of Tytler's translation of St. Marthe's work. Michel describes the episode in St. Marthe's life:

"His researches [were] so successful that he cured his young son by remedies of his own prescribing after [his son] was given over by physicians [as lost]. Being then entreated by friends to communicate such curious discoveries to the public, he comprehended them in this poem."*

St. Marthe's poem paints a grim picture of child-care practices in the

---

*Spelling and punctuation of quotations have been modernized.

sixteenth century. Children at birth, were often bathed in icy water to harden them to cold. The *Paedotrophia* protests against this abuse:

"The Germans used, a race inured to cold,
To war, to labor from the cradle bred. . . .
The new-born child, yet reeking from the womb,
They took to what oft gave him to the tomb;
Lest he should from his father's strength decline,
They plunged him shivering in the freezing Rhine. . .
And taught him thus, from childhood, to defy
The cold and frost of an inclement sky,
The force of dreary winters to despise. . . . "

"The Germans grown more wise, as more refined,
And doomed, no more, to ignorance of mind,
For ages have their barberous cure despised
And all condemn what their rude sires devised.
A method, how superior! learning gave,
To bathe the infant in the tepid wave."

To protect the child from cold, St. Marthe recommends swaddling:

"Remember too, that only by degrees
His tender skin endures the cooling breeze:
Expose not, recent from the womb, the child,
Except to gentle heat, and seasons mild;
Lest ills succeed, lest penetrating cold
Benumb his limbs, and of his joints take hold.
As when a Libyan traveller must defy
The inclement seasons of an arctic sky,
Unused to face the blustering North and West,
He wraps his body in a woolen vest,
Head, limbs, and feet, defends with cautious art,
In double folds involving every part;
So, from relaxing baths, still keep in mind
That you more open every pore will find,
And more unfit to bear the cooling air:
For this, in powder, finest salt prepare,
To anoint his skin, and all his joints around,
Constringing thus what bathing had unbound.
Nor then forget that wrappers be at hand,
Soft flannels, linen, and the swaddling band,

To enwrap the babe, by many a circling fold,
In equal lines, and thus defend from cold."

Powdering newborn babies with salt, the ancient practice mentioned by von Louffenburg, was also endorsed by St. Marthe. Tytler, in his notes on the poem, says that "perhaps the method recommended by Dr. Underwood [the eighteenth-century physician] may be preferable: to mix salt in the bath." By Tytler's time, however, the "ancient method of swathing children with tight bandages in now justly laid aside." Children could be protected from cold without swaddling cloths which, as Tytler comments, "by pressing too hard on the soft blood vessels, either impede or entirely stop the circulation." But St. Marthe, writing before the discovery of blood circulation, even with the best intentions and advice available could only record the balanced opinion of his time. Lawyerlike, he sought the middle ground.

Since many physicians asserted that a cure for epilepsy was to hang a peony around the neck of the patient, St. Marthe recorded that prescription in his book. He also repeats the idea that hare brains rubbed on the gum would soothe the pain of teething.

"What infants suffer when they breed their teeth.
What causes so much pain and often death?
I'll tell: for while they make their way, they gnaw
With latent teeth and pierce the tender jaw,
Sharp humors enter, e're the tooth appears
And the soft gum incessant grinding tears. . . .

"He [the infant] strives to help himself, but strives in vain,
The nurse's help must ease him of his pain:
In a hare's brain, his little fingers dip
Or what Sicillian bees from roses sip."

From the time of Hippocrates, teething had been seen not only as a discomfort but as a major threat to infant survival. Hippocrates described "the breeding of teeth" as being the source of convulsions and fever, a diagnosis endorsed by the majority of physicians into the eighteenth century. Most of the problems attributed to teething in the past seem to have been problems of weaning. Teething and weaning often took place at about the same time since a mother breastfeeding her child did not like to be bitten. At weaning, the child was taken off a balanced diet of mother's milk and put on a standard infant diet of pap and prechewed table scraps.

Much of the ulceration and discoloration of the gums which early medical writers attributed to teething seems to have been a symptom of infantile scurvy. Infants were not generally fed fruits or fresh vegetables due to superstitions and the belief that they tended to upset the infant's digestion.

Most of St. Marthe's prescriptions were derived from folk medicine: "When the child at once is weak and loose/ [suffering from diarrhea] White poppy seeds into the purge infuse."* Other treatments seem closer to magic: "Bull's gall mixed with cummin seed" is one of several recipes St. Marthe offers for the cure of worms. For epilepsy he suggests powdered ash of human skull.

Despite St. Marthe's success in treating his own son after the physicians had failed, he still recommended professional help over much of the folk medicine in use at that time:

> "Call the physician to your aid; advise
> With him, and do not think yourself too wise;
> Do not to every idle tale attend,
> Nor on old woman's recipes depend."

It was not uncommon for infants to be fed only at the parents' meal times regardless of the infant's needs. On this subject, St. Marthe falls squarely into what would now be called the "demand feeding" camp:

> "The hours for suckling it I do not fix.
> Nature in that must guide the nursing sex.
> When by its cries it calls you, do not spare
> Your labor; nor be loath your breast to bare."

In his observations on child-raising psychology, St. Marthe also seems contemporary.

> "And since all human happiness depends
> On that to which the mind enlarging tends,
> If you delight a prosperous child to see,
> With honor thriving, and from danger free,
> Direct this emanation of divine,
> Lest his unguarded youth to vice incline.
> And that you may, with more success, overcome

*The use of opium to treat severe diarrhea is still valid.

> The seeds of sin, imbibed even in the womb,
> Urge him when slow, exhilarate when sad,
> Check if too forward, or inclined to be bad,
> But still by gentle means, and not use force,
> Lest he, too much diverted from his course
> And still compelled, should lose both health and growth,
> Turn heavy, negligent, and sink in sloth."

Discipline with a gentle hand, correcting the child according to the child's needs and encouragement are what St. Marthe is recommending here. Like his advice on nursing, his opposition to cold bathing and his condemnation of old wive's tales, his view of discipline was centuries ahead of its time.

In 1655, a second French author, the physician Claude Quillet, produced an equally popular work on child care, *Callipaediae, or An Art How to Have Beautiful Children*. Commenting on at least one reason for its popularity, the anonymous translator of the first English edition (1710) observed in his introduction that "'Twas not likely that the *Callipaediae* would long remain unattempted [for translation]. . . the title being so promising for sale."

The motives that led Quillet to write his poem were somewhat different from those of St. Marthe and are an interesting story in themselves: In the 1630s, the abbess and several nuns at a convent in Loudon, France, claimed to be possessed by a devil sent to them by a popular priest, Urban Grandier. In the course of the ensuing *procés*, or trial, Quillet defended the priest, openly asserting his disbelief in the nuns' claims. Despite his efforts, Grandier was convicted and burned and Quillet had to take shelter in Rome. It was during this period of exile that he wrote the *Callipaediae*, including in it everything he believed would appeal to the public. In addition to a brief coverage of child care, the book contains passages on beauty, love, sexual relations, marriage, travel, astrology and life generally.

The whole package was apparently intended as a vehicle to guarantee wide circulation of some scathing verses on the subject of Cardinal Mazarin, who, along with his predecessor Cardinal Richelieu, Quillet believed to be the power behind Grandier's trial. Mazarin, probably preferring to keep a clever man on his side, made peace with Quillet, offering him an abbacy. Quillet, in gratitude, cut the offending verses and added a few lines praising his new benefactor.

Even with its political purpose achieved, however, the book continued to be popular. The principal theme stated in the title – how to have beautiful children – seems to have touched on a basic parental desire. Quillet's method for achieving beautiful children is clearly in the line of the modern proponents of eugenics. The way to have beautiful children, he proposes, is to start out with healthy, young and beautiful parents.

Near the beginning of the *Callipaediae*, Quillet offers a description of the ideal parents, the most perfect of which were found in France:

"There beauteous Nymphs you view whose sparkling eyes
Shine like Pandora's, ere she left the skies,
Nor is their size too short, nor yet too tall,
But straight and of a middling stature all,
Nor gross, nor meager, for it pleases none
To see the strutting flesh or starting bone.
Clean are their limbs, erect their forms and bright
Their charming faces as the morning light.
See how their fronts in shining arches rise,
How white their skin, how keen their killing eyes.
Their cherry lips with balmy odors blessed,
Their ivory necks, behold, their snowy breasts,
But the chaste Muse forbids to speak the rest. . . .

"Not only in a Nymph, kind Nature shines,
But in our manly youth's severed lines.
The softer graces those, the stronger these,
As those the Youth, so these the Virgins please.
A sanguine look adorns the beardless Male,
And never does his equal temper fail.
Nor stained his face, nor is his color wan,
But fresh and fair as when the race began.
A graceful shade around his temples grow
And thence in curls adown his shoulders flow.
Firm are his joints; the well-proportioned frame
Agrees and is in every part the same."

Quillet also describes the mates who are unlikely to produce handsome children. His list includes the ugly, the dirty, the impotent, those with gout, epilepsy, stones or consumption.

"For, if the generative seed's defiled,
The Father's hurt's transmitted to the child.
Ill habits and diseases thus are nursed
In the weak frame, and he with life is cursed."

Quillet further opposes marrying the young to the old, a common practice in an age when the old had control of most of the available wealth:

> "Nor does she, when she sees his riches, dread
> The spotted issue from his loathsome bed.
> Though crippled are his limbs, his head reclined,
> And age forbids him to increase his kind.
> By choice or else compelled, she plies her charms
> To the cold circle of his withered arms."

May-December marriages were often "compelled" by parents anxious to be rid of an unwanted daughter or to secure economic benefit.

In other cases, the problem was that the mate might be not too old but too young:

> "Nor with green girls should beardless boys be joined.
> The body comes not forward like the mind.
> No juice as yet the genial vessels swells
> But scattered in the growing man it dwells."

Semen, like mother's milk, was believed to be whitened blood and was thought to be scattered throughout the body prior to sexual relations or, as in this case, prior to maturity.

After the selection of a mate, marriage follows. Quillet's description of the rite has a charm and earthy humor that remainds one of Breughel's painting of the *Wedding Feast*.

> "The Rite's performed, the Nymph's no longer coy,
> But like the Bridegroom burns to taste the joy.
> The cheerful Parents load the festial board
> And empties for the Bride the golden hoard.
> The Father most, with a dilated soul,
> Deals freely to the guests the flowing bowl.
> The table's with inverted glasses spread,
> And the gay Lass the measured round is led.
> The venal harper tears his laboured strings
> While the glad house with bridal blessings rings.
> The Bridegroom steals a pledge of future bliss
> And oft he mixes with his mirth a kiss."

Then, the feast over, the couple retires to bed:

> "Now to the Bride, the naked Bridegroom turns,
> And to begin the marriage combat burns.
> 'Come to my arms, my love, my life, ' he cries,
> While trembling by his side the Damsel lies.
> 'The unwelcome crowd are gone, the field is ours,
> Oh, waste not with delay, these precious hours.
> Come to my arms and *Hymen's* happy fight
> And give to love and me the blissful night.'"

But suddenly, at this romantic moment, Quillet breaks in with advice for the couple (these next seven lines are quoted from a subsequent translation made two years later, in 1712, by the poet Nicholas Rowe):

> "Hold, furious Youth — better thy heat assuage,
> And moderate a while thy eager rage,
> For if the genial sport you now complete
> Full of the fumes of undigested meat,
> A thin, diluted substance shall thou place
> Too weak a basis for a manly grace
> To rise in figure just and dignify the Race."

Quillet's book goes beyond this point and becomes one of the earliest sex manuals. He describes the supposed relationship between sexual method and the likelihood of conception:

> "You, yet fond Wives, who love the rapturous bliss,
> To feel the close embrace and biting kiss,
> Too gamesome at the sport, the work you spoil,
> Too quick rebound, and when you work, you toil.
> You heave too fast, the flowing seed prevent
> And the male vigor with vain force is spent. . . .
> If in its cell, the seed, thus shaken, sticks
> The Foetus cannot, for your frisking, fix.
> Both yield in vain what Nature would supply
> And the loose parts in scattered masses lie."

This reflects the ancient belief that the male created the child out of the

totality of his semen — if some of it was lost, the child would lack something.

Before discussing anatomy, Quillet includes this disclaimer:

"Hence, ye Profane! We write this not to you
Who, in hot lust, our harmless verse will view.
You'll lewdly Nature's hidden works survey
Or scoff the sacred womb where once you lay."

His description of sexual anatomy is a mixture of fact and mythology.
A physician, Quillet understood anatomy, but he only speculated about the
function of the different organs. When discussing the ovaries and fallopian
tubes, he explains that the left side produces daughters and the right side
sons, continuing:

"An oblong pipe is at the bottom placed,
By which the virile nerve is oft embraced:
The seed is darted to the womb by this
The center of the Mother's pain and bliss.
'Tis called the neck and in the strong embrace
It shuts, with wondrous art, the parent place,
Lest the hot Youth too far should wildly rove
And ravage the forbidden fields of love.
When the Male seed has past this narrow room
It meets the Female in the sucking womb.
Where clinging arms the expected juice compel,
It darts and lodges in the gaping cell.
For as, with joy, the famished paunch receives
The grateful food which Nature's wants relieves,
So the glad womb repletes her empty maw,
And both their fill with greedy suction draw.
Light motions hence, and nimble hips, destroy
The tiller's pains and mar a fruitful joy. . . .

"What shall we here of wicked postures say?
When lovers with inverted dalliance play
Nor take the joy as Nature bids the bliss,
But to the pillow [the buttocks] turn the balmy kiss.
What Monsters spring from such impure delights?
What hideous forms? What foul Hermaphrodites?
But the chaste Muse forbids me to declare
What the chaste Wife would blush to do, or hear."

The aim of Quillet's book was not only to produce a beautiful child but, more explicitly, to produce a male child. Males he terms "the strength and glory of a race;" females, though "necessary," were at best "fair monsters."

Quillet describes the care and feeding of the mother before birth, warning the mother against excessive exercise, too much dancing and the dangers of fast driving in coaches. The birth is attended by a midwife. Soon after, the baby is swaddled.

> "He's swathed, but see the swath be not too hard.
> Oft from the Nurse's negligence arise
> Humped-backs and bandy legs or crooked thighs;
> And if in careless folds, the Babe you wrap
> You'll bend the figure and distort its shape."

Quillet argues for maternal breast feeding rather then the use of a wetnurse, condemning those who "with a hopeful beauteous Offspring blest,/ Forget themselves, and hire unwholesome Breasts."

Quillet covers children's ills in a cursory way, referring the reader to his predecessor: "And who that ever read thy verse divine,/ Thou great St. Marthe, will e'er be pleased with mine?"

He concludes his poem with a section on children's education, extolling the virtues of travel and offering witty comments on the inhabitants and customs of different nations.

Quillet's poem on child care was not the last of this tradition. Other verses, for the most part minor, continued to appear. One of the last of these works, entitled *Infancy or the Management of Children*, (written and published between 1774 and 1776 by Hugh Downman) went through seven editions to 1809. By that time, however, prose had become the dominant form in child-care writings. Today, Downman's book seems more a curiosity than historically significant.

Books of didactic poetry on child care had been only one of several sources of information available to parents. There were, in addition, prose works both for the general public and for doctors and midwives. Though all these works were written during the same era (1450-1750), each genre had its own slant on child care.

CHAPTER 2

The Child of the Physicians

The earliest medical work written after the advent of printing was a book on the care of children, Paolo Bagellardo's popular *Book on Infant Diseases* (1472). To read the treatments Bagellardo offers is to savor the spirit of fifteenth-century medicine — occasionally useful but more often quaint or sinister. In some cases it resembles black magic. Here for example, is his treatment for convulsions:

> "Prepare a bath for the infant made from boiling down the heads of young pigs or gelded sheep or young goats until they melt. Make a decoction of their meats and then put the child in the bath. After this, make an ointment of the aforementioned oils [and apply it to the neck of the child]. I have also heard that oil of white lilies or hyssop works."

While this strange recipe was considered appropriate to a mysterious disease like convulsions, Bagellardo had only slightly less esoteric advice to cure bedwetting. He begins sensibly enough:

> "It saddens parents when infants or boys beyond three years of age wet their beds regularly, not only every few days, but continually every night — and not only up to the age of five or six, but sometimes even into puberty.
> "[Here are some of the] remedies which have been recommended by the authorities and are true:
> "Beware of coldness of temperature, of food and drink. . . make sure the child sleeps comfortably, make certain that the child gets moderate exercise, make certain that the child does not become accidentally upset or disturbed by anger or unhappiness."

Bagellardo then goes on to list a number of other treatments for bedwetting, presumably for use in recalcitrant cases. One cure he attributes to Dioscoridies, the Greek herbalist of the first century A.D., "Grind and drink cerebrum of hare" is reminiscent of the ointment for teething. Two other cures from Fidelis   "lung of kid goat, eaten and made into a plaster" and "bladder of young breeding sow, ground and drunk" — and one by the great Arab physician Rhazes (c. 900 A.D.), "dried and powdered cock's comb, scattered over the bedwetter's bed without his knowledge," are wild. Even when Bagellardo speaks from experience, however, his recommendations strike the modern reader as fanciful.

"I know from experience that the flesh of a ground hedgehog prevents the passage of urine if it is administered frequently." Avicenna and Rhazes concur on this, he points out. The "skin of a hen's stomach, dried and pulverized, also removes nocturnal bedwetting marvelously."

What is worth noting is not only the dependence of medicine on ancient authority, but also the vast number of cures offered. Physicians were ready to try *anything* that promised relief, since they were often helpless in the face of plagues, and even simple ailments were misunderstood without modern methods of analysis.

Opium, which had been a part of medicine since the time of the Sumerians (before 4000 B.C.) was formally reintroduced into Europe by Paracelsus in 1521 (in a tincture with powdered gold and pearls, which suggests something of the value placed on it). By reading Bagellardo, however, we discover that even before 1521, in the absence of the pure drug, "our common people give infants a little of the stuff called 'Quietness'," a decoction, or boiled-down extract, of black poppies or poppy seeds.

Bagellardo became the first of many doctors to say that he did "not approve at all" of dosing children with opium to make them sleep and that it should not be given "except upon urgent necessity." Nevertheless, the existence of one really effective drug in a time of hare's brains and ground hedgehog, made its use irresistible. Over the protests of dozens of generations of physicians, opium remained a popular method of quieting babies until the twentieth century when its distribution was brought under government control.

Swaddling, the wrapping of infants in cloth bands, was another means of keeping children quiet. Yet it had a more popular purpose in the eyes of the parents. Bagellardo describes the use of swaddling to force the child's body into a proper shape.

After the child is born, it is to be bathed in warm water, sometimes slightly salted after the manner of the Greeks.

"The midwife should cover the infant's head with a fine linen cloth in the fashion of a hood. Then, placing the infant in her lap, its head towards her feet, she should raise its arms and, taking a soft linen cloth, she should wrap its breast and bind its body with three or four windings of the band. Next she should take another piece of linen or a little cloth and draw the hands of the infant straight forward so that the infant acquires no humpiness, and then, with the same bands, bind and wrap the infant's arms and hands so that they will become correctly shaped.

"Next she should turn the infant over on its breast with its back raised upwards and take hold of the infant's feet and make its soles touch its buttocks so that the knees will be properly set. Then she should straighten the infant's legs and with another band and little cloths bind and wrap up the legs and with yet another band and little cloths wrap up the hips. Next she should take the entire infant and roll it in a woolen cloth or garment like a cape lined, in winter, with sheepskin or, in summer, a simple linen cloth will suffice.

"Put the child in a mild room, fairly dark so that the infant will not be blinded by the light and cover it over with a light covering, wrapping a piece of linen around its head but being careful not to cover its face so that it does not suffocate.

"And then let it sleep."

Suffocation was common. Infants were often wrapped so tightly that they could neither breathe nor turn their heads to let out fluid when they drooled or vomitted.

Bagellardo's work remained typical of medical texts through the time of William Harvey. Describing the impact of Harvey's work, Robert Willis (editor of the Sydenham Society edition of Harvey's *Works,* 1847) paints a sharp picture of medical practices of those years:

"The appearance of Harvey's book on the Motion of the Heart and Blood seems almost immediately to have attracted the attention of all the better intellects among the medical men in Europe. The subject was not one, indeed, greatly calculated to interest the mass of mere practitioners; and had it been a book of receipts it would have had a better chance with them."

The "better intellects" of the medical profession also produced works on child care. One of these, Bartholomaeus Metlinger, created an excellent book *A Regimen for Young Children* issued in 1473, only one year after Bagellardo's.

Reading Metlinger, we sense the kind of balance and craftsmanship that is largely missing in the earlier work. Even in his quotations from the ancients, Metlinger selects what is practical and sensible. Here, for example, is Metlinger paraphrasing the Galen passage quoted earlier:

"Healthly children have good habits and do not complain. When children cry or lie awake, they are unhealthy and we should, therefore, consider their health and take care of them in such a way that they do not lose it. It is worthwhile to take care to maintain children's virtue not so that others will call them virtuous, but so that their health will be maintained.

"If children are angry or upset or lie awake, this is a sign of the beginning of fevers and diseases. If children sweat, or lie still and unmoving, it makes them pale and destroys their natural body temperature.

"You must observe the child with great care to see that they should have no irregular movements. When they whine or cry or are angry or lie still, it is necessary to find out why and to try to turn the child [that is, to turn the course of events].

"Galen says a child cries because something hurts him, or they are troubled from external causes, or they are wet with urine, or they want to go to stool, or they are too hot or too cold, or they have too many clothes on, or they have lain too long, or are lying in unclean covering. All these things should be considered and whatever is wanting should be provided for the child. Most important, their linen should be kept clean. When one would comfort or quiet a child, it can be done in these ways: First, one puts the mother's breast in his mouth, for when one gives the child the breast, all his troubles are put aside, [secondly] with song for a mild voice reaches his heart, and thirdly, one softly rocks the cradle.

"It should also be known that when children begin to creep around the floor and reach after things, one should make for them a little pen of leather so that they do not hurt themselves. And finally, one should not leave them long and unprotected."

Metlinger, in general, avoids the more bizarre remedies, placing his faith primarily in salves and poultices. For pockmarks, for example, he recommends a "white salve," prepared from equal portions of "litharge [lead monoxide], burnt calves' knuckles, chick pea meal, rice flour, and melon seeds, finely powdered and mixed with linseed." This salve was to be applied in the evening and washed off each morning with a small bag of bran "wet with water in which violets or poplar leaves have been boiled."

When Metlinger recommends (as a treatment for running ears) cleaning with cotton and the use of an astringent (made from boiling ground acorns, that is: tannic acid) and an antiseptic (wine: dilute alcohol), his prescription is valid wilderness medicine. When he points out that "children frequently have warts, glands and other growths," he goes on to say that "it is unnecessary to advise about them as they largely disappear as children grow up." If this does not occur, "one must have advice." At a time when medical men were largely unable to cure illnesses and traded on their ability to offer convincing explanations of diseases, the advice that a problem should be left to heal itself is the mark of a knowledgeable physician.

Metlinger deals with the feeding and care of small children, saying that their meals should be kept light while they are growing with "mush and milk" provided between meals. "Sweat baths are not healthy for them and they should not be bathed in cold water. . . which hinders growth. . . . The child should never be bathed, on a full stomach."

"We should be diligent to instill good habits; as Aristotle says: 'You should teach your children to be industrious as a habit. They should avoid anxiety, anger, ill humor, fear, sadness, and they should not be kept awake too much. You should give them what they ask for and avoid what makes them unhappy. You should bring them up to be obedient to their father and mother and reverent to God. Good habits make for good nature in the complexion [personality or character] .' That is why Avicenna [The much noted Arabian physician, c.1000 A.D.] says, 'Bad habits point to a bad streak in their nature. Anger, being headstrong, sadness, fear, coldness, anxiety and bad temper make for stubbornness, and all these things are a beginning of many diseases. Also, becoming accustomed to good habits is important for both body and soul.' As Aristotle says: 'The soul of a child is like a clean slate on which nothing is written, on it you may write what you will.' Therefore, a child with bad habits should be slowly and regularly be accustomed to good habits by kindness and punishment until the character becomes better.

"It is to be known that children should not be punished too severely. Valerius [first century Roman author] in his second volume writes about one Mancilio Torquato who drove his son out of the house because he had taken money secretly. The son, in grief, went and hanged himself."

" . . . Parents should look after their children, and Valerius writes about the son of King Antioch who was mad with forbidden desire for his stepmother. His father saw this and looked to it that another woman should be brought to his son and so avoided a great evil.

"Note that a child of six years should be given to a teacher so that he will learn something. King Octavius has written that he educated his son in knightly exercises and his daughters learned embroidery on silk, and so though they had from birth and inheritance what they needed, they learned to be as industrious and wise as if they had lost everything, or could seek such riches through the exercise of such virtues. But children should not work all the time but should have recesses for recreation."

Metlinger's images drawn from the life of the wealthy were more than simply fairy-tale examples. They reflect the audience for his book. In the fifteenth century, illiteracy restricted access to child-care books so that only the middle and upper classes could read them.

Historically, the middle class has had the leisure and money to attend to its children's needs and to seek professional advice. This class has always provided the natural market for books on how to raise children.

Ninety years after Metlinger, in 1563, *The Children's Book* by Felix Wurtz, a Swiss surgeon, again used images derived from the life of the wealthy to illustrate the proper handling of children:

"To clear this with a comparison: if the hands are kept clean because their work is about silk, fine linen, laces of gold or silver, is not man more precious and worthier to be kept clean than all of these?"

Wurtz's book received wide distribution throughout Europe and became far more popular than Metlinger's. An English edition was published in 1689. It is in some respects more radical than the earlier one because, unlike Metlinger, Wurtz not only offered advice about child care but also criticized many of the practices of his time. On swaddling, he remarked:

"I have seen both mothers and nurses to bind and tie their children so hard for pity sake [it] made me weep. . . . Young tender children are not able to speak or complain against those which deal roughly with them. . . .

"Some used to lie the children behind the hot oven whereby the child may soon be stifled or choked, not regarding whether the heat doth not cause a pain in the body or head, supposing only that if the child be but laid behind the oven, then it is well cared for."

Noting that children's mouths should not be scrubbed "with wool or rough linen" as a cure for thrush, he added, "Children must not be kept long naked or wet." Some mothers or nurses feed children hot pap "which burns their mouth, tongue, etc." or offer it in hot spoons which "burn and cut" the mouth. These are all basic, and yet they appear to have been largely unknown. The image of child care we receive from Wurtz is almost one of children caring for children. For example, when the infants were swaddled in tight, neat little bundles, it was not uncommon to toss them around.

"Some parents hath that ill and base custom, they flit with one hand the child upwards and catch it with the other. . . [as a consequence of which the children] usually take frightings in their sleep [remembering this treatment].

"I have seen a Father taking his little boy by the shoulder and threw him upward. The sport pleased the boy very well, desired his Father to do it again and again; this pastime pleased Father and Son for a while but one time the boy being flung too high and turning in that, flinging out of his Father's reach, fell down behind his Father who was not able to stop him then in his fall. This sport was turned into lamentation."

Among the child-training devices used in the past was the "standing stool," which kept the child standing or sitting upright on a chair sometimes for hours. On these devices, Wurtz was vehement:

"Touching the standing of children: there are stools for children to stand in in which they can turn round any way; when Mothers or Nurses see them in it, they care no more for the child, let it alone, go about their own business supposing the child should be well provided [for] ; but they little think on the pain and misery the poor child is in in that standing. . . . I wish that all such standing stools were burned and that never any were made by reason of the great misery that children endure from such standing, for I hold these stools a mere prison or stocks for poor infants. I do wonder sometimes what merciless fool that was who invented that rack at first to make a child stand an hour in that tub. I found many times that when such children overstood themselves in that tub, they sunk down where they lay a long time and there lost their strength, which were brought to me afterwards to recover and cure them. Children should not be made to stand before they are half a year old and be strong enough in their sinews."

Wurtz, a surgeon, talks knowledgeably about the strain on the back muscles caused by forcing children to sit before they are ready.

Wurtz also describes the running stool. "There are running stools for children in which they not only stand but go also: in these stools, the children can hold out longer because they can also stir and move in them." But even these stools, he felt, were only the lesser of evils.

In a book by an Italian, Omnibonus Ferrarius, published fourteen years after Wurtz, in 1577, there are illustrations of the running stool and of one of the chair stools that forced the infant to sit. (Page 24) The child in the illustrations is about two years old, yet the devices were clearly intended for infants. As Ferrarius says in his text, a child of two "is quite capable of walking, talking and eating on its own."

During the sixteenth century, a child was considered an infant until he was six or seven because he was still dependent. A child of any age less than six was approximately the same creature to artists; only the size differed. After the age of six, unless a child was middle- or upper-class and to be educated, he or she went to work at an adult trade and could be drawn as a miniature adult.

Many of the child-raising practices of this period, like the arts, seem to deny the physical reality of children. Compelling a child to sit upright before he was ready, or to stand before he was ready, both seem to deny the limitations of the baby. Even swaddling, with its attempt to shape the curved limbs of babyhood into the straight limbs of the adult suggests an effort to give babies adult form beginning, as Bagellardo proposed, immediately after birth.

While Wurtz did not flatly oppose swaddling, so long as "the child be not tied or packed too hard," he proposed as "a fit garment for children to wear in their cradles" a long shirt or smock with an attached hood.

"The cap and sleeves should be all of one piece or sewed together, for a cap of itself and sleeves apart, though they cover the parts they are made for, yet the child is not covered all the way. But if the cap and sleeves be sewed together as one piece, it is the best way. . . [and] though the child puts his hand out of the cradle, yet are his arms covered. . . . His clothes should be made wider [than the child] that they may fall on one another and lie double. . . . This in my opinion is a proper garment for a child."

Another 165 years passed before William Cadogan wrote a letter, *Essay on the Nursing and Management of Children* (1748), to a Govenor of the Foundling Hospital in London proposing a similar garment. In medical history, it is generally considered that the end of swaddling and the start of modern child care began with the proposals Cadogan made in

that letter. From this perspective, the truly advanced quality of Wurtz's book may be appreciated.

*   *   *

The rather franciful and magical systems of Bagellardo and others, and the essentially pragmatic approach typified by Metlinger and Wurtz, existed without open conflict until the mid-seventeenth century. These divergent ideas were united by a common analysis of medicine: the humors theory which held that the world was composed of four elements: earth, water, air and fire. In sympathy with these elements, there were in the body four corresponding colored biles or fluids: black, green, yellow and red (blood), each of which corresponded to an emotional disposition. A man with too much black bile would be diagnosed as melancholic, a man with too much green (phlegm) as phlegmatic and so on. Even a pragmatist such as Metlinger when opposing giving wine to children before puberty ("before twelve in women and fourteen in men") offered the reason that children's nature required "moistness in the extremities from which they grow." Since the nature of wine was "hot and dry," it tended to disrupt childish constitutions.

After William Harvey's discovery of blood circulation (1628), the growth of medical knowledge accelerated. Three times, in 1645, 1649 and 1650, three different physicians "discovered" rickets. Diphtheria, mentioned even before Harvey, began to be systematically described. Thomas Sydenham, "the English Hippocrates," described chorea (a nervous disease also known as *St. Vitus's dance*) and measles in detail. In the face of these and other discoveries made by the pragmatic physicians, the old humors theory began to collapse.

Attempts were made to develop a new mythology based on Harvey's discoveries. When Daniel Whistler, the first writer on rickets, explained the cause of the disease (in fact, a vitamin deficiency), he attributed it to a misproportion in the blood between the clotting factor and the serum. However, neither this nor any other scheme gained widespread popularity. The one exception was a theory propounded by Walter Harris in his work, *A Treatise on the Acute Diseases of Infants* (1689). A successful doctor and appointed physician to William III, there is very little to separate Harris from a dozen other medical writers of his time. What makes Walter Harris's compendium of infant diseases different from others was his advocacy of a theory first proposed by the French physician Franciscus Sylvius de la Boe (in a posthumous book of 1674). De la Boe postulated that many diseases of infancy were caused by acidity. Since the author was, however, a believer in opiates, he did not pursue his ideas on acidity to their logical conclusion. Harris was quite prepared to take that last step. As Harris puts it:

"The antecedent and more distant causes of the diseases of infants, however numerous or various they may be, all center at last in one immediate cause, viz. in an acid prevailing through the whole habit [body]. . . . I make no scruple to assert that the diseases of infancy are very few in their kind and differ only in degree from one another. . . . In short, all the complaints of infants spring from an acid as their common source."

If the disease was acidity, the cure was obvious – an antacid:

"[There are] medicines of a perfectly mild nature which efficaciously absorb any prevalent acidity, subdue any preternatural commotions in the humours, and perform the function of anodynes both effectually and safely. Such are crab's eyes and claws, oyster-shells, cockel-shells, bones of the cuttle-fish, egg-shells, chalk, coral coralline, pearls, mother of pearl, both kinds of bezoar, burnt hartshorn and that of the unicorn, bole Armeniack, sealed earth, bloodstone, etc. . . . If in such a variety of testaceous medicines almost of the same nature any of them were to be preferred to others for their virtues, I would chiefly recommend common oyster-shells, as they are found on the seashore, after they have been long exposed to the sun and ripened, as it were, by his kindly beams."

The active ingredient in all these items is calcium carbonate.

G.F. Still, the pediatric historian, lists eighteen editions of Harris through 1742. His influence was felt even longer. Michael Underwood's *Treatise on The Diseases of Children* (1784), the most comprehensive work on pediatrics in the eighteeneth century, continued to show the impact of Harris's theories.

The extended popularity of Harris seems to have been due in part to the fact that his prescriptions did little harm. If oyster shells accomplished nothing else, at least they tended to slow down the deadly flow of opiates with which many physicians regularly drugged their infant patients.

This mixture of pragmatism and medical alchemy was the nature of pediatrics during the first three centuries after Gutenberg. The advice of poets and physicians was, however, augmented by texts prepared for a third group, the midwives.

CHAPTER 3

The Child of the Midwives

The early books on midwifery seem more modern than the poetic or pediatric child-care texts of the same period. Written in the vernacular rather than in medical Latin, midwives' manuals were unpretentious works communicating the essentials of a practical craft to a readership that included both professional midwives and the lay public.

Midwives varied in competence. A few were skilled professionals like Catherina Schraders (b.1655), who practiced until she was ninety. Schraders compiled a record admirable even by modern standards, delivering more than four thousand infants including 42 pairs of twins and 3 sets of triplets, losing only 90 infants and 15 mothers. Many of the losses occurred, as Dr. Isidore Snapper wrote in a recent essay, from "complications which even today might imperil the life of a fetus."

Nevertheless, Schraders, if not unique, was certainly exceptional. Practicing in the countryside remote from the anerobic organisms and streptococci of the urban hospitals, she was well trained by her neighbor Dr. Hendrik Van Deventer, author of a classical obstetrical text. More common were the many midwives who had only the rudiments of training at best. Like many of the physicians, they were more involved in creating excuses for their failures than in attempting to remedy them.

Eucharius Roesslin's *Rosengarten* (1513, in English titled *The Birth of Mankynde*) was one of the earliest and most popular midwifery books. The introduction to the English edition (translation by Thomas Raynaldes, 1604) comments on the reception the work received when first available to midwives.

"Let not the good midwives to offended [though I have called some midwives indiscreet, unreasonable and churlish] for verily there is no science but that it hath its apes, owls, bears and asses which, as above all others, have most need of information and teaching [yet] will kick and whine against such as would reform or reduce to any better way than they have been accustomed to in times past. And this I do say because at the first coming abroad of this present book, many of this sort of midwives moved either of envy or else of malice or both diligented and endeavoured them[-selves] very earnestly by all ways possible to find the means to suppress and abrogate the same."

The biology presented in the midwives' manuals is not essentially different from that presented in the medical texts of the period. In Roesslin, for example, blood circulation is described in the traditional, pre-Harvey terms:

"[The heart and arteries] have two contrary motions: the one is enclosing itself and the other is opening itself which sort of movings we call the beating of the pulse. When the arteries do open themselves, they attract, draw or suck in fresh air to temper the heat of the body withall. . . . But when they close themselves, they do expel misty fumes and hot breaths and unnatural vapors."

The understanding of biological processes is similarly alchemical: The "mettals" of which man is made derive from "four principal [mines] in the body of man," the first being the mine of blood, the liver, the second the heart, the third the brain and the fourth the stones or testes. It was in the testes that the output of the other three was mixed and "whitened" into seed, both semen and mother's milk being considered blanched blood.

"And here we shall understand that most commonly always when . . . nature is disposed to make a transmutation of any matter, this she cannot do unless she have a mine, shop or workhouse wherein, by continual circulation of the matter transmuted, she may bring her purpose to pass.

"[And] this transmutation of blood into sperm is not only in color but also in properties and absolute perfection. What greater miracle is there wherein we may knowledge and behold the omnipotency of God."

Roesslin covers fetal biology in a craftsmanlife manner, showing even the different positions in which infants are found: cavorting in the

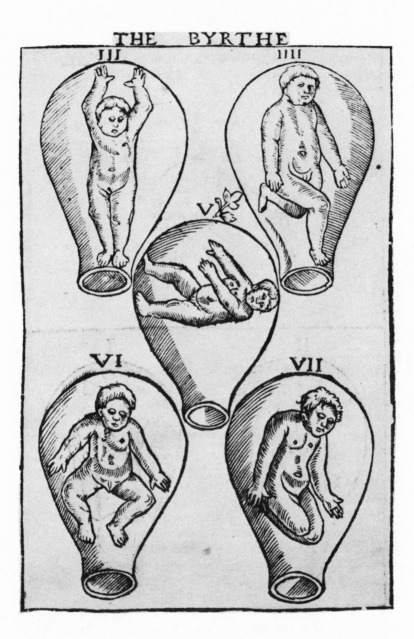

womb, singly and as twins. His infants are however, always more mature
than real infants.

Roesslin describes a delivery stool in which the mother sits to deliver
her child through an opening in the front (which, some feel, is an easier
and more natural position for the mother than is today's prone posture).

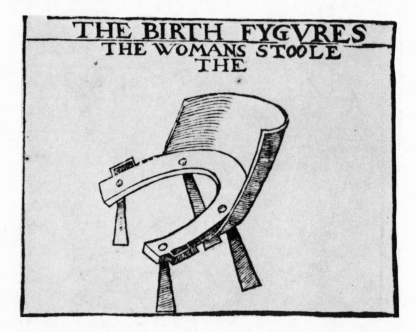

Midwives' guides also commented on nursing. Again, Roesslin is a
conservative, sticking primarily to physical requirements, but other writers
were more imaginative. Jacques Guillemeau in a 1609 book entitled *The
Happy Delivery of Women* included a description of the selection of a
wetnurse. She should, of course, be healthy, between 25 and 35 years of
age, of middle stature, with a "light and rosy complexion" and a "broad
large breast." He then adds this stipulation: "Especially she should not
have red hair."

Guillemeau describes at length five considerations in the choice of a
nurse: her birth and parentage (she must be of good stock), her person
(health), her mind, her milk's quality and her child. Under each heading
he lists specifics:

"She ought to be of good behavior, sober and not given either to drinking or gluttony, mild without being angry or fretful, for there is nothing that sooner corrupts the blood of which the milk is made than choler or sadness; and therefore she should be merry, playing and singing to the child, dandling and using him gently, and one that will not refuse to give him the breast at any time for fear lest he cry. She must likewise be chaste, not desiring after her husband's company and much less a stranger's, because carnal copulation (as Galen says) troubles the blood and so by consequence the milk . . . [and] the Nurse thinking only to take her a little sport may thereby prove with child . . . ."

"Let her be sage, wise, discreet that she may take care of her little one and not lay him in any place where he may endanger himself to be either sick or stifled. For there are more Nurses than should be which are such beasts and so careless who having their children such in the night as they lie with them in bed do oftentimes fall asleep upon them and so stifle them."

The wetnurse was a staple of virtually every household that could afford one.* Even as late as the mid-nineteenth century, few European mothers who could afford a standin suckled their own children.

Guillemeau urged that the child be kept "dry and clean" and that he be changed on a soft pillow placed in the nurse's lap, "the doors and windows being close shut and having something about her to keep the wind from the child. . . . If he be very foul, she may wash him with a little water and wine lukewarm, with a sponge or linen cloth." Even with the best intentions, it was virtually impossible to keep a fully swathed child clean and dry, and the practice of swaddling had not yet been set aside.

As did Wurtz, Guillemeau protested against swaddling's abuses:

"Some swathe the child's body hard to make him have a goodly neck and to make him seem the fatter, but this crushing makes his breast and ribs which are fastened to his backbone stand out so that they are bended. . . and that causes the child to be either crump shouldered or crooked breasted."

A more revealing description of the practice and the attitudes behind

---

*Romeo and Juliet, written approximately contemporarily with Guillemeau, contains such a nurse. Likewise, Shakespeare's reference in Jacques's speech on the Seven Ages of Man (from As You Like It) portrays the infant not with his mother but "mewling and puking in the nurse's arms."

the popularity of swaddling is contained in a later book, *The Expert Midwife*, by a Scottish physician, Dr. James McMath. This was written in 1694,
long after Guillemeau and Wurtz.

> "Let his arms be wrapt up in his bed, straight down close along his
> sides, the thighs also, legs and feet equally extended, and bound down
> together that they may lie more straight and not turn crooked or wry
> and grow firm also and stable [so that] he may be able in time to raise
> himself, stand up on his feet and come to go upright, with a soft linen
> between to hinder their galling, having also a stayband pinned on each
> side [of] the blanket to keep its head steady, and so its whole body
> being thus equally contained in swaths and in a straight figure from
> top to toe, due and decent, for mankind may thereby [be] rightly
> conformed and perfited, its bones made firm and stable."

Notice that midpassage as the child is swathed up and pinned down, the
baby, who started out as "he" is transformed into "it." There are few other
descriptions of swaddling that symbolize as clearly the degree to which the
child, once swathed, became an inert thing, the passive recipient of his
parents' or his nurse's will.

One of McMath's contemporaries, John Pechy, saw physical and
moral freedom as equally dangerous. Swaddling, he held, was vital "lest
the infant move its hands and feet too freely and [thus] distort its bones
which are very flexible." But swaddling was only a part of the overall
training of the infant.

> "Do we not see that young lions and bears, when they are young, can
> be made so tame as to obey the very nod of their keepers, whereas if
> you let them alone till they are grown up, they will forever remain fierce
> and wild. Why then should the mind of a child be not so trained? . . .
> Anger shows itself first by crying and the like and therefore you should
> endeavour to nip this animosity in the bud, and they that will not be
> reclaimed by admonition must be disciplined by the rod that in time
> to come they may be fit to perform the offices of a man."

Science in the service of morality has remained a popular theme in books
on child care to this day.

Midwives, in addition to their role in parturition, played the part of
marriage counsellors, handling problems from impotence to infertility. In
fact, a source of the popularity of their manuals was surely the sexual
anatomy described therein. Henry Bracken's *The Midwife's Companion*

(1737) is one of the most vivid texts on the subject and begins with the traditional notice:

> "Now I come to the act of generation which is an affair that everybody naturally desires to know and I heartily wish this account may not, at any time hereafter, fall into the hands of the lascivious or wanton libertine. Guard it, I beseech Thee, O divine Architect! from such unhallowed lips.
>
> "In the act of generation, the pleasure is so exquisite as to alter the course of blood and animal spirits which at this time move all these parts which before lay still: the clitoris, or penis of the women is erected, which by its fullness of nerves and exquisite sense affords unspeakable delight. The glands of the womb being pressed by the neighboring parts pour forth a liquor to facilitate and make easy the passage of the penis, or man's yard, and to increase the pleasure. The neck of the womb (or rather the passage to it) contracts and embraces closely the yard. The fibres of the womb contract themselves and open its mouth, which is at other times closely shut, and this is for the reception of the man's seed."

It is possible to regard this passage simply as a piece of salacious writing but that would be incorrect. These are, in fact, the anatomical terms of the period. This is post-Harvey, and the function of the organs is no longer described in the alchemical terms of Roesslin but in the fundamentally mechanistic terms of modern biology.

In reading Bracken we are dealing with the blunt realities of modern medicine. Discussing ectopic (extra-uterine) pregnancy, for example, Bracken says that there is not in such a case "any method to save the poor mother's life, which is a very deplorable circumstance." No herbs and no excuses.

In 1676, Anton Leeuwenhoek using a self-made microscope had discovered bacteria. Like Harvey's discovery of blood circulation, the impact of Leeuwenhoek's work was immediate — the beginning of modern biology. We can note the change in Bracken's account of the process of conception:

> "The seed impregnates the egg, which from being transparent becomes opaque or dark in color. It is afterward covered with a thick yellow substance which presses it on all sides and thrusts it out through a little hole in its middle so it falls into the orifice of one of the *Tubae Fallopianae* which dilates suffciently for its passage to the womb.

"There are other notions about the manner of conception but I think them so wide of the truth that I do not now take the trouble of writing them down."

He includes a description of sperm: "There are such enormous numbers of little creatures, like so many tadpoles, swimming every way in the male sperm of all animals as is really a very amazing sight." But he comments that the actual mechanism of fertilization is not clear. Even that admission is a sign of progress.

Bracken heaps contempt on the popular device of amulets, hung around the neck as cures and preventatives. A typical amulet, taken from Culpeper's *Directory for Midwives* (c. 1650, in print as late as 1762), might contain "male peony root gathered in the decrease of the moon [and] magistery of coral [powdered with] leaf gold." Bracken says of the practice that amulets "may comfort and relieve the nervous system. . . but as to be servicable in forwarding the teeth [he is speaking of teething amulets] . . . [it] is mere stuff and nonsense, fit only to amuse the credulous and ignorant part of mankind who (God knows) are too often carried away with false appearances and unintelligible jargon."

Bracken concurs with Walter Harris on the importance of acidity as the basis of infant ills. He seems to express the ambivalence of medicine at a time when physicians knew more than they could persuade their patients to accept. Bracken's description of swaddling illustrates his difficulty: On one hand, he supports swaddling, yet he uses images not far removed from those that would later be employed by the next generation of physicians to condemn it.

"That the bodies of infants will admit of almost any form is plain to anyone who has been to the East-Indies where the Chinese custom is to lace or swaddle the feet into very small compass, nay even till they are almost crippled. And if the foot, which is naturally a hard part, be capable of receiving any form we please, how much more will the trunk yield to our demands when the proper swathebands are applied."

By the mid-eighteenth century, the ambivalance regarding swaddling — the clear understanding of its defects set off against the equally clear desires of parents to shape their children and of nurses to demonstrate their expertise in this practice — was finally resolved. Physicians began advocating that swaddling be abandoned altogether. In 1754, a book appeared in France (an English translation followed a year later) that offered a sample of this new approach. M. Brouzet's *Essay on the Medicinal Education of Children* was one of the earliest books of a new genre, the comprehensive guide to child care, written in prose and intended for parents, not primarily for midwives. It combines the medical and moral advice of writers such as Metlinger and Wurtz with the practical advice on birth and related matters contained in the midwives' manuals.

> "The Chinese who crush the feet of their girls, the savages who flatten the heads of their children, those who bore their noses, endeavor to enlarge their nostrils, to lengthen the opening of their eyes, pull the beard up by the roots, draw out the teeth, &c. have the same authority [that is, tradition] to allege if anyone condemns their practice. From these general excuses, made by ignorance and prejudice, people are led to practices which it is essentially necessary to reform. . . .

> "The cries of the [swathed] infant. . .the fleeting redness shown on the skin, the suffocations and violent coughs to which they are subject are but too often the fatal effects of compressing the breast whatever precautions are taken; the sides which are soft have nothing to support them within, but the play of the diaphram and lungs must be sensible. . . of the impression of these ligatures. . . . It is also very improper to fasten the inferior extremities the one against the other, for by this means the feeble articulation of the thigh is sometimes disordered by placing the toes at too great a distance. Many women carry this dangerous custom to an excess and imagine that the feet are better situated in proportion as the toes are placed outward and the heels inward — in a position neither natural nor favorable.

> "In short no inconvenience can attend the leaving of the members of an infant merely at liberty."

From the length and detail of Brouzet's protest against it, we can judge how commonplace swaddling remained even as physicians began to turn against it.

Perhaps the primary influence in the eighteenth century leading to a new attitude towards the child was the discovery of "nature." In earlier times, underneath all the discussion of humors and the biological speculations, the world had been inexplicable. Harvey's discovery of circulation had offered some hope that nature could be understood, but Isaac Newton's work was more impressive. His analysis of the principles of gravitation and motion were more than physical descriptions; they were the invisible made visible. One can feel the excitement of the period captured in Pope's couplet: "Nature and Nature's laws lay hid in night / God said: Let Newton be! and all was light." Through the use of his mind, it seemed, man could become, like God, all-knowing. It is this emotion that lies behind the contempt with which Brouzet treats the ignorant:

"There are people who imagine that infants would walk on all-fours if care was not taken to have them swathed. Such opinions can only arise in the mind of ignorant and lazy speculatists for it is easy to demonstrate anatomically that the articulation of the head with the neck, that of the bone of the arm with the shoulder blade, and that of the knees are contrary to this kind of progressive motion. The form of the face indicates that the natural attitude is that of an erect posture [and] this position is so dependent on the conformation of his members that he takes it of himself though even no care be taken to bring him to it."

As Newton had demonstrated, the place to learn the laws of nature was in the study of nature. The natural history of the time, however, left something to be desired. Brouzet quotes Buffon, the great French natural historian and a man whose work involves a strange mixture of acute observations and imaginative fantasy, on the subject of infant care among the Africans. Buffon reports, Brouzet says, that the infants were not swaddled and "began to walk at two months old, or rather to draw themselves forward on their hands and knees. . . an exercise that at length gives them such facility in running in this manner that they move almost as fast as if they were on their feet." Obviously, Buffon perceived the Africans as something only quasi-human. Brouzet, however, did not concur. That argument, he says, "proves nothing against what we have advanced, for this situation is not less forced." Brouzet, arguing in the fervent tones of reformers everywhere, was living in a world whose widened horizons offered too many examples to the contrary:

"The Icelanders, the modern Greeks and many other people never swath their children; the Siamese, the Japanese, Negroes, the savages of Canada, those of Virginia, Brazil and most of the people of South America lay their children naked on beds of cotton suspended [hammocks] or put them into a kind of cradle covered and adorned with skins. . . . The Icelanders do not procure even these slight conveniences, yet there is scarcely found among them a person lame or hump-backed and their children walk at four or five months old. . . .
"[Animals put their young in] a warm and tranquil place shaded from the light. . . . Silence, an obscure light, air, air a little warm and rest are [what is] necessary to infants in the first hours after birth."

Much of this is incorrect. The "savages," the American Indians, often swaddled their children.

More important than its accuracy is the force that Brouzet's argument derives from a general belief in the rightness of nature and natural methods of child care. The behavior of animals was here given a moral force; man was urged to model his own practices after animal behavior. The natural child had, thus, been introduced well before Rousseau was to popularize the idea.

Brouzet's faith in natural methods of child care was carried a bit farther than most of us would care to take it today:

"Children should be washed oftener than once a day; they should not be suffered to lie in their urine and excrements; and care should more particularly be taken of the parts next to their linens. Infants are commonly washed in warm water; there are, however, some nurses who clean their children in their own milk; but it is better to lay aside this custom because the milk leaves a cress [crust] on the skin. . . . Sometimes too they make use of their spittle, but warm water to which may be added a little wine when there is a slight inflammation to be removed appears to be preferable. I have seen women in Provence who regularly caused their children to be licked by dogs that were very fond of this employment. Animals, 'tis true, clean their young so well and their tongues seem so soft and proper for it that it seems natural to procure the same assistance for infants. The observations that have been made on the cure of scabs and ulcers by the assistance of the saliva and tongue of dogs point out the use of this remedy in these disorders of the skin and authorize the advice we give of making use of it to cure that of infants."

Brouzet's book is one of the comparatively few early works that goes beyond infancy and covers child care, if briefly, up to puberty. His remarks on adolescent boys are astute and charming:

"Scarce does he feel the first effect of virility than he perceives with astonishement that his voice grows every day deeper and hoarser; his surprise is accompanied with supineness and natural timidity; he flies from society and domestic company and is pleased with none but youths of his own age; the children with whom he was before amused begin to grow troublesome. He trembles before those who are complete men, whose conversation and actions commonly too little favor the desires with which he is filled. In a word, he is in a kind of intoxication proceding from the strength, liveliness, swiftness and multiplicity of his ideas."

At such an age, Brouzet affirms, education is a critical matter, and the boy should be given a "suitable turn [towards] religion, society, and the employment for which [his heart and mind] are destined."

The manuals written for midwives focused on practical aspects of child care, offering advice far less romantic than that proffered by poets and less wildly theoretical than that given by many physicians. In their deepening understanding of child care, the works of the first three centuries reflect the gradual accumulation of factual knowledge about the child. The first overall theory of child care was, however, not to come from a poet, physician or midwife, but from a man who had little interest in the real problems of the child, the philosopher Jean Jacques Rousseau.

PART TWO

Nature and Religion

(1750-1900)

"The first object of Education is to train up an immortal soul.

"The second — but second at an immeasurable distance — is to do this in the manner most conducive to earthly happiness; never sacrificing either the interests of the future world to those of the present, or the welfare of the man to the inclinations of the child."

MELESINA TRENCH (181-)

CHAPTER 4

The Child of Nature

"Observe nature and follow the path she traces for you. She exercises children continuously: she hardens their temperaments by tests of all sorts, she teaches them of happiness, of what pains and saddens. The teeth in piercing [the gums] give them fever, the sharp colic gives them convulsions, they are suffocated, plethora corrupts the blood, many illnesses breed in them and they break out with dangerous erruptions. Nearly all of infancy is filled with sickness and danger, the greater part of infants perish before their eighth year.

"These tests make infants earn their strength and it is only afterwards that they can make use of life, that life becomes secure. That is the secret of nature. Why are are you set against it? Don't you see that by thinking you can improve on it, you destroy her labors and hinder the good effects of her care?"

This philosophy, ennuciated in *Emile* (1762) by Jean-Jacques Rousseau, offered child care its first systematic theory: the vision of the child as an unspoiled creature of nature, the offspring of the noble savage. Roughly seventy years earlier in *Some Thoughts Concerning Education* John Locke had a similar vision when he proposed the toughening of children by contact with nature:

41

"Children [should] not be too warmly clad or covered, winter or summer. . . . [The child's] feet should be washed every day in cold water and [one should] have his shoes so thin that they leak and let in water whenever he comes near it. . . . I doubt not but if a man from his cradle had been always used to go barefoot whilst his hands were constantly wrapt up in warm mittens and covered with handshoes, as the Dutch call gloves, I doubt not, I say, but such a custom would make taking wet in his hands as dangerous to him as now taking wet in their feet is to a great many others. . . .

"I should advise him to play in the wind and sun without a hat [though] there would be a thousand objections made against it."

Locke's theory of infant feeding also seemed to derive something from the natural vision of animals hunting for their food, never sure of when their next meal would be found:

"When custom has fixed his eating to certain stated periods, his stomach will expect victuals at the usual hour and grow peevish if [it passes without a meal]. . . . Therefore, I would have no time kept constantly to for his breakfast, dinner and supper but rather [have them] varied almost every day."

Though Locke's writings became popular, their impact was limited. *Some Thoughts Concerning Education* was a long essay full of random and often contradictory advice. It lacked a dominating theory of child care.

It fell then to Rousseau, the most gifted political image-maker of the eighteenth century, to develop a unified and convincing philosophy of childhood:

"All things are good as they come out of the hands of the Creator, but everything degenerates in the hands of man. He compels one soil to nourish the production of another, he blends and confounds elements, climates and seasons, he mutilates his dogs, his horses, his slaves; he defaces, he confounds everything: he delights in deformity and monsters. He is not content with anything in its natural state, not even with his own species. His very offspring must be trained up for him, like a horse in his menage, and taught to grow up after his own fancy like a tree in his garden."

Like much of *Emile*, this was closer to diatribe than to reason, but it was effective in the context for which it was written: eighteenth-century France where, for those who could afford it, social life consisted of elaborate artifices and amusements surrounding the court of Louis XV. Nature is an ideal backdrop against which to contrast society:

> "In the social order, in which the respective places of the individual are fixed, everyone must be educated for that [role] which he is to fill. . . .
> "In the natural order, all men being equal, their common vocation is the possession of humanity."

Rousseau, however, clearly understood the impossibility of raising men outside society and expecting them to function in it:

> "Without this [training] matters would be still worse than they are and our species would not be civilized but by halves. Should a man, in a state of society, be given up from the cradle to his own notions and conduct, he would certainly turn out the most preposterous of human beings. The influence of prejudice, authority, necessity, example, and of all those social institutions in which we are immersed would stifle the emotions of nature in him and substitute nothing in their place. His humanity would resemble a shrub growing by accident in the road which would be destroyed by the casual injuries it must receive from the frequent passers-by."

Rousseau's natural child was different from Locke's. What separated them was the difference between the ideas of nature in England and in France. In England, ideal nature might be represented by a landscaped park; in France it took the form of a formal garden. Locke had tried to put the child into nature; Rousseau imposed nature on the child. If the child, as Rousseau said, was to be inured "to the rigors of the seasons, the climate, the elements. . .to hunger, thirst, fatigue," it was not simply a matter of health; it was a matter of morality:

> "It is customary to bathe an infant in warm water. That is the first concession to the effeminacy of the parents. As the child grows stronger, the water's temperature should be reduced until you finish with icy water, summer and winter alike."

Rousseau's prestige and literary skills helped to spread the dangerous idea of icy baths for children. His position on swaddling, however, was more beneficial. Arguing vehemently against it, he described the swaddled infant as so bound up in stay bands that "even the head itself is rendered immobile." He noted: "One would imagine that the nurses were afraid that the poor creature would have the appearance of being alive.... In countries where no such extravagant precautions are taken, the people are tall, robust and well-proportioned. Whereas, on the contrary, those where infants are thus treated swarm with hunchbacks, crooked-legged, lame, rickety and deformed persons of every kind."

However much Rousseau may have approved of a free child in theory, he could not abide one in practice. Witness his comment on infant demands:

"If we consider the state of childhood in itself, is there in the world a more feeble and helpless being, more exposed to the mercy of everything about it, that has more need of pity, assistance and protection than an infant? . . . What then is more disgusting and contrary to the nature of things than to see a child, imperious and refractory, commanding everyone that comes near it and impudently usurping the tones of master over those who have only to leave it and it must die?"

Rousseau solved his own child-raising problems by abandoning his five illegitimate children in a foundling home, presumably as soon as they began to make demands.

Parents, for Rousseau, were to be the surrogates of nature, as harsh and disciplined as nature herself.

"The child who needs only to desire a thing to obtain it is led naturally to imagine himself the proprietor of the universe. He looks upon all mankind as his slaves and when anything is, at length, refused him. . . [he] esteems such refusal an act of rebellion."

Rousseau opposed Locke's belief that the child should be reasoned with. Though the theory was in vogue, Rousseau commented, "The success of it . . . does not seem to recommend it." Firmness and consistency were the keys. If "sometimes a baby is threatened and sometimes cajoled, [we make] him a servant or master." As a result, the child develops those unruly "passions" falsely attributed to his nature. "First the child's tears are prayers but, if one is not careful, they soon turn into orders."

It is ironic that Rousseau's suggestions were endorsed so enthusiastically by physicians since the philosopher made his feelings about doctors explicit:

"I never call in the physician for myself so I will never trouble them for Emile [the ideal boy, used as an example in the book].

"I know very well the physician will not fail to take advantage of that delay. If the child dies, he was called too late. . . if he recovers, it is the doctor who saved him.

"For want of knowing how to get well, a child should learn how to be sick as this is one of the arts of nature. When a beast is sick, it suffers in silence and keeps itself still: and yet we do not know that brutes are more sickly than men. . . .

"The only useful part of medicine is the hygiene."

The medical profession, however, adopted Rousseau's ideas. One of the most popular books of the late eighteenth century, William Buchan's *Domestic Medicine* (1769, and 19 later editions in Britain and the United States) took positions on swaddling and cold bathing much like those Rousseau proposed:

"How little deformity of body is found among uncivilized nations. So little indeed that it is vulgarly believed that they put all their deformed children to death. The truth is, they hardly know such a thing as a deformed child. Neither should we if we followed their example. Savage nations never think of manacling [swaddling] their children. They allow them full use of every organ, carry them abroad in the open air, wash their bodies daily in cold water, etc. By this management, their children become so strong and hardy that by the time our puny infants get out of their nurse's arms, theirs are able to shift for themselves."

By the late eighteenth century, under the first wave of industrialism, society had become brutal. By contrast, the world of the primitive looked pure, simple and unspoiled — in a word, romantic.

Only the first section of Buchan's book deals with child care, "the period of our lives [when] the foundations of a good or bad constitution are generally laid." In this relatively short section he takes the time to draw examples from the primitives and to comment at length on social conditions:

"Mothers of the poorer sort think they gain a great deal by making their children lie or sit while they work. In this they are greatly mistaken. By neglecting to give their children exercise, they are obliged to keep them a long time before they can do anything for themselves*

---

*One of the earliest comments on the connection between poverty and physical or mental retardation.

and to spend more on medicine than would have paid for proper care while it can never supply its place. To take care of children is the most profitable business in which the poor can employ themselves: But alas! it is not always in their power. Poverty often obliges them to neglect their offspring in order to procure the necessities of life. When that is the case, it becomes the interest as well as the duty of the public to assist them. Ten thousand times more benefit would accrue to the state by enabling the poor to bring up their own children than for all the hospitals that ever can be erected for that purpose."

In a footnote to that paragraph, Buchan proposed economic incentives to reduce infant mortality.

"If it were made the interest of the poor to keep their children alive, we should lose very few of them. A small premium given each year at the year's end would save more infant lives than if the whole revenue of the Crown were expended on hospitals for that purpose. This would make the poor esteem fertility a blessing whereas many of them think it is the greatest curse that can befall them."

Bribing the poor to keep their children alive was a step of sorts towards the development of social responsibility. Buchan's arguments are mercantilist, not religious; the poor are seen as a national resource. When Buchan talks of "benefit to the state" and raises the image of "our puny infants," contrasting them with the "strong and healthy" children of the savages, he values an increase in a healthy population as one would the accumulation of gold. The poor and even infants had roles to play in the politics of economic competition.

"[If] Mothers suckled their own children. . . it would prevent the temptation which poor women are laid under of abandoning their children to suckle those of the rich for the sake of gain, by which means society loses many of its most useful members and mothers become in some sense the murderers of their own offspring. I am sure I speak the truth when I say that not one in a hundred of those children live who are thus abandoned by their mothers. For this reason no other should be allowed to suckle another's child till her own is fit to be weaned. A regulation of this kind would save many lives among the poorer sort and could do no hurt to the rich. . . . "

So common was the nurse among the middle-class readers of Buchan's book that it was actually seen as credible that the survival of the human race depended on her, whatever the fate of her own offspring:

"It is folly to imagine that any woman who abandons her own child to suckle another for the sake of gain should feel all the affections of a parent towards her nursling; yet so necessary are those affections in a nurse that, but for her, the human race would soon be extinct."

If the children of the poor died, it was beginning to be seen, at least in part, as a failure of society as a whole. True, infant deaths had always occurred, but in rural areas deaths had occurred largely out of the sight of the middle class. In the expanding cities of nineteenth-century Europe, the shocking rate of infant mortality became all too clear. To understand life in those cities (and, for that matter, even in the early years of our own century*) it is necessary to grasp the incredible facts of the widespread practice of infanticide. A recent article by William Langer (1972) offers us a startling view of the subject:

"The easy methods of committing infanticide included dosing the baby with gin or opiates; starvation and strangulation were often resorted to, and cases of a skull being broken by a hairbrush were by no means unknown. . . . Of all procedures, the most unobjectionable was simply to leave an infant at some church entrance or in a secluded doorway, in the hope that perhaps someone would rescue him. Most of these abandoned children died quickly of exposure or starvation.

"In the eighteenth century it was not an uncommon spectacle to see the corpses of infants lying in the streets or on the dunghills of London and other large cities. . . .

"[Newspaper clippings from the 1860s and the report of the Select Committee on Protection of Infant Life in 1871] tell of dead infants found in rivers, canals and drains or lying under bushes in parks and fields."

Hogarth's *Gin Lane*, while certainly exaggerated in its combination of events, is for the most part an accurate depiction of infant mortality among the poor.

Against this grim reality, Rousseau's vision of the child of nature takes on new meaning. His was not a carefully thought out and researched

*In our own century, Margaret Sanger's work on birth control made one of its earliest arguments the necessity of stopping widespread infanticide.

GIN LANE.

thesis on the nature of infant life but rather a retreat from the growing chaos both caused and revealed by the Industrial Revolution and the massing of population in the new industrial centers.*

Eighteenth-century advice on child care was continually tied to specific examples and applications in the wider world. On even such a simple subject as exercise, Buchan expresses this broader concern:

> "Many people imagine it a great advantage for children to be taught early to gain their bread. This opinion is certainly right. . .provided they be so employed as not to hurt their health or growth, but when these suffer, society in place of being gainers are real losers by their labor. . . .
>
> "There are. . . various ways of employing young people without hurting their health. The easier parts of gardening, husbandry or any business carried on without doors are most proper. These are employments that most young people are fond of and some parts of them may be adapted to their age, taste and strength. . . .
>
> "One needs only look into the great manufacturing towns. . . [to] find a puny degenerate race of people, weak and sickly all their lives. . . . Art and manufacture, though they [are] the riches of a country, are by no means favorable to the health of its inhabitants."

Children, he says, "should not be set to work too early. . . . Every person conversant with horses or other work animals knows that if they be set to hard labor too soon, they will never turn out to advantage."

Regardless of these protests, children were to enter the mines and mills for another century and a half as younger siblings were dosed with opiates or gin while their mothers worked.

At the end of the section of *Domestic Medicine* that deals with child care (which, with an additional short section on infant diseases, constitutes about 10 percent of the book), Buchan summarizes his advice in 25 rules for parents and nurses. The first three rules deal with feeding. A mother should suckle her own child if possible or, failing that, should get a wet nurse. The next two rules are that a child should be kept clean and not too warm. Eight following rules again deal again with feeding. The parent is warned not to overfeed the child at birth and to use pap rather than wine, sugar or spices. Suckling alone is sufficient for the first three or four months; the child should be weaned gradually and his food kept simple —

---

*In the reign of George III alone (1760-1820), the population of Britain rose from 7.5 million to better than 14 million. It was approximately halfway through this period, 1798, that Malthus penned his *Essay on the Principle of Population* predicting inevitable famine for mankind.

animal and vegetable, not fruits and roots — and the child is to be fed as is necessary: "Children require to eat oftener than adults." Children, Buchan says, must be allowed exercise. The nurses should amuse the child and not let it cry. Care should be taken for "erruptions and looseness" in the child. The child should not be forced to sleep but be permitted to sleep as he pleases. These last two suggestions are apparently aimed at restricting the use of drugs; the next rule carries the same message: no medicine should be administered unless the child is ill.

Of the last five suggestions, four deal with the child in a social sense. He should not be sent "too early to school nor confined to any mechanical employment within doors." Schoolmasters should not keep the child at work continually but should permit breaks for recreation. The best place to raise a child is in the country; in any case, he should get open air. Weak children require special care in their handling. And, last, a "mother should never abandon her child solely to the care of a mercenary nurse."

These suggestions, along with other comments in the text including the statement that "the cold bath does as much mischief as good" and the statement that diseased parents rarely have a healthy child, constitute much of what was known about infant care in the mid-eighteenth century.

Even the middle class was not immune to the temptation to abandon unwanted infants. Infants were sent out to the countryside, to so-called "baby farms" where these matters could be managed more discreetly. When Buchan speaks of a mother "abandon[ing] her child *solely* to the care of a mercenary nurse," he may be referring to this arrangement. As early as Walter Harris's *Acute Diseases of Infants* (1689), this system had been little more than an organized system of infanticide:

"The Rector of a Parish, twelve miles from London. . .told me that his Parish, which was not small either in its bounds or number of inhabitants and was situated in a very wholesome air was, when he first came to it, filled with suckling infants, and yet in the space of one year, that he had buried them all, except two and one of his own. . . and that the same number of infants being soon twice supplied, according to the usual custom of hireling nurses, from the very great and almost inexhaustible City, he had committed them all to their parent earth in the very same year."

Other children (according to the article by William Langer previously quoted) abandoned and assigned to parish workhouses, were handled by similar nurses "who were universally detested and nicknamed 'killing-nurses' or 'she-butchers' because no child ever escaped their care alive."

In his *Essay on the Nursing and Management of Children* (1748), William Cadogan speaks out against nursing-out in similar terms. "The ancient custom of exposing them to wild beasts or drowning them would certainly be a much quicker and more humane method of dispatching them." Nevertheless, such protests had little efficacy as long as the wider social problems of population and poverty remained unsolved.

The foundling hospital movement began with a sea captain, Thomas Coram, who was horrified at the number of babies abandoned "to perish in the streets." With the assistance of a number of well-placed ladies, Coram petitioned the Crown to establish a home for infants and, in 1741, the London Foundling Hospital was opened. It was promptly swamped with so many applicants – women fought at the gates to gain admission for their infants – that the number of admissions had to be sharply curtailed.

Foundling hospitals were subsequently opened in other cities. Even these institutions, were often not much better than the baby farms. The mortality rate fluctuated between 80 and 90 percent, most infants dying in the first few days.

Buchan describes one of these hospitals, a physically lavish establishment – he calls it a "palace" – and says of the treatment offered there:

> "When I took charge of a large branch of the Foundling Hospital in Yorkshire [at Ackworth], I found that the children at nurse had till then been attended by the county apothecaries who, sure of being paid for their drugs, always took care to exhibit them with a very liberal hand. Every cupboard and every shelf in the house was filled with phials and gallipots. Under such treatment, half the children died annually."

By his own account, simply by forbidding the use of drugs (which would have been mostly opiates used for child control), Buchan was able to cut the mortality rate down to one in fifty.

The experience gained in the foundling hospitals served physicians of the eighteenth century well. Buchan in Ackworth, Cadogan in London and George Armstrong in his Dispensary all had the opportunity of observing great numbers of infants under a variety of treatments and conditions, and all three came to similar conclusions about the effects of cold and poverty on infant survival. Armstrong is, in this regard, a heroic figure. He opened and supported his Dispensary for the Infant Poor, the first infant care clinic in England, largely out of his own pocket and with his own labor. His comments on treating children speak to us across the years. When explaining why some doctors dislike treating infant patients, he says, "I know that there are some of the physical tribe who are not fond of practicing among infants. . . . "

"If you ask a boy of three of four what is the matter with him, he will very likely either give you no answer at all or one that you can make nothing out of. If you ask whether his head aches, perhaps he will say, Yes. If he has a pain in his stomach, Yes. And if you ask him twenty such questions, he will probably answer in the affirmative, while, perhaps, he has no pain anywhere. It may possibly be sickness that he takes for pain, not yet knowing the distinction between the two."

Armstrong recommends asking the parents or the nurse in such cases for clues from which the trouble can be deduced.

The labor of supporting the clinic exhausted Armstrong. Approximately fourteen years after it had opened, it closed. But by that time, the need for such a clinic was demonstrated and another soon opened to replace it.

If Buchan, Armstrong and Cadogan can be said to have represented the pragmatic side of what was being learned about infants, Michael Underwood can be claimed as representative of the professional side. Perhaps the most technically brilliant and certainly the most thorough eighteenth-century physician, his work, *A Treatise on the Diseases of Children* (1784 and later editions), reflects the limitations of learning when it is derived from relatively few experiences, no matter how intelligent the observer. While the pragmatists were content to let their observations speak for themselves, Underwood constantly tried to mix evidence with the prevailing medical theories — to the disadvantage of medicine.

Morality constantly enters his descriptions of medical problems, not in the socially specific way of Buchan, but in an abstract, theoretical vision of society:

"I cannot help suspecting that wherever any neglect of parental duties may exist, whether in regard to suckling or superintending the management of their children that does not arise from want of health or some equally warrantable excuse, it can only be charged to the depravity of the age which insensibly corrupts the taste and perverts the judgment of many who wish to do well. And depravity of manners, when once become general, has ever been considered a symptom of falling empire."

This is an echo of Rousseau's "Let mothers nurse their babies, and a general reform of morals will happen naturally;" not surprisingly, Underwood is a great follower of Rousseau. The epigraph of his *Treatise* is from the philosopher: "The mother wants her child to be happy immediately and she is right. If she is wrong, it is in her methods and it is necessary to enlighten her." The true heritage of Rousseau was not the introduction of moral philosophy into child raising; it was his notion that the professional is the person best equipped to tell a mother how to raise her child.

The split between the professionals and the pragmatists was especially pronounced on the subject of cold: "I cannot agree with Dr. Armstrong," Underwood says, "who thinks that the rich lose fewer children than the poor because they are kept warmer."

When Underwood discovered that the French editor of his works had altered his advice on cold bathing, he was outraged:

"Monsr. Le Febure de Villebrune, in his translation of this work into French, has added a chapter upon baths in which he highly extolls the warm-bath and as strangely controverts the idea of the probable good effects of cold bathing, and even makes use of a long chain of arguments against it deduced indeed from an ingenious theory and supported by quotations from the ancients who practiced, however, in a different climate. The shortest and, perhaps, the best reply to this mode of specious reasoning might be given in the mode of Diogenes to Zeno whose arguments against the probability of motion Diogenes laconically refuted by hastily getting up and walking across the school. We have, in like manner, only to point to the numbers of children and young men who have been rendered strong and healthy merely from the prudent use of cold baths and may defy any man to produce the like instances of its opposite effects when made use of with the cautions which every powerful remedy requires."

The cold bath was a moral as much as a physical treatment and medicine was still entangled with philosophy: "It is the province of art to superintend nature and not only to guard over her exercises but so to watch over her as to ensure the accomplishment of her intentions."

Underwood represents the limit of establishment medicine at the turn of the nineteenth century. He was capable of accepting new ideas like Cadogan's infant smock but was unwilling to give up past theories.

The conflict between the pragmatists and the professionals was not simply a conflict over cold baths but over the whole approach to medicine. In the following debate on whether teething was or was not a disease, we can see the lines being drawn. Underwood writes:

"Some writers indeed, and particularly Dr. Cadogan and Dr. Armstrong, seem to think. . . that teething is scarcely to be ranked among the diseases of children. They have imagined that children would cut their teeth with no more danger, if otherwise healthy, than adults who often cut their wise teeth [wisdom teeth]. . . at an advanced age without any difficulty and always without hazard. They likewise observe that many children get their teeth easily. But this argument must suppose the healthiest and best nurtured children to be in all respects in the same circumstance with adults, which is by no means the case as they are liable to fever, dangerous purgings and even convulsions from causes that would in no wise affect the latter. . . . I have therefore no doubt but the time of dentation ought to be ranked amongst the most dangerous to infants, and the greatest attention ought to be paid to it."

In this passage note that the verb Underwood uses to describe Armstrong's and Cadogan's relationship to facts is "observe." The word he applies to their theories (in other words, the word that describes *his* relationship to them) is "argument." A debate was developing between those who investigated facts and those who still affirmed that the route to truth was through rhetorical logic.

Despite the attention physicians and philosophers had finally directed toward child rearing, abuses and neglect of children continued in this period often in the name of morality. The advent of foundling hospitals could scarcely counteract the effects of wholesale abandonment of unwanted babies. Icy baths and overdoses of opiates would be recommended for many more years.

In the absence of scientific theory, religion was yet another influence on child care not to be denied.

CHAPTER 5

The Moral Child

If Rousseau's philosophy of the child was ambivalent (on one hand stressing the child's natural perfection, on the other hand arguing for parental strictness to educate him for society), the Puritan theology admitted no such contradictions. The Protestant vision of the child was clear: unless a child was educated to knowledge of God and virtue, he would be eternally damned for the innate wickedness of his soul.

The Rev. John Robinson wrote of this vision of the child in his essay *On Children and Their Education* (c. 1600):

> "Grace is [not] derived by natural generation but by the supernatural covenant with believers and their seed confirmed in Christ, and by Godly education on the parents' part. . .so where it follows not, usually the negligence and indulgence of the parents, and always the parties proper rebellion is the cause thereof, as we may see both in the Word of God and in daily experience. . . .
>
> "[We sacrifice to devils our sons and daughters] if we either neglect in instructing them, or [in] praying to God for them, or walking exemplary as we ought before them, or correcting them duly, or any other such means as by which the seeds of grace may grow and prosper in them."

In the tradition of the Catholic Church, the child's soul was only briefly in peril. The child was considered to be a heathen — non-Christian without hope of entry into heaven — until baptism, which took place a few days after birth at the latest. In much of Protestant tradition, the emphasis was on the rational choice of salvation, made as a conscious commitment to Christ, which could take place only after a period of indoctrination. Thus, the child could and did, in effect, remain a heathen until his sixth year or later.

The extreme pressure placed on parents to guarantee their children's conformity to the adult standards of religious behavior was reflected in the severity of their discipline. "Children's wills and selfishness," Robinson wrote, must "be restrained and repressed."

"Children should not know, if it could be kept from them, that they have a will of their own. . . [nor] should these words be heard from them, save by way of consent, 'I will' or 'I will not.' And if it be suffered to sway [to their demands] in small and lawful things, they will hardly be restrained in great and ill matters. . . .

"It is much controverted whether it be better in the general to bring up children. . . under the severity of discipline and the rod or no. And the wisdom of the flesh, out of love to its own, alleges many reasons to the contrary. But men say what they will or can — the wisdom of God is best and that saith that 'foolishness is bound up in the heart of the child which the rod of correction must drive out.'. . . And surely there is in all children, though not alike a stubborness and stoutness of mind arising from natural pride which must, in the first place, be broken and beaten down that so the foundation of education being laid in humility and tractableness, other virtues may, in their time, be built thereon."

As wealth and worldly success were seen as manifestations of God's grace and favor under Protestantism, the well-brought-up religious child was another indication of parental virtue. A sinful child could be seen as one index of the parents' lack of virtue.

A parent who could be condemned for the sins of his offspring necessarily had an ambivalent attitude towards his or her child. While that did not make children "to be no blessings or to be lightly esteemed," Robinson wrote, "yet should they [the spiritual dangers] moderate our desire of them [i.e. desire to have them] and our grief for their want [i.e. for lack of them] ."

"One or two [children] proving wicked will break our tender hearts more than all the rest will comfort us. . . . as in the natural body there is more grief in the aching of [one] tooth than comfort and ease in the good sound state of all the rest. . . . "

"After coming into the world through so many dangers, they [children] come even into a world of danger. In their infancy, how soon is the tender bud nipped or bruised by sickness or otherwise! In their venturesome days, into how many dangers do they throw themselves in which many perish, besides those into which God brings them, and that all life long! Above all others, how great and many are the spiritual dangers both for nourishing and increasing the corruption which they bring forth into the world with them and for diverting them from all the goodness which God's grace and man's endeavours might work in them!"

In such a world of peril, there was little room for love. Robinson's comments are particularly astute when it comes to eliminating one of the hazards to strict upbringing: the grandparents.

"Love rather descends than ascends: as streams of water do. . . . Hence also is it that grandfathers are more affectionate towards their children's children than to their immediates, as seeing themselves further propagated in them, and by this means proceding on to a further degree of eternity, which all desire naturally if not in themselves yet in their posterity. And hence it is that children brought up with their grandfathers and grandmothers seldom do well but are usually corrupted by their too great indulgence."

Even with its hostility towards affection, what we can sense in this passage is a greater awareness of the complexity of the relationship of parents to children. It leads towards the beginning of a new understanding of child psychology.

"Many bodily diseases are hereditary; and so are many spiritual. . . .

"The child ofttimes, by feeling the evil of his father's sin, is driven. . . into the contrary evil. Thus a covetous father often makes a prodigal son; so doth a prodigal a covetous."

If these comparatively humanistic observations are part of Puritan thinking, the underlying philosophy of the child as a heathen might be interpreted as a view of the child as inately evil. Some of the more unpleasant consequences of this view may be observed in a pamphlet published in London in 1709, John Banks's sermon entitled *A Rebuke to Unfaithful Parents and a Rod for Stubborn Children*. By "unfaithful," Banks means lacking Christian faith.

"The Fear of the Lord is the Beginning of Wisdom, and a good understanding have all they that do thereafter, not only in things appertaining to this life, but in those which concern that which is to come. . . And therefore stand in awe of him as trueborn Children who have known weeping and Godly sorrow. For they that will not endure the Chastisements of God, in this wise, by his Rod are Bastards and no Sons: for every Son whom he loveth, he chastiseth. . . .

"They that have learned Fear of the Lord and how to perform their Duty to Him in order to walk in the Way of Truth and Righteousness, they are also taught by the Light and Grace of the Lord Jesus Christ and guided by His wisdom how to teach and train up their Children in the Way of Truth and Righteousness, as those will find that begin and use care and diligence in so instructing them while they are yet in their young and tender years. . . .

"For anyone to say to his Child (as I have observed), *Go boy and do so and so*, and the Child to answer *I will not* again and again yet no correction offered: Whether this tends to learn Children due subjection to their parents, I leave you to judge. . . .

"Are not such Parents as these void of a good and right understanding? . . . The Rod of God is for their backs who (through a foolish pity) are ready to say: *I cannot find it in my heart to whip my child*. What! hast thou not a heart and mind to do thy Child good?"

If you "neglect of making use of the rod in time," Banks says, you will weep when they grow "wild and wicked." But what was *in time?*

"As soon as you perceive they understand what offence they are corrected for, and in [like] measure know what they should not and what they should say and do, and how they should be good and not evil."

In this respect, John Banks appears to differ from the often quoted account of child raising given by one of his contemporaries, Susannah Wesley, the mother of John Wesley, founder of Methodism. Susannah was prepared to start discipline even before children could reasonably be expected to understand their acts. "When turned a year old (and some before), they were taught to fear the rod." As a consequence, "the most odious noise of the crying of children was rarely heard in the house, but the family usually lived in as much quietness as if there had not been a child among them."

We may reasonably wonder, reading Banks or Wesley, if parents were as severe with their children as these texts would indicate. Banks comments:

"Some are ready to make an apology to excuse themselves from correcting their children, saying there is a great difference in the nature of children. That is true, so there is of parents also. . . . Some will be more gained upon by words fitly spoken in the fear and wisdom of God than others will be by corrections."

He advises against disciplining children in anger (some parents "provoke their children to wrath because they correct them in their passion"), though it has rarely been easy for a parent to discipline a child when the heat of the moment has passed.

By the mid-eighteenth century, the start of the Industrial Revolution had made some of the Protestant merchants, who were fearful of losing their purchase on salvation, wealthy. In a time of prosperity and social change, there was less reason to endorse the harsh practices that had seemed so appropriate when Puritanism was struggling for survival.

One writer who reflected the change was James Nelson. It was wholly appropriate that this man was not a minister but an apothecary, that is, a man of science. His book *An Essay on the Government of Children* (1753) was one of the most popular guides to child care of its time and is one of the first comprehensive works, giving equal weight to the child's physical and moral needs. Even before Rousseau's *Emile* (but not before his *Discourse on the Arts and Sciences*, 1750, where the idea of the noble savage first appears), Nelson asserted that nature is "our best, our surest guide" in the handling of children, propounding the virtues of hard beds and advocating cold baths, the colder the better.

Yet Nelson was not extreme. While he approved of "inuring" children to cold in principle and agreed with Locke on the virtues of light clothing, he admits that he "cannot help being of [the] opinion that it ought not to be begun with [but should be arrived at] by degrees."

"It is easy for my readers to see that I am an advocate of warmth and that I not only recommend it as yielding great comfort to infants but esteem it highly necessary and useful to them."

It is, however, in the area of moral government that Nelson is most provocative and it is on this subject that he concentrates most of his efforts.

On Children: Children vary but "children, while young, may be compared with machines which are or should be set in motion or stopped at the will of others."

On Child Control: "Love and fear are the two great springs of human action."

On Good Upbringing: Good upbringing "implies such a government of our children as tends to regulate their conduct by making their actions what they ought to be."

On the Necessity for Authority: "The basis for government is authority. . . . Cities, armies and kingdoms are all sustained by it and so too must private families be. By authority, I do not mean that stern brow, that trembling awful distance... that favors more of the tyrant than of the parent. No, I mean a rational yet absolute exercise of the degree of power necessary for the regulating of the actions and dispositions of children till they become wise enough to govern themselves."

The string of images underlying the last paragraph does more than describe parent-child relations; it offers us a picture of the industrial revolution brought home. Images of authority are images of the state, cities, armies, and kingdoms. Yet when power is put into effect, the vocabulary is that of the engineer. The father runs his "machine" child, "regulating" the "degree of power" efficiently, using neither more nor less than is necessary, until the child achieves that final aim of engineering and becomes automatic, self-regulating. The images of power still belong to the state but the reality of power is in the hands of the engineer.

The obsession with authority is also an omen of the future. In a medieval family where the father could kill a willful child and be within his rights, the subject of authority was not generally raised except, as Metlinger did, to reprimand its excesses. As the parents of the Industrial Revolution were cut off from their roots and as society made claims on their children, restricting parental rights over them, authority became a problem. The parent, feeling himself lost and powerless, increasingly attempted to assert his vanished authority over his children. By Victorian times, the loss of authority was more than a problem, it was an obsession.

Nelson reflects this increasing intrusion of the state into family life in a paragraph on how long it takes to produce the self-governing child. Some children, he says, can achieve the necessary knowledge at fifteen, some at twenty and some at thirty. "There is but one way of ascertaining the length of time our authority should be exercised in its full force [and that is] settled by the laws of our Kingdom, viz: till the age of twenty-one."

On Punishment: "Severe and frequent whipping is, I think, a very bad practice; it inflames the skin and puts the blood into ferment and there is besides a meanness, a degree of ignominy attending it which makes it very unbecoming. Still there may be occasions that will render it necessary, but I earnestly advise that milder methods be first tried."

Nelson, however, did recommend punishment before children had reached the age of speech or reason, arguing that the first principle of human nature is self-love. "Reason, the second principle, opens only by degrees."

Moral education, at this point, had transcended its religious roots and was based on a mythology of nature in the service of society. Child raising had become a science.

*   *   *

By the turn of the nineteenth century child-care literature was still religious in tone but its moral force had been diluted. One work, *The Importance of Domestic Discipline* (1807) by Daniel Tyreman, reflects this change. The framework is traditional morality, according to which "pampered children grow profane and prodigal and bring destruction upon themselves and their sinful parents." Yet when the author details methods of carrying out discipline, severity is lacking.

"Parents should indeed first rule by authority, and convince their children that they will be obeyed. But children may be reasoned with much sooner than most parents suppose; and therefore this mean[s] ought to be next used. Even a child of four years of age, feels its native prerogatives and resists the hand that would force it into motion like an insensible machine. We naturally revolt from oppression, and as naturally wish to know why we are to do this, and not to do that. Reason with your young charge as soon as it can understand your language, and you will most generally succeed. Point out the evil of the action you are condemning, place it in various lights till you see that it is felt, then a remorse will follow which the keenest pains occasioned by the rod will never produce. – A pious friend of mine has four sons. Like other children, they often do wrong. The father used to employ the rod, but a better acquaintance with human nature, taught him to lay it aside, and to adopt other measures infinitely more effectual. The little offender is called into his father's closet, and the door is shut so that no one may overhear what is said; for we naturally resist reproof that is given before others, and feel a propensity to justify ourselves. The pious father begins to inquire the reason of his conduct, in order that he may show that circumstances were not sufficient to justify the crime. He then informs him how sinful the action is in the sight of God; when he has silenced the young offender, he falls down upon his knees, and makes his son do the same; and there he confesses the sin before the all-seeing God, and implores mercy for his son, and weeps over him, till his heart begins to relent, and he bursts into tears also, and feels his crime most acutely. — This method is most effectual. It secures the two grand aims at which parents ought always to aim, I mean, filial fear, and filial love. Many parents are dreaded, but not loved. But it is difficult to say whether my friend is more feared or venerated — for their love rises to a sort of veneration. Such a mode of treatment suits all dispositions. This will awe the most inflexible mind, and affect the tenderest. 'Go ye and do likewise.'"

Tyerman senses the end of authority over children. He notes:

"Schoolboys, when they see falsehood [bonded] to power and force, they think themselves released from the compact of truth with their masters. . . . Thus schoolboys hold no faith with their schoolmasters, though they would not think it to be dishonourable amongst one another. . . . We do not think that these maxims are the peculiar growth of schools; in private families the same feelings are to be found under the same species of culture; if preceptors or parents are unjust or tyrannical, their pupils will contrive to conceal from them their actions and their thoughts."

The child is not to be punished unjustly. In a sense, law has entered the family, and the adult and the child are equal and mutually involved in a social contract in which each has obligations to the other. Puritan parents, by contrast, had a contract with God to bring up moral children according to immutable law.

If parent and child are equal, it is more the result of reducing the status of the parent than of elevating the child. From this point it is only a small step to the modern idea of parents and children as pals.

Thoughts on Education by "A Parent" (Melesina Trench) published a few years later (181-) shows us clearly the place religion had in the life of middle-class women at that time. It is the period of Jane Austin, and the author's style is not unlike that of the parson's daughter:

"The first object of Education is to train up an immortal soul.

"The second — but second at an immeasurable distance — is to do this in the manner most conducive to earthly happiness; never sacrificing either the interests of the future world to those of the present, or the welfare of the man to the inclinations of the child, errors not dissimilar in complexion, though so awfully different in the importance of their results.

"This simple position seems so evident as to require neither repetition nor enforcement; yet experience proves how little it is acted upon in Education; and among those who do act upon it, how many discover a strange species of false shame in confessing their motive.

"When *Mrs. K.* boasted to *Miss M.* in a confidential moment of her daughter's accomplishments, the latter, a sincere and high-minded woman, seeing how exclusively the embellishments of life had superceded all else in her friend's estimation, ventured to hint that the great object of Education was paramount to these.

"*Mrs. K.* 'Oh, yes, I know what you mean, the great object is her making a good marriage.'

"*Miss M.* "Not exactly. So many unmarried women are eminently useful in walks where wives and mothers can seldom tread; and the balance of happiness so equal that I cannot feel very anxious to ensure the marriage of my young friends.'

"*Mrs. K.* 'How stupid I am! You mean by the great object, living in the best company.'

"*Miss M.* shook her head.

"*Mrs. K.* 'Oh then, you mean the power of amusing yourself at home.'

"In short, when *Miss M.* explained, by hinting somewhat of her religious instruction — that Education of the heart which prepares for a higher existence — she was listened to with evident ennui; and a certain degree of restlessness in her fair auditor showed the desire of terminating a conversation derogatory to *Miss M's* understanding."

This is the status of religion among the class that patronizes child-raising books, ennui. Mrs. Trench goes even further in making the situation explicit: "Any person who ventures, except in the pulpit, to speak with the openness of *Miss M.* is considered (unless mildly set aside as a Methodist) as either half fool — or, an untutored *Parson Adam*-ish sort of person, regardless or ignorant of the common usages of life."

Mrs. Trench goes well beyond simply remarking on the absence of religion in the education and interests of her contemporaries. She gives advice on how to reincorporate religion into the life of children. In her advice on these matters she is a shrewd observer. The advantage of religion in her eyes is pragmatic. Religious education "simplifies the apparently complicated task of education. . . . An affectionate mother [who heeds the Gospel]. . .would be in no danger of following those rash philosophers who advise us to trust implicitly to Nature. On the contrary, she would vigilantly eradicate those vices to which she knows our nature is prone, though some of them may shoot up in the most brilliant and beautiful colors, for the graces of infancy reflect a charm on its very faults."

Melesina Trench forms a bridge between the earlier religious writers on morality and the Victorians. Her concern is religion and her advice is scaled down from pulpit pronouncements to the tranquil domesticity of a middle-class home. "Parents spoil the child, she says, by their own "self-indulgence."

"In the great preparatory school called human life, we are continually required to practice the virtues of patience and self denial. From the dawn of observation, in our very cradles, the temper may equally be spoiled by neglect—severity—or a timid, slavish indulgence. The real wants of an infant should be supplied the moment they are known. To supply them before they are announced by tears and cries will often wholly prevent those whimpering and noisy habits so injurious to children and so distressing to their parents. . . .

"An infant should ever be addressed with mild cheerfulness and treated with that uniform kindness of which it appears conscious. . . . [If we deny them something, our denials should be] good humored, prompt and decisive. We ought not excite false hopes or create suspense. We ought not to associate the idea of our displeasure with that of privation. But 'let your No,' says Rousseau, 'be as a wall of brass, which the child with all his endeavours shall not be able to shake.'"

Rousseau's influence continued to be felt in the early years of the nineteenth century, though no longer as dogma. As Mrs. Trench suggests (when warning us against those "rash philosophers who advise us to trust implicitly to Nature"), Rousseau had become simply one among many sources of advice.

Thoughts on Education goes considerably beyond moral instruction and offers advice in a number of areas, ranging from "humanity to animals" and manners to teaching children courage (courage, Trench says, is natural, but cowardice is acquired). The author is not of the opinion that all children are blank slates for the parents to write on.

"Difference of temper. . . is observable in a few days after our birth. While nature is so various, an unbending systematic education will too often prove no better than a bed of Procrustes. . . .

"The education of the heart must begin in the cradle. . . . Much depends on the choice of a nurse or the conduct of those mothers who, when it is possible, undertake that endearing office. One of a serene temper is preferable to those noisy, laughter-loving, loquacious dames so often applauded by parents for their high spirits."

Mrs. Trench is opposed to physical punishment. The population has been educated "these thirty years" without the use of a rod or cane, these are "reserved for the sons of the nobility or gentry." She is equally against shaming children for their errors.

On good health, she says:

"The physical habits most favorable to firmness of mind and body are well known. Healthful exercises, open air, cold bathing – plain diet – a country education – and youthful companions – all contribute their share to the attainment of these valuable qualities."

Melesina Trench's work is not only prophetic of the modes of child raising that were to become common in the Victorian era, but is also one of the earliest books on child care written by a woman. The influence of women in this area was to become substantial, and the reasons are already plain in this early work. Unlike physicians, who derived their theories from intermittent contact with sick children, women had the day-to-day opportunity to observe – and observe sympathetically – the natural process of growth in their offspring. Books written by women rarely included the ill-founded or unfounded theories proposed by Rousseau and some physicians. Mothers were not in a position to give advice and then depart before its consequences were felt.

Long after the moral severities of the Protestant Reformation had diminished into the quiet, moderate form propounded by Melesina Trench, the central heritage of Protestantism remained. In the simplest sense it is reflected in our belief that the role of the parent is to educate the child and in our feeling that the parent is responsible for what the child becomes.

CHAPTER 6

The American Child

"Now God hath seen good to call the line of election so as that it doth (though not wholly and only, yet) for the most part run through the loins of Godly parents. There are, it is true, elect children who are not born of elect parents, but they are few (if any) elect parents without elect children. . . .

"Parents be exemplary. Walk before God in your houses with a perfect heart. Let us be careful in our families to walk so that our children may see by our examples how they ought to walk and please God. That if they will but be and do like unto their parents, they shall certainly be blessed forever. . . . If your children see you holy and faithful to the interest of God and of Jesus Christ and every way exemplary, doubt not of it but in God's time they shall receive of your spirit."

Prayer for the Rising Generation (1684), written by the New England theologian Increase Mather, (1639-1723), father of the famed preacher Cotton Mather, marks a new note in the relationship of parent to child. The child is no longer the simple heathen or wicked being. He may, in fact, be "elect" when his parents are not. If the child is wicked, it is largely his parents' fault. "There is nothing more fatally destructive and ruining to the souls of children," the elder Mather says, "than a bad example in parents, especially if they be such as pretend to religion."

The child has become a reason for the parents to perfect themselves. In some cases, the parents apparently preferred to perfect their children *instead* of confronting their own sins:

66

"There are great complaints (and too great cause) concerning the rising generation in New England, whereas the fault is very much in parents in that they are no more exemplary. Your children take notice of your pride, your sensuality, your worldliness, your unmortified passions, and that doth woefully scandalize and harden them against the blessed ways of Christ. . . .

"Men should not think with themselves (as some do) if their children do belong to God, then He will convert them [the parents] whether they pray for it or no, but should be therefore stirred up to the more fervency in cries to heaven for the blessing promised."

The blessed child who provides an example to his parents is an image with deep roots in the American experience. In the new world, there was a need to keep every child alive. Colonial success depended on an increasing labor force. The American family, consequently, has been child-centered to a degree that would have seemed remarkable in Europe.

Child-centered did not mean that the lives of children in New England were pleasant. Religion played a harshly restrictive role in their care, even before birth. In one pamphlet by John Oliver of London, *A Present for Teeming American Women*, published in Boston in 1699, the author addressed the "big-bellied women" of the New World in these terms:

"[In lying in it] is common [to] get linen and other necessaries for the child; a nurse, midwife, entertainment for the women who are called to labor, a warm convenient chamber, &c. . . But all these may prove miserable comforters, they may perchance need no other linen shortly but a winding sheet and have no other chamber but a grave, no neighbors but worms. . .[if] they are delivered. . . with God's curse [and] not with His blessing."

Increase Mather's son, Cotton Mather, developed this same theme more explicitly in his *Elizabeth in Her Holy Retirement* [1710] :

"It is a child of God that you have now within you. What a consolation [for your pain] ! It is a member of His mystical body which is now shaping in secret and curiously to be wrought.

"Sobriety must accompany this holiness. Indeed the unborn infant will be naturally and powerfully and profitably affected by the sobriety of a holy mother. The passions or the surfeits of the mother make a strange impression on the infant: yea, on the soul of it. Be temperate in all things. Keep your mind in all the undiluted serenity that is possible. In your meats, drinks, rest, use enough, but nothing too much. This temperance will dispose you to wait upon God in a due frame for His favors and your offspring will enjoy the good effects of it."

This is sound medical advice, which is not surprising since Mather had an interest in medicine and had been one of the first to endorse smallpox inoculation.* Nevertheless, he emphasized not the child's body but his soul.

Children were raised on religious catechisms and pious verse, such as this from Benjamin Bass's *Parents and Children* (1730):

> "If I BELIEVE in JESUS CHRIST
> Then I shall be forever blessed;
> But if I flight that Savior kind
> My misery will never end."

Children were treated to sermons. *A Child of Light Singing in the Valley of Death* (1726) from Cotton Mather is presented below with original punctuation and emphasis:

> "Oh ye, *Lambs of the Flock*, you are once more, with all possible solemnity, now called upon. *Come, ye Children, Hearken to me! The Shepherd of Souls*, is waiting to hear the Bleats of your *young Souls*; Longing to hear such a petition as that; *Let thy tender Mercies come unto me, That* I *may live!* Be aware of this; as young as you are, you are in the *Valley of the Shadow of Death*. Yea, while you are lambs of the flock you may be called forth unto the *Slaughter. Death* takes not people according to their seniority. Though the *Old* are *Half Dead*, yet the *Youngest* of you may *Dy* [sic] before the *Oldest*; and they that have *Marrow moistening of their Bones*, may be laid in Ashes, as soon as those whose furrowed Face and shaking hand may show them *Decaying, and waxing old, and ready to vanish away.* Oh! 'Tis time, 'tis time, that you be sure of the *Good Shepherd*."

"Children," Mather exhorts, "the thing demanded of you is this: that you give yourselves up to your Saviour as unto your shepherd. . . [and] that all the rest of your life be a course of obedience to him."

In early American history, there are few texts that deal with the purely secular side of child raising. *Health, a Poem* written by the English

---

*This was not cowpox vaccination, discovered by Edward Jenner (1798), but inoculation with the smallpox virus itself, a hazardous operation.

physician Edward Baynard in 1719 (revised several times) was reprinted in Boston in 1724. Only a portion of the poem deals with child care, but the work is interesting for its attempt to convert the theories of Locke's *Some Thoughts Concerning Education* (1693) into verse. "Let reason guide you," Baynard writes, "let all the passions of the body be subject to her [control]."

> "She checks all rashness and gives time
> To think and rethink each design.
> Those that do this before they act
> 'Tis rarely seen repent the fact.
> This makes an easy, quiet mind
> (The greatest blessing of mankind)
> And he that in this bliss does share
> Enjoys a ray of heaven here.

> "Fly all excesses, first take care
> Of wine and women to beware.
> Sport, dally, tattle with 'em rarely
> And marry not a wife too early.
> Stay till you've grown and joints are knit
> And you have reason got and wit."

Baynards's advice may be traced to Locke's statement, "It seems plain to me that the principle of all virtue and excellency lies in a power of denying ourselves the satisfaction of our own desires where reason does not authorize them."

Baynard paraphrases Locke's enthusiasm for a natural diet: "New milk and rice, bread, corn and roots, / Fresh sallets [salads] and fresh gathered fruits, / Sweet butter, oil and well-made cheese" and warns against spiced meats. He also advocates cold baths and supports another of Locke's notions:

> "Sometimes let your feet get wet
> But in your wet shoes never sit."

His comments on infant care are brief. He advises against bedding "youth" with "aged bones" or the "fat." The aged "suck" the youth out of the child. The overweight:

> " . . . sweat and overheat the child

>By which a good cool habit's spoiled
>For in a moderate temperature
>The welfare of the child secure.
>In short, observe, the tender young
>Should be well-nursed but laid alone."

Although Baynard's statements on physical care are scanty, his comments on child psychology are astute:

>"But above all, take special care
>How children you afright and fear
>In telling stories of things seen:
>Sprite, Demon and Hobgoblin.
>Hence they'll contract such cowardice
>As ne'er will leave them all their lives
>And then the ideas of their fears
>Continued into riper years
>Can by no reason be suppressed
>But of it they'll be so possessed
>They'll swear and quake, and start and stare
>And meet the Devil everywhere."

Baynard discusses exercising ("swimming's best" [and] "next to swimming, riding's good") and avoiding cold drafts ("A crack or crevice in the wall / Hurts more than doth an open hall.") and argues at length against alcohol. In an appendix to the poem, he offers a satirical view of doctors and of their reliance on opium as a cure-all:

>"Opium, alas. . .
>May lull a disease
>By a seeming false peace
>Yet these physic allies
>Use such fallacies
>And fail us so common
>We can't depend on 'em.
>So, as to a cure,
>There's none to be sure.
>Those other specifics [drugs]
>Have no valid effects
>But the getting of fees
>For a promise of ease
>(Much like the South S——)."

The last line is a reference to the South Sea Bubble (1720), one of the first stock manipulation scandals.

Samuel Phillips's *Advice to a Child* (1729) was fundamentally an attack on the sins of youth. Phillips is unique in his scrupulous detailing of all of the vices to which young people are prone. His book, in fact, is as organized as a sociology text and begins with the following outline of his major points:

> "I.   It is the wicked practice of some young people to entice others to sin.
>
> II. It greatly concerns young people to see to it that when they are enticed to sin they don't consent.
>
> 1. What are the sins which young people most commonly entice one another to sin?
>
> 2. What inclines some young persons to entice others to sin?
>
> 3. How, in what manner, or by what methods do young people entice one another to sin?
>
> 4. What arguments do they make use of?
>
> 5. When, at what times, do they more especially entice one another to sin?
>
> 6. How does this appear to be a wicked practice?"

The picture painted by Phillips's descriptions of the sins of youth is more realistic than anything rendered in the sermons. On "the sins which young people most commonly entice one another to the commission," he first names the sins of "tippling and frolicking:"

> "There are, alas for it!, some younger as well as elder persons who thirst after strong drink and will leave their honest calling and spend hours together at the tavern. Now such persons are very *fond of company* and will sometimes take no small pains so to prevail with some others to go with them, or to tarry still longer, if they find 'em at the *house* just now mentioned. And this meeting and drinking together is sometimes attended or followed with mad *frolicking*, such as excessive vain laughter and that accompanied with antic behavior. And this is not always confined within the walls of said house, but oftentimes appears abroad. Yea, it is sometimes discovered by giving reins to their horses after they are mounted as well as to their tongues, *both* of which it would well become 'em to *bridle*. And the truth is the *Club* sometimes breaks up in a quarrel; becoming inflamed with drink, they forget their late friendship and because of some little affront which, at another time would not, perhaps, be resented, they

seek to vilify, reproach, abuse, yea, would be glad to destroy one another. . . .

"Idleness alone is a sin very provoking unto God. . . moreover, idleness is a *leading* sin; such as are idle are seldom, if ever, only idle; and to be sure this is true with respect to such persons who waste away their time over their cups, for these misspend their *money* as well as their time. . . .

"I may add that where immoderate drinking prevails, there oftentimes gaming and laying wagers takes place. These persons because they can't endure to labor with their hands are very fond of getting money easily and quickly. . . .

"And I shall take this opportunity to make mention of *another* bad custom which prevails especially with such people whether elder or younger who love to frequent taverns, and that is of *swapping horses* or *other creatures.* . . . Observe, I don't say that it is *absolutely* unlawful for people to make an exchange of horses or other creatures; it may sometimes be a great kindness to both parties; but I say for any to make a trade and business of it, and spend their time in riding about and visiting taverns on purpose to tempt people to trade and traffic with them, designing all the while to overreach them in the bargain and rather than fail to speak falsely in the matter. . .what can such traders expect but to be held in contempt and distaste among men?"

On the subject of "fornication" and "uncleanness," Phillips comments that "It is the manner of many young people to *entice* others to these sins. . . . It is too evident by the *fruit* that this has been much practiced."

On the sin of theft, Phillips comments that young people "sometimes prompt one another to knavish methods in their dealings, and to cozen people under a show of honesty. . . . Some of them have learned to cheat betimes and are very free to communicate their hellish skill to some few at least of their intimate acquaintances that they may follow the same course."

He details at length other sins including lying, cursing, profanity, profane merriment, disobedience to parents and elders, insulting ("put[ting] a slight on") their elders, extravagance in attire and the penchant to embrace erroneous principles and pursue strange beliefs.

They lure each other by "a smile accompanied with a nod, a becking [beckoning] with the hand, a touch of the foot. . . whisper" and other secretive signals. They meet "when they have a convenient opportunity because no eye seeth them," including in the evenings and even after Sunday "lecture."

*   *   *

As early as 1643, when New Amsterdam was less than twenty years old and had less than five hundred people, Saint Isaac Jogues noted that a score of nationalities were represented and eighteen different languages could be heard in the streets. A multilingual town is, in all but size, a city with the characteristic urban toleration of differences and appreciation of liberty. Parents enjoyed drinking, dancing and social gatherings of a non-religious and nonpolitical nature. The children were permitted games, and there was ice skating on the Broad Street canal.

Further south, in Pennsylvania, William Penn and the Quakers were also tolerant of individual liberties. By the mid-eighteenth century, Philadelphia had become a center of scholarship to rival Boston, particularly with regard to medicine. It was there in 1772 that the American edition of William Buchan's *Domestic Medicine* was published and went through several editions, the contents largely unchanged from the English original discussed earlier (Pages 45-50).

Promptly after the American Revolution a new work on child care appeared that reflected the fresh spirit of independence. Enos Hitchcock's *Memoirs of the Bloomsgrove Family* (1790), the story of an imaginary exemplary family, was written in two volumes, the first dealing primarily · with physical care, the second with moral guidance.

After the manner of European books dedicated to royalty, Hitchcock dedicated the book to Martha Washington: "Permit me, Madame, to felicitate you on your elevation to the rank which you hold in this rising empire, and to assure you that, with your illustrious consort, you bear an unrivaled sway in the hearts of a grateful country." Hitchcock's volumes are one of the first child-care books written specifically for women, emphasizing "the Dignity and Importance of the Female Character."

A minister, Hitchcock was concerned with moral guidance, but his approach was in the Deist mold of the Founding Fathers rather than in the Puritan tradition. The primary authorities for his beliefs on child care were Locke and Rousseau with their interest in the child as a creature of nature. Locke's emphasis on self-control particularly influenced Hitchcock.

"It was the maxim of these worthy parents [Mr. and Mrs. Bloomsgrove] that in every stage of domestic education children should be disciplined to restrain their appetites and desires. They thought, therefore, that they could not begin too early to check the desire which children have for gewgaws and toys and to accustom them to restraint and self-command. . . .

"In a world like this and with passions like ours, what can be more useful and necessary than the power of restraining our appetites? The objects of sense which surround us on every side are suited to awaken desire and desire pushes us on to gratification; but this cannot always be attained. The preservation of health and of tranquility often forbid it. . . . To acquire an early habit of restraint must, therefore, be useful to us as long as we are conversant with those objects.

"This command over ourselves will become easy by custom; and it will not be difficult to graft in on children where proper authority has been maintained. Parents are the natural guardians of their children and their reason should be employed to control, restrain and direct the appetite of childhood."

The authority of parents over children was not to be employed capriciously. "To cross children in things perfectly indifferent has the appearance of capriciousness, and tend[s] to sour their minds." Restraints must be reasonable not only in terms of the parents' demands but also in terms of each child.

"In laying restraints. . .some regard must be had to the particular constitution of childhood. Those of feeble or slender make require more indulgence in their food, exercise and in the punishments which are found necessary than those of a firm, robust habit of body. Many a fine child has been ruined by imprudent management."

Hitchcock realistically suggests that parents cannot reasonably expect themselves to be perfect. He emphasizes not the ideal of child care but its real problems:

"Every man to whom the care of children is committed is not a Rousseau nor is every child an Emilius or Sophia [Rousseau's ideal children] ; neither are we aerial beings that we should subsist on sentimental diet: application of labor, or some kind of employment is *necessary* for most people and proper for all. It is humiliating, I confess, that we are obliged to spend so great a part of [our] time in procuring the means of supplying the perpetual wants of a body we must soon throw away, but, degrading as it may seem, it is unavoidable, and it is the more necessary as the organs of the corruptible mass are the only vehicles of the intelligence within. . . .

"We must take children as they are, induced with a variety of humors, dispositions and propensities, and endeavour to make them what we wish them to be, consider the circumstances which actually surround them and not figure to ourselves an imaginary situation in which we might suppose education could be carried out to advantage. Fine-spun theories may amuse the vivid imagination, but it is practice only that makes perfect."

Memoirs of the Bloomsgrove Family, is written like an early novel, as a series of letters in which the imaginary Bloomsgroves raise their ideal children, Osander and Rosella. The children are allowed the cold air and wet feet advocated by Locke as a method of strengthening them. The natural child has come to America.

"Cleanliness, air and exercise, she [Mrs. Bloomsgrove] considered as the stamina of health and therefore let them play in the open air. She was less fearful of cold than of heat and had them temperately clad both summer and winter; by varying their dress but little with the seasons she preserved a regular temperament of the body. This idea she probably received from Mr. Locke. . . .

"Little Rosella is suffered to wet her feet while at play on the green in the back yard where runs a murmuring rill conducted from a distant fountain. The rose and the lily bloom on their cheeks while they slide on the ice which this little current affords in winter till their feet become wet with the snow which melts upon them. The tender mother is pained at the sight. She has almost forgotten the period of such amusements and shivers with the cold she thinks they endure. She is about to call them in, but they play on the snow and ice without appearing to have the sensation of cold. Their own feelings, said Mrs. Bloomsgrove, are the best standard for them; why should I call them in on account of the cold since they seem not to perceive it?"

Learning from nature is a continuing theme in the *Memoirs*. Rosella tumbles into a freezing brook and is discovered to be cured of some minor complaint. Mrs. Bloomsgrove is promptly seized by a vision of the benefits of cold bathing.

Locke's belief in a natural diet is also adapted to Hitchcock's book:

"Food should be plain, nutritive and in plenty, and. . .the interval between meals should not be distant or formal with children, whose whole constitution digests rapidly. . . .

"Osander ate little else than bread, milk, roots and vegetables until nearly five years old. He was not confined to set meals but ate when he was hungry and drank when he was dry, unless those appetites appeared to be the effect of caprice or were excited by seeing others eat, for children are imitative beings. In that case he is tried with a piece of dry bread or fair water; if the appetite is not strong enough for these, it is a false one."

At the age of five, Osander was permitted to sit at the table, but he was rarely given meat until he had reached six or seven.

Emphasis on moral education began in infancy. We can substitute a more modern term, socialization, for the older term, education, which Hitchcock uses.

"The success of education depends on the steps which are taken in the early stages of life. . . . The foundation of it is laid at the breast: there the future temper and disposition commences. . . .

"In America, there are comparatively few mothers so unnatural as, of choice, to put their children out to nurse. Some, indeed, there are who do this from a love of ease or of fancied superiority to the drudgery of giving sustenance to their helpless offspring to whom they have given existence. It should be considered that the obligations between parent and child are reciprocal and if neglected by the former, it can hardly be expected that they will be fulfilled by the latter. If the voice of nature is not strengthened by habit and cultivation, it will be silenced in its infancy and the heart will perish, if I may so express myself, before it is born."

"In the first seven years of life," Hitchcock notes, "we gain more knowledge than in the same term during any other part of life." Children should be taught by their parents' example.

"Children should be taught to submit to necessity, that is, to bear any unavoidable pain with patience. . . . Happy it would be for children if their parents were more generally possessed of this quality. Precept would then have its influence and more powerful example would not fail to persuade."

Fear was not to be used to curb a child's behavior, and frightening them with ghost and hobgoblin stories was to be avoided. If the children were afraid of something, their fears were to be taken seriously.

"Whatever objects affright them, unless they are such as should warn them of real dangers, she [Mrs. Bloomsgrove] reconciles them to by rendering them familiar: this is done by degrees with a great deal of management and with an air of pleasantry. . . ."

The proper method of education was reward and punishment with corporal punishment reserved for rare cases of obstinacy:

> "[When] Osander violates his word, his papa expresses as much surprise as indignation, and tells him, 'If you were not quite young, such an action would be very disgraceful, and if you should do the like again, you would render yourself contemptible in the eyes of everyone.' . . .
>
> "Children who are taught to be frank and candid, if they find they can always be so without danger, never think of dissembling but when they are conscious of having done wrong; and then, if they can find as much security and more comfort in confessing than in dissembling, they will be candid and honest. . . .
>
> "There is a meanness which sometimes appears in children that does not belong to nature; it is either caught from example or inspired by injudicious management. This is sometimes the effect of too great severity [so that] their spirits [are] broken by too great restraint and they become sheepish. In others, it may arise from having the views crossed and the pursuits checked where there has been an unconquerable thirst for some particular object. From whatever cause, the effect is most unhappy. It damps the noble ardor of mind which is a spring of worthy actions and should be cherished with great care."

Hitchcock's time, aptly named the Age of Reason by Thomas Paine, had a great faith in the possibilities and liberating power of rational thought and discussion. Reason was the force lifting men not only from their own superstitions but also from the past erroneous and brutal methods of child care.

Hitchcock's view of the rigid authoritian family of the past may be contrasted with that offered by James Nelson. While the English writer had argued that "the basis for government is authority. . . . Cities, armies and kingdoms are all sustained by it and so too must private families be," Hitchcock's image of authority is post-revolutionary: "It is with families as it is with states: they have been too busy with laws and too remiss in education. They contrive methods to punish, not to prevent crimes."

Education is the keynote of Hitchcock work. With the mastery of self-control and patience, it is the foundation of rational family life. "In forming and preserving the morals of youth, two things are especially to be regarded. They are the pernicious effects of bad company and bad books." Hitchcock offers the example of Misander, the boy gone wrong:

> "Loose and dissolute companions proved the bane of Misander; and these are the most formidable enemies a young man is in danger of.

From the very nature of social union, he will study to be assimilated to his companions, and they will strive to make him so, for without likeness there can be no complacency. Under the ruins of such connections lies buried many a promising youth, the hope of his parents; many a splendid genius, the pride of human nature. . . .

"It is with books as it is with society: they are the occasion of much good to the world and vehicles of great mischief. Bad company and bad books have a similar effect on the mind: they corrupt and debauch the heart while they please the fancy. . . .

"[Mr. Bloomsgrove] took care to keep from their [Osander's and Rosella's] sight when quite young the wicked trash with which the world abounds. The free access which many young people have to romances, novels and plays has poisoned the mind and corrupted the morals of many a promising youth, and prevented others from improving their minds with useful knowledge.

"I do not mean to pass an indiscriminate censure on all writings of this stamp but on a permissive and indiscriminate use of them. . . .

"[Mr. Bloomsgrove] collected for them the writings of the best poets, historians, travels, characters, geography, elements of natural philosophy, and books of taste and elegance, miscellaneous, moral and entertaining. He used. . . [to have the children] give him some account of the books they had read. This method made them read with attention and recollection."

This vision of child raising — the creation of a good child by isolating him from evil influences — is at least as old as Galen. It was to become one of the dominent themes of child care in America. The parental ambition for purity expressed through raising a pure child, the child as a second chance, is an idea that has not yet disappeared.

*   *   *

By the beginning of the 1800s, the enthusiasm for the natural child advocated by Locke and Rousseau was beginning to be replaced by a skepticism about the practical effects of their theories. This was evident not only in the works of such religious writers as Melesina Trench (with her caustic remarks on "rash philosophers who advise us to trust implicitly to Nature") but even in the commentaries of some of their admirers in the medical profession. Rousseau particularly was selected for criticism. In the introduction to a German book on child care, C.A. Struve's *A Familiar View of the Domestic Education of Children* (German, 1797; English, 1800), the translator Dr. A.F.M. Willich commented:

"Emilius has obtained a higher degree of credit and authority than any other production of a similar kind. . . . It is not only the most complete and systematic treatise on the subject but likewise contains the most exhalted ideas which are, as it were, derived from the very bosom of Nature.

"The works of Milton, Locke, Addison and other English writers, though containing many valuable observations relative to the physical education of youth, do not afford us any connected series of rules by which so important an office in society may be regulated. . . .

"[Quoting a contemporary, he adds:] 'Now, though I have freely acknowledged that the system of this ingenious philosopher in many respects merits commendation and if pursued in some of its branches will probably be attended by beneficial effects, yet it is interspersed with such absurdities as will cause a smile in the countenances of the judicious.'"

By the 1820s Rousseau's authority was almost entirely discounted in the United States. William P. Dewees, a professor of midwifery at the University of Pennsylvania, reflected the new attitude. In his *Treatise on the Physical and Medical Treatment of Children* (1825), Dewees not only criticized Rousseau's ideas but even ridiculed the philosopher.

"We have tried [in this book] to avoid speculation by appealing to experience or to reason and have not permitted ourselves to be seduced into the diffuseness of Jean Jacques. . . .

"[We cannot rely on] preconceived notion [which] prescribes rules for that which it would be desirable to attain rather than that which is practicable, hence the many Utopian notions of Jean Jacques Rousseau."

Reading Dewees, we see that by the 1820s, medicine had progressed far beyond the work of even such a generally knowledgable physician as Michael Underwood a quarter century earlier. The past as a source of authority was gone. On the subject of maternal impressions (that is, the widely-held belief that what a pregnant mother saw or read could affect the child), Dewees remarks bluntly: "The origins of this belief, it is true, are coeval with our earliest records, but its antiquity should not entitle it to the least force."

Even the popularity of a treatment was, for Dewees, no proof of its virtue. Dewees quotes Struve on the ill effects of cold bathing and on the fatalities it led to in practice* and comments generally, "Conformity to usage, though a more rational mode is constantly presented for their imitation [is no excuse for bad child-care practices] ."

As far as middle-class Americans were concerned, by the 1820s swaddling was virtually a forgotten practice. Dewees, warning against it, has to define it first "for those who have heard of 'swaddling' but who know not its meaning."

Although past advice was rejected when it was obviously in error, it could be put to use when the advice was found credible. Dewees quotes a mid-sixteenth-century poem, *The Nurse*, by soldier-poet Luigi Tansillo, on the subject of wetnurses who ate heartily but unhealthily: "Say, will the nurse her wanted banquet spare / And for your infant stoop to humbler fare?" Even old beliefs which were wrong in more subtle ways (like the idea that a child could absorb the character of the nurse who suckled him) found their way into Dewees's generally rational book.

Though primarily a technical author, Dewees was not beyond advising on the moral side of child care:

"Let her [the mother] then in early life convince herself that an awful [awesome] responsibility attaches to the title of 'mother,' and that if she enters into holy marriage with heedless haste and without weighing the nature and importance of the duties she voluntarily imposes on herself, she will but too certainly discharge them without pleasure, if not without reprehensible neglect."

The reciprocal obligations between parent and child of which Hitchcock had written are here reflected, but the child is a "responsibility" in almost puritanical terms. There is no more of Robinson's, "It is natural for parents tenderly to love all their children till they see where God bestows his [favor] ." By the early nineteenth century, all children were considered equally perfectable, and it was the responsibility of the parents — more exactly, the mother — to guarantee their proper upbringing.

The life of the child is vividly portrayed by Dewees in his extended section on the design and management of the nursery. After roundly condemning those parents whose nurseries are "usually selected from the

---

*Struve, in his *Familiar View*, attributes cold bathing to the English: "Cold bathing, so generally practiced by the English, has lately been introduced into Germany; but that nation, after having by experience ascertained its injurious effects, has now in great measure relinquished this practice."

other rooms because it is 'handy', or because it is the only one that can be spared," he describes the nursery as it should be:

> "The nursery should be spacious, with a high ceiling, and perfectly dry; that is, it should not be exposed to the operation of any cause that may render it damp, as on a ground floor, too much shaded by trees, or placed beyond the influence of the sun. Its windows should be tight and the walls dry; the floor should be of wood that will be quickly dry after being wetted for the purpose of cleanliness; but the utmost care should be taken not to hasten this process by placing ignited charcoal in its center. . . . It should be so situated that the doors shall not open immediately on staircases or should this unavoidably be the case, the head of the stairs should be secured by latticed half doors so constructed by having the slats placed perpendicularly, that the child cannot climb upon them and so defeat their object.
> "The windows should have cross bars placed before them."

Details continued through shuttered windows — "carpets in cold weather are decidedly useful" — and the virtues of having a two-room nursery so that the child could be moved from one to the other as the stale room was aired.

> "The nursery should be as free as possible from air-holes or crevices, that the children may not be exposed to partial draughts of air; and that the air of the room may be preserved in winter of a pretty uniform temperature. Attention to this will enable the children to play in every part of the room without injury; and it will also prevent the desire to crowd round the hearth, which will diminish the risk of their clothes taking fire, or doing themselves other injury.
> "Too much care cannot be taken to guard against the accident of the clothes taking fire; there is but one security against this when an open fireplace is the means employed for warming the room, namely by dressing the children in worsted garments, at least the outer ones. . . .
> "It is also wrong to permit children to run about the nursery barefoot or in their stocking feet, especially if the floor be covered either by carpet or mat, as it every now and then happens that they run into their feet, needles, pins, nails, glass or other sharp substances that may be concealed in the substance of the floor covering.
> "The introduction of glass into the nursery should be avoided as much as possible. . . . "

Compare this description of a nursery with the one offered by Struve in his *Familiar View of the Domestic Education of Children*. His basic requirements for a nursery are the same as those repeated by Dewees: dryness, cleanliness, sun and air. But Struve was writing in Europe, where the problems of managing these requirements were different:

> "In the large towns, though every attention be paid to the cleanliness of houses, it is nevertheless difficult to introduce pure air into apartments, as narrow lanes and filthy courts cannot but contaminate the air in their vicinity."

Prior to the work of Louis Pasteur and Robert Koch relating disease to germs, contagion was generally considered a matter of good and bad air, and that concern is reflected here. Struve is discussing child raising in an urban world of confined spaces. The nursery Dewees proposes, on the other hand, accepts as a precondition a kind of comfort and spaciousness available to the average American family that existed only at the upper edge of European society.

The house was to be kept warm. Dewees advised that charcoal was too dangerous (in an improperly vented stove it produces stove gas, i.e. carbon monoxide) but praised the virtues of Lehigh coal in an open hearth and suggested that the nursery temperature be kept at 66 or 67 degrees by means of a thermometer. By the first quarter of the nineteenth century, then, we have arrived, among many American families, at a facsimile of the modern home. Dewees continues:

> "The nursery should be the purest place in the house, as well as the one in which the children should most delight to be. It should therefore never be made a place of punishment by banishing children to it for any little delinquency or inadvertence they may have been guilty of — but, on the contrary, a temptation should constantly present itself in the nursery, by making it a place of amusement; children will then bear being placed there without considering it a place of confinement or one in which they are to experience privations.
>
> "Among the proper provisions of a nursery we should reckon a small backgammon table, with men, but without dice. Children, as soon as they are capable of comprehending the subject, should be taught draughts or checkers. This game is not only highly amusing, but is also very instructive, as it calls forth the resources of the mind in the most gentle as well as in the most successful manner. It becomes a source of endless amusement, as it never tires and always instructs.

"Battledore or shuttlecock is also a proper game for the nursery; this gives great agility as well as great vigor to every muscle in the body. It exercises with but little fatigue; it gives great practical accuracy to the eye and to the hand while the mind is agreeably amused. . . .

"A rocking-horse of good size should also be an appendage to a nursery — this article, however, should be considered as a luxury, or it will become abused by becoming too familiar; it should therefore only be introduced occasionally, and that as a reward for good conduct. This will teach children to find their seat upon a saddle much easier than they would otherwise do when they are placed upon the back of a living horse.

"Slates and pencils afford much employment as well as amusement to children — it gives them the habit of making letters and figures very early, as well as calls forth their imitative powers in rude attempts to copy any of the objects of nature or of art which may present themselves. For the same reason, we would indulge children in the use of paper and lead pencils."

A vision of practical utility still lay underneath children's amusements. Struve had written of manual labor that "it is wise to accustom children as early as possible to a certain regularity in their transactions and thus to unite the spirit of order with that of industry" and that the parent should "combine with every kind of labor the idea of utility, or at least of attaining a certain end, so that young people may always know the ultimate object of their pursuits."

Similarly, Dewees describes "dissected maps [jigsaw puzzles] and Chinese puzzles, or tanagrams" as "very acceptable and highly useful: they exercise the memory, elicit ingenuity, excite a laudable ambition and give the habit of patience or perseverance." Building blocks, nine-pins, balls and other amusements are also mentioned. Caution should be observed that toys are not "sharp-edged or pointed as they can "serve no possible use, and may be productive of serious mischief. We have known the loss of two eyes from pointed instruments, and a number of severe wounds from sharp ones."

By 1825, the technology of child care had made considerable advances. There was an expanded awareness of objective facts about children's needs. The role of the parent as nursery manager was increasingly shaped by the professional even to the selection of the games a child should or should not play.

The child of nature was replaced by the child of society.

CHAPTER 7

The Correct Child

"Certain men and boys were employed to examine them [empty bottles] against the light, and reject those that were flawed, and to rinse and wash them. When the empty bottles ran short, there were labels to be pasted on full ones, or corks to be fitted to them, or seals to be put upon the corks, or finished bottles to be packed in casks. All this work was my work, and of the boys employed upon it I was one. . . .

"No words can express the secret agony of my soul as I sunk into this companionship; compared these henceforth everyday associates with those of my happier childhood. . . and felt my hopes of growing up to be a learned and distinguished man crushed in my bosom. The deep remembrance of the sense I had of being utterly without hope now — of the shame I felt in my position; of the misery it was to my young heart to believe that day and day what I had learned, and thought, and delighted in, and raised my fancy and my emulation up by, would pass away from me, little by little, never to be brought back any more — cannot be written."

That is, of course, Charles Dickens, writing in *David Copperfield* (1869). It is certainly autobiographical; he had spent a part of his youth working in a blacking factory.

84

Our images of Victorian childhood are still shaped by the genius of
Dickens. His descriptions are most often of orphans and small children
surrounded by middle- and upper-class adults who are generally eccentric
or grotesque, and by lower-class figures either sinister and aggressive or
good natured but helpless. Victorian society was polarized into these two
worlds with the child caught between them — the only individual in society
with real alternatives yet powerless to determine his own future.

In Dickens, the world is an evil place for children. Education, as he
portrays it, is either inclined towards the "facts-facts-facts" school described in *Hard Times* where the child is encouraged to give the "definition
of a horse" or towards the progressive, almost Montessorian learning-by-
doing approach utilized by Fagin to train his boys as pickpockets in *Oliver
Twist*.

Religion for Dickens is no longer a moral force for the protection of
youth. It has become, like patriotism, the last refuge of a scoundrel. In
David Copperfield, when David runs away from the factory, his stepfather,
Mr. Murdstone, comes to David's aunt's house where the boy has taken
refuge.

"'[David] has been the occasion of much domestic trouble and
uneasiness. . . . He has a sullen, rebellious spirit, a violent temper, and
an untoward, intractable disposition. Both my sister and myself have
endeavoured to correct his vices, but, ineffectually. . . . '

"'It can hardly be necessary for me to confirm anything stated by
my brother,' said Miss Murdstone, 'but I beg to observe that, of all
the boys in the world, I believe this is the worst boy.'

"'Strong!' said my aunt shortly.

"'But not at all too strong for the facts,' returned Miss Murdstone.

"'Ha!' said my aunt. 'Well, sir?'

"'I have my own opinions,' resumed Mr. Murdstone. . . 'as to the
best mode of bringing him up; they are founded, in part, on my knowledge of him, and in part on my knowledge of my own means and
resources. I am responsible for them to myself, I act upon them, and
I say no more about them. It is enough that I place this boy under
the eye of a friend of my own in a respectable business. . . . '

"'But about your respectable business. . .' said my aunt. 'If he had
been your own boy, you would have put him to it, just the same, I
suppose?'

"'If he had been my brother's own boy,' returned Miss Murdstone. . . 'his character, I trust, would have been altogether different.'"

This passage parodies Victorian morals. The child is "sullen, rebellious [and] violent," so the proper place for him is in a "respectable business." This contradiction is Dickens's way of revealing Murdstone's hypocrisy towards the stepson he wants to be rid of. The author exposes a society which assumes that business — any business that is middle class — is respectable.

The reliance for guidance is no longer on God or the Scriptures but on a knowledge of "my own means and resources" — something irrefutable relative to mere Biblical text. The vehicle of salvation for the Victorians was society, a society made omnipotent by the machine, where values of right and wrong were easily assessed in terms of economics.

Dickens, the novelist, dealing with human eccentricities and social horrors, is not necessarily the best guide to the actual conditions in Victorian society. To break through our stereotypes of the period, it is necessary to look at something more typical of the real life of the times. Here, for example, is one fictionalized account of a young family beginning to set up house in New York City, in *How We Raised Our Baby* (1877) by Jerome Walker, M.D.:

> "We were married in Illinois and I, Robert Matthews, brought my wife to New York. Though *my* acquaintances were many, it was long before Lena could feel exactly 'at home' for she had lived for years with her parents in the old homestead. The youngest of seven children. . . .
> "My salary was a moderate one, but enough for two and a servant."

What Walker is describing here is a most important fact of urban life: its isolation from the structure of family, community and tradition, typified by rural life. Instead of being tied into a culturally static, self-stabilizing matrix of family and social ties and beliefs, the individual is isolated. He lives less frequently in a house, and more often in apartments — in units that set him apart. After the birth of their child, Walker's couple gets the following advice from the doctor:

> "'In one sense you are very fortunate in not having a nurse at this time — you are saved meaningless or hurtful suggestions. The ignorant woman believes in giving molasses and water, or a little gin. The more intelligent (?) will advise some medicine.'"

The best nurses, Walker says, are connected with hospitals, but they are few in number. Eventually, the couple hires a nurse:

> "I started out to hunt up a nurse [and] met our washerwoman on the

stairs [who said] she would send up her sister, the Widow Flynn, a woman who had raised a family of her own.

"The widow arrived, a large, muscular, stolid-faced woman [who] took off a musty-smelling shawl and bonnet and, seating herself, asked for the baby, some water, a towel and soap.

"The widow soaped the child and [then rubbed] it briskly with a rather coarse towel. The little one was screaming. . . . [When it was] suggested that if a little oil were rubbed over the body and a softer towel used, the baby could be cleansed sufficiently for the first washing [,] Mrs. Flynn replied that 'she ought to know — hadn't she had nine children of her own, and where could anyone point to finer children? and she would thank people to let her alone.' Well, I thought, they are the sturdiest, dirtiest set of youngsters I have set my eyes on — and is mine to be like them? Heaven forbid!"

What is worth noting here is the comparative helplessness of the parents before the ministrations of the nurse.

When the husband returns, he sees the nurse giving the baby molasses and gin, the baby screaming and the mother protesting to no avail. The nurse has taken possession of the house.

"[Mrs. Flynn] showed unmistakable evidence of having taken some of the medicine which she had recommended for the 'poor baby's little stomach.'"

She is dismissed and replaced with a new and better nurse.

The physician, the voice of science and pragmatism, explains to the novice parents: "Find out that a baby isn't a mere machine."

The husband visits Mrs. Quick's Wetnurse Agency at 620 Second Avenue, where "Mrs. Quick informed me that when the nurses obtained places, their own babies are cared for in institutes for children." In one of the few references made in child-care books of this period to the fate of the wetnurses' own babies, Walker comments that most of these children die.

Walker goes on to describe the attempt to found a home for children. The woman in charge, Mrs. Morrel, proves to be a shrewd administrative in-fighter whose other attributes are brutality and incompetence. Finally, she is sent packing "but only to take charge of a half-orphan asylum in another county. Her chief recommendations to that place, so it seemed, were — first, that she had quite an extended experience in a nursery, and second, that she was introduced to the trustees."

Walker's inexperienced family is preyed upon by businessmen

promoting baby foods, drugs and formulas for children. Magazines are used to spread the message. Walker describes *The Herald of Health*: "It was evident that the editor had some pecuniary interest in the sale of Dick's Celebrated Graham Crackers, Thompson's Dessicated Milk [and] Wheeler's Health Rejuvenator." The creation and distribution of advice and products for child care had become an industry and the baby, through his mother, a customer.

One magazine, however, *Babyhood*, which began in December, 1884, and remained in print into the early years of this century (the name continued under different management into the 1920s) represented the best in progressive child-raising thought. Walker, as well as approximately fifty of the most popular pediatricians (Holt, Chapin, Yale, Meigs — the last noted for his research into the chemistry of milk) and medical specialists were regular contributors to the magazine.

Some discretion was exercised in printing advertisements. A few of the products are still in existence today (Ivory soap, Baker's cocoa, Armour's beef extract) and others, while of questionable worth ("Nutro-lactis: To Nursing Mothers we offer a free sample of Nutrolactis which enables nursing mothers whose supply of milk is scanty or of poor quality to have a copious flow of rich milk in three days."), appeared plausible at the time.

The range of materials covered by articles in *Babyhood* was vast, from the use of opiates ("Parents should never, under any circumstances, assume the responsibility of prescribing the drug for their little ones!") to the problem of detecting food coloring and other additives. (The description of chemical tests to be used on suspect foods, particularly candies, was written before the Pure Food and Drug Act). "Baby Days in the Wigwam," described child care among the Indians ("Indians love their children fondly, constantly, and will make any reasonable sacrifice for them. . . . Our Indian policy. . .is one of national dishonor."); "Hereditary Mental Traits and How to Meet Them in Training Children" provided ante-natal and post-natal precautions to guard the health of the child.

A series of articles by one of the editors of the magazine, Marion Harland (pseudonym for Mary Terhune) was subsequently reprinted as a book under the title *Common Sense in the Nursery* (1885). Harland's book is the product of a time that is proud of the progress it has made. She looks back on "Mrs. Gamp," the image of everything that was wrong with child raising in the past: "a matron of mature years or an acrid spinster of the same date." She might be describing Walker's Widow Flynn:

"Baby, an unschooled rebel, was vociferous in protest against his share

of torture decreed by the monthly nurse and winked at by the licensed
physician. . . .

"[Mrs. Gamp] swathed the yielding abdomen and ribs in bands of
linen and flannel pinned as tight as her sinewy fingers could draw
them."

This is a description of swaddling, still in use in some quarters a century or
so after Cadogan, Buchan and the others had argued against it and perhaps
fifty years after some had claimed it had been abolished.

The period Harland is describing, when the swaddling took place, is
apparently the 1850s. Another ancient practice acquired renewed popularity
at that time:

"The torture of the cold bath is abolished in nurseries where common
sense and humanity hold sway.

"When my first baby was born, twenty seven years ago [1858], the
rage for the cold plunge bath was at its height. Having known for
myself the discomfort of such immersion. . . I resolved that my boy
should never suffer [it].

"I bathed him myself and, under the playful pretext of nervousness
in performing under the eyes of others a task to which I was not
accustomed, I used to lock myself up with him in our nursery while
washing and dressing him. My conscience flinches slightly to this day
in recollection of the deception practiced on an exemplary matron
who one day asked me how my baby 'liked his cold dip every morning.'
I answered that he had 'never objected to it.' I had not the moral
courage to avow that I washed him in tepid water.

"Times have changed, and nursery fashions with them. Let us be
thankful — and progressive."

Harland devotes eight pages to the subject of "Baby's Bath." It is
worth quoting for the attitude expressed about the relationship of the
Victorian mother and child. Underlying this passage is not so much the
sentimentality of Dickens as a real warmth and sensuality. It compares
favorably with the clinical approach used in baby books of our own time.

"Tie around your waist a soft flannel apron that has been washed
several times. A half-worn flannel shirt, cut open at the back and
hemmed down the sides, is excellent for this use. It must be wide
enough and deep enough to enfold the child entirely. The tub should
be perfectly clean and not more than half full. Baby soon learns to

flourish his naked limbs in the water, to splash and beat with hands and heels to his and your delectation. The exercise is good for the growing child, and can hardly be indulged freely if the water rises so near the brim as to dash over upon the carpet. . . .

"Set [a low table] with a tub on it upon an old rug or square of oil-cloth spread to protect the carpet, and fill the tub, as has been said, halfway to the top with water before stripping the baby. Undress him rapidly, talking cheerfully and soothingly to him to allay impatience, should he delight in the prospective process — to quiet nervousness, if he dreads it. . . .

"When he is quite clean, and has had a brief frolic in the waves he has churned into yeast, lift the child to your lap, having laid a soft towel (warmed in winter) on the flannel apron. . . . Should the child resist the motion to remove him — and the chances are that he will — do not yield, but try some form of consolation. A toy, a game of bo-peep behind the flannel folds, a flow of chirruppy talk accompanied by prompt removal from the tempting tub, will usually bring him to reason.

"Lose no time in enveloping the child in the warm folds of the flannel apron. Two towels ought to be used in drying him — a soft one to absorb the moisture, another somewhat coarser, but not harsh, to rub him gently until the skin is suffused with a glow. When perfectly dry, his flesh sweet and pure with the exquisite lustre imparted by bath and friction, he is the most kissable object in nature. Nevertheless, do not delay to dry him. He is more likely to take cold now than before the exercise that has given both of you such delight, and for an hour or so thereafter he should be kept indoors and shielded from draughts."

While husbands were busily striving to make their way in the ruggedly competitive world of nineteenth century economics, wives apparently focused a good deal of their attention and sensuality on the only unre-pressed (and, in fact, encouraged) emotional relationship of the period, the interplay of mother and child. The fact that this article was printed in a popular magazine and was reprinted in a book, suggests that it was an accurate reflection of the way many mothers felt on the subject.

The magazine offered the readers opportunity for rebuttal in letters to the editor. This measure of feedback was one assurance that an author would, in short measure, hear of the practical effects of his suggestions rather than continue, as have so many authors of books before and since, to lecture in a void.

In 1898, *Babyhood* reprinted an article and rebuttal together from another magazine (*Christian Union*) that offers us a view of this process. It is especially interesting to us today since the author of the rebuttal was Mark Twain.

The story on which Twain commented was the tale of a two-year-old boy, "a cheruphim [sic] if ever there was one on earth," who, on arriving at two years of age, became "a handful."

"On that day, Junior, who had hitherto been obedient to the ukase prohibiting him from touching anything on his father's writing-table, entered the library, where that personage was at work, marched audaciously up to the desk, snatched an open letter from under the busy fingers, and threw it upon the floor.

"'Now, 'ook, Papa!' ejaculated the cheruphim, locking his fists at his back and putting up his lower lip in a defiant pout that made him into the loveliest picture his mother had ever looked upon.

"'Junior is a naughty boy!' said the father, judicially. 'No, Mamma!'" — for she stooped to recover the paper — "'Junior must pick it up and put it on the table.'

"'Ont!' uttered the angel smiling.

"'My lamb!' (deprecating) from the mother.

"'Pick it up, sir!' (magisterial) from the father.

"Both Johns [junior and senior] have bright brown eyes. They meet now with a dangerous flash, as when two rapiers strike full on the edges of their blades.

"'Junior — 'ont —pick — it — up!' The pout was angry; a small heel rang sharply on the hearth.

"John, senior, pulled open a drawer and took therefrom a strip of whalebone that might have been tossed there after the fall dressmaking was over. Mother and child had seen it once before on a dreadful November afternoon neither of them had forgotten. They recognized it immediately, the one with paling, the other with reddening, cheeks. A sibilant sigh cut the awful hush that fell upon the three at its appearance. The father answered it:

"'My dear' (in ominous composure), 'I am going to see this thing through. You had better leave the room.'"

The mother pleads with the father, embracing him, and the father twists "himself loose from her embrace and strikes her full in the face, his own enflamed with rage." Junior tells mother "Go 'way, bad Mamma!" and she leaves Junior to be whipped, after which Junior "picked up the

letter with his teeth, crept in the same dog-like fashion to his father, and
laid the prize on his boot!"

This was the original story, a case of the "terrible twos" we might
say today, and full of interesting Victorian details: the two-year-old striking
adult poses, the alliance of mother with child against father and child with
father against mother, and the question of why the father keeps a whip in
his desk.

Mark Twain's rebuttal includes the only time he mentioned his wife
in print:

"I have just finished reading the admirably told tale entitled 'What
Ought He to Have Done?' in your No. 24 [of *Christian Union*, where
it was first published], and I wish to take a chance at that question
myself before I cool off. What a happy literary gift that mother had!
and yet, with all her brains, she manifestly thinks there is a difficult
conundrum concealed in that question of hers. It makes a body's
blood boil to read her story!

"I am a fortunate person, who has been for thirteen years accustomed,
daily and hourly, to the charming companionship of thoroughly well-
behaved, well-trained, well-governed children. Never mind about taking
my word: ask Mrs. Harriet Beecher Stowe, or Charles Dudley Warner,
or any other near neighbors of mine, if this is not the exact and
unexaggerated truth. Very well, then, I am quite competent to answer
the question of 'What ought he to have done?' and I will proceed to
do it by stating what he would have done. . . had [he] been me, and
his wife. . .my wife, and the cub our mutual property. . . .

"[When John junior threw down the paper] John, senior — meaning
me] would not have said. . .'Junior is a naughty boy.' . . . He wouldn't
have aggravated a case which was already bad enough by making any
such stupid remark — stupid, unhelpful and undignified. . . .

"No — he would have kept still. Then the mother would have led the
little boy to a private place, and taken him on her lap, and reasoned
with him, and loved him out of his wrong mood, and shown him that
he had mistreated one of the best and most loving friends he had in
the world; and in no very long time the child would be convinced, and
be sorry, and would run with eager sincerity and ask his father's
pardon. And that would be the end of the matter.

"But, granting that it did not turn out in just that way, but that the
child stood out against reasoning and affection. In that case a whipping
would have been promised. That would have a prompt effect upon the
child's state of mind; for it would know, with its mature two years

experience, that no promise of any kind was ever made to a child in our house and not rigidly kept. So this child would quiet down at this point, become repentant, loving, reasonable; in a word, it own charming self again; and would go and apologize to the father, receive his caresses, and bound away to play, light-hearted and happy again, although well aware that at the proper time it was going to get that whipping, sure."

The proper time is an hour or two later, by which time "both parties are calm, and the one is judicial, the other receptive."

The mother administers the spanking. "The spanking is never a cruel one, but it is always an honest one. It hurts. If it hurts the child, imagine how it must hurt the mother. Her spirit is serene, tranquil. She has not the support which is afforded by anger. Every blow she strikes the child bruises her own heart."

"You perceive that I have never got down to where the mother in the tale really asks her question. For the reason that I cannot realize the situation. The spectacle of that treacherously-reared boy, and that wordy, namby-pamby father, and that weak, namby-pamby mother, is enough to make one ashamed of his species. And if I could cry, I would cry for the fate of that poor little boy − a fate which has cruelly placed him in the hands and at the mercy of a pair of grown-up children, to have his disposition ruined, to come up ungoverned, and be a nuisance to himself and everybody around him, in the process, instead of being a solacer of care, the disseminator of happiness, the glory and honor and joy of the house, the welcomest face in all the world to them that gave him being − as he ought to be, was sent to be, and would be, but for the hard fortune that flung him into the hands of these paltering incapables."

If Twain's attitudes and methods of child discipline do not exactly match the free ruffian liberality we might expect from memories of *Tom Sawyer* and *Huckleberry Finn* (1884, about a year before the first publication of this rebuttal), it is because we do not sense the common morality underlying both Twain's fiction and his home. Twain's heroes, like Dickens's, may be outside society because of their youth, but they have their own tribal ethic (Tom Sawyer's band of pirates with their blood oath) and punishments for violations of the tribal code of behavior.

Even the position of the child outside society has opposite meanings for Dickens and Twain. Compare David Copperfield on the road from

London to Dover, robbed and gradually stripped of his clothes, at the mercy of the world until he finally arrives at the security of his aunt's house, with Huck Finn, secure only on the raft, endangered every time he comes to land. For Dickens, society represents security and ultimate morality; for Twain, morality is individual, outside society.

Twain's own spanking of the child is not because the child violates a social code but because he violates a personal one:

> "The mother of my children adores them — there is no milder term for it; and they worship her; they even worship anything which the touch of her hand has made sacred. They know her for the best and truest friend they have ever had, or ever shall have; they know her for one who never did them a wrong; who never told them a lie, nor the shadow of one; who never deceived them by even an ambiguous gesture; who never gave them an unreasonable command, nor ever contented herself with anything short of a perfect obedience; who has always treated them as politely and considerately as she would the best and oldest in the land, and has always required of them gentle speech and courteous conduct towards all, of whatsoever degree, with whom they chanced to come in contact. . . . "

The mother is the child's friend as well as being responsible for his behavior. It is this vision of the parent-child relationship that Twain feels to be so acutely threatened by the image of arbitrary authority presented in the original story.

The vision of the essential decency of parent-child relations is also evident in one of the most popular books on moral guidance, Jacob Abbott's *Gentle Measures in the Management and Training of the Young* (1871). The book argues against corporal punishment, but unlike many other texts with the same intention, it offers a number of specific suggestions on the maintenance of household authority without the use of the rod. "The rod," as Abbott says, referred to in the Scriptures, "is used simply as a symbol of parental authority" and not as a prescription of method. Its use in society is an atavism:

> "In savage or half-civilized life. . . it is certainly better that [a mother] should whip [her boy] when he runs away than that he should be bitten by serpents or devoured by bears."

Authority, however, is the means by which we structure life, and parents are always confronted by "the necessity of bringing up children *in complete subjugation* to their authority," both to protect and to shape them.

> "Every parent will find that this principle is a sound one, and of fundamental importance in the successful management of children — namely, that it is much easier for a child to do what he does not like as an act of simple submission to superior authority, than for him to bring himself to an accordance with the decision by hearing and considering the reasons. In other words, it is much easier for him to obey your decision than to bring himself to the same decision against his own will."

It was not, in Abbott, that this authority should be used arbitrarily. In a long series of anecdotes, he argues for explaining to the child the reasons why a given decision has been made. He is strongly in favor of the child's understanding the consequences of his actions and is, in this regard, prophetic of the "logical consequences" doctrines of Rudolf Driekurs:

> "If the penalty annexed to the transgression is made as much as possible the necessary and natural consequence of it, and is insisted upon calmly, deliberately, and with inflexible decision, but without irritation, without reproaches, almost without any indications even of displeasure, but is, on the contrary, lightened as much as possible by sympathy and kindness, and by taking the most indulgent views and admitting the most palliating considerations in respect to the nature of the offense, the result will certainly be the establishment of the authority of the parent or guardian on a firm and permanent basis."

Ultimately, reasoning can only be carried so far, and, in the end, Abbott's faith is placed in a "calm, quiet, gentle, but still inflexible firmness in maintaining" parental authority.

His description of the ideal parental method parallels almost exactly Twain's description of his wife and the vision of the parents of "John, junior:"

> "How seldom do we see a mother's management of her children regulated by a calm, quiet and considerate decision which thinks before it speaks in all important matters, and when it speaks, is firm: and yet, which readily and gladly accords to the children every liberty and indulgence which can do themselves and others no harm. And on the other hand, how often do we see foolish laxity and indulgence in

yielding to importunities in cases of vital importance, alternating with vexatious thwartings, rebuffs and refusals in respect to desires and wishes the gratification of which could do no injury at all."

The child is a person, not to be arbitrarily thwarted by the willfulness of the parents; the natural energy of the child must not be repressed:

"You may stop the supply of force [natural energy], if you will, by refusing to give them food; but if you continue the supply, you must not complain of its manifesting itself in action. . . . To give children food and then to restrain the resulting activity, is conduct very analogous to that of the engineer who should lock the action of his engine, turn all the stop-cocks, and shut down the safety valve, while he still went on all the time putting in coal under the boiler. The least that he could expect would be a great hissing and fizzling at all the joints of his machine; and it would only be. . .the escape of the imprisoned force [through the looseness in the joints] that could prevent the repression ending in a frightful catastrophy.

"Nine-tenths of the whispering and playing of children in school, and of the noise, the rudeness, and the petty mischief of children at home, is just this hissing and fizzling of an imprisoned power, and nothing more.

"In a word, we must favor and promote, by every means in our power, the activity of children, not censure and repress it. We may endeavor to turn it aside from wrong channels — that is, to prevent it manifesting itself in ways injurious to them or annoying to others. We must not, however, attempt to divert it from these channels by damming it up, but by opening other channels that will draw it away in better directions."

This was written well before Freud, yet we can already see the imagery he was to use in describing the id, the irrepressible energy of personality, the mind as a force of nature not to be tampered with, or as a steam engine, the most visible symbol of power to the Victorians.

Abbott holds as well another Victorian belief, the vision of childhood as a kind of Eden, a time to be allowed freedom, to be protected from society. In book after book, we find stern warnings against beginning the education of the child too soon. Richard Sharpe Kissam's *Nurse's Guide* (1834) advises that while moral cultivation may properly begin in childhood, "it is otherwise with regard to mental cultivation in its more extended sense":

"The brain, which is the apparatus of the mind, does not arrive to complete organization until about the seventh year. Before this time no task involving any great degree of mental *effort* should be imposed. Children have a certain aptitude for learning the elements of all kinds of knowledge, far superior to the adult. This no doubt is the provision which the God of nature has instituted to prevent or render unnecessary a long continued effort of the child's mind. . . . Children learn by imitation. . . . If the reasoning capacity of the child be urged to action [before the mind has acquired facts to reason upon,] then the exercise of the reasoning faculty produces injury. . . .

"Thinking acts on the brain in the same manner a blister does on the skin. If a child be allowed to think too long, the blood which goes to the brain will produce a kind of irritation there which is apt to lead to inflammation, sometimes terminating in dropsy of the head. . . . The consequence is the brain is soon worn out."

Ten years later, in an English book reprinted in the United States, Mrs. Barwell's *Infant Treatment* (1844), we see similar advice to the effect that "weakness and disease" arise from "a premature use of the brain. . . . If the mind is worked much [during childhood] a deficiency of. . . energy is sent to the frame and. . . the natural process of growth is checked." The body is again an engine, with a limited amount of energy available for growth, sexuality, mental and muscular activity. Anxiety about loss of energy through misuse of any of these functions obsessed Victorian popular medicine.

The Victorians were the first to become enraptured with numbers (it was seen as bookkeeping applied to society), and through their gradually accumulating statistics a picture of society emerges. In the American edition of *Infant Treatment*, the editor, Dr. Valentine Mott, offers some statistics in the introduction that are worth considering: In Britain, from the period 1730-49 to the period 1810-29, infant mortality fell from 74.5 percent to 31 percent. On the other hand, in Boston, from the period 1811-20 to 1831-39, infant mortality *increased* from 27 percent to 43 percent. Even if these figures are not accurate, (reliable statistics for 1730 would be difficult to acquire), the trend is clear. Even as Britain was gaining ground, the United States was losing it.

The explanations Mott offers for these statistics are many. He says that in the United States we "undervalue" human life. But the validity of this explanation is doubtful; it was not in the United States, after all, that baby farms and infanticide were organized into a profession. Mott also claims the rising infant mortality is the result of climate, American climate being more extreme than that of Europe. Digestive diseases carry off children in summer, he says, and respiratory diseases in winter. But how can one explain the fact that, as he asserts, Southern cities had a *higher* infant mortality rate than Northern ones, despite their more temperate climate?

In fact, the rise in infant mortality in America paralleled increasing urbanization. Industrialism, common on both sides of the Atlantic, was shaping urban cultures. American cities, however, did not resemble Victorian European cities with their expanding networks of charitable institutions and social services; they resembled eighteenth-century European cities, overcrowded towns filled with urban poor and factory workers. By the 1840s, slums crowded with Irish immigrants (fleeing potato famines) were appearing in commercial and industrial centers.

As the poor crowded into older neighborhoods and shantytowns, the middle class began a flight to open land (the countryside was then still within city limits). While the children of the poor were compelled to work or starve, middle-class children were educated as consumers and indulged accordingly. As Charles Dickens observed in *American Notes* (1842), the American middle class and even some factory workers enjoyed a lifestyle that would have "startled" his European readers.

Mrs. L. D. Tuthill, the American author of *Joy and Care, A Friendly Book for Young Mothers* (1855), criticizes the doll-like environment into which privileged children were put:

> "When the boy is permitted to go out of doors to play, allow him due freedom. . . .
>
> "Making sand pies and building stone bridges and mud houses are fascinating amusements though not the most cleanly, and when young children are indulged in them, they are not to be punished for soiling face, hands and clothing.
>
> "Although you cultivate habits of neatness, do not make your boy a bond slave to them.
>
> "Those fine painted pets [children] who are constantly 'dressed up' like dolls in a shop window are much to be pitied."

In one of the letters that make up Mrs. Tuthill's books, the proud mother writes her "aunt" [the author] that, at age three, her son has already begun to read. Mrs. Tuthill comments, *"Confinement to books* would inevitably destroy his health, enfeeble his intellect and injure his moral character. . . . Let a child enjoy his childhood," she adds. "Never tell a child to act like a man."

> *"Give him* [the child] *the impression, and carefully keep it up, that*

you are conferring a favor on him, a great favor by instructing him and not that he is doing you a favor by learning. Do not *force* a child to learn."

This is far from the seventeenth- and eighteenth-century children, who had to be disciplined and educated into adult salvation.

The subject of the isolation of children in the world of the well-off was approached by another author, Alfred Donné, in a French work that received considerable attention in English, *Mothers and Infants, Nurses and Nursing* (1859, English 1860). Children, he pleads, need companions.

"It is well to seek companions of their own age for children − to make them play together and accustom them early to live in the society which suits them. . . . The solitude in which certain children in high life live, who are not allowed to associate with those they meet in the public walks and who have not any comrades around them with whom they can frolic and abandon themselves is a lamentable circumstance. The constraint in which they are kept give to their solitary sports a monotony and sadness which fatigue and weary them. They become shy and formal and their body soon feels the effect of the limited activity allowed their tastes and natural instincts. Never having to contend with the wills and caprices of children the same age, to exercise their faculties and their address in the presence of companions sometimes superior to themselves − sharing neither their sports, their vexations nor their pleasures − finding around them no physical or moral resistance proportioned to their strength and age − they become imperious and pusillanimous, effeminate in body and mind and they learn nothing of the life which is suited to children. . . .

"I repeat it, children must live as much as possible with children. They mutually form and develop each other. . . . Children brought up alone are melancholy. . . . It is thus that those irritable temperaments are formed which are accessible to a host of nervous affections so common in society."

Parents and children − isolated in varying degrees by the formation of an industrial society with social units of gigantic scale (cities and factories as opposed to villages and workshops) − were not only susceptible to the good advice offered by Tuthill, Harland and the contributors to *Babyhood*, they were equally vulnerable to bad advice. Isolated in the home with the baby, the mother had little but her child on which to focus her attention. His perfection or lack of it became fascinating. As a result, a number of innocent universal childhood behavior traits began to be branded as bad habits and depravities. Among the most popular of these was masturbation.

In *Maternity, A Popular Treatise for Young Wives and Mothers*, Tullio Suzzara Verdi, M.D., put forth this popular 1870 advice:

> "We wish we could be silent on a vice [onanism] as repulsive to our self-respect as this; but we feel that it is this very silence which permits this vice to grow, by default of proper warning and education. . . .
>
> "The problem of 'onanism' is much more common and more extended than anyone is willing to believe; it is common in the adults of both sexes. This vice is acquired very early in life, even before the tenth year of age. . . .
>
> "Mothers, generally, delude themselves upon the pretended innocence of their children, particularly of their girls; yet it is our painful duty to state that our experience as a medical man has taught us that very few are exempt from it.
>
> The apparent symptoms that indicate the practice of the vice are general emaciation in spite of good appetite; intellectual langor and inaptitude to work; a nervous susceptibility; palpitations: shortness of breath; panting at comparatively little physical effort; melancholy; inclinations to solitude; headaches; derangements of digestion. These phenomena vary in individuals according to their constitution; and, in the beginning, are so very slight as to escape notice of the parents. If the victim, however, fails to appreciate these warnings, and continues in the fatal practice, the symptoms become very grave indeed and are as follows. . . . "

Verdi's list includes general langor and depression leading to absent-mindedness, loss of memory, giddiness, "eyes constantly encircled by a livid halo," dilated pupils. The individuals become:

> "indifferent to objects that interest others, indifferent to the opposite sex [and] they are troubled by voluptuous dreams and by night emissions; they become timid and faint easily. . . . In man, spermatorrhoea [a common, though vaguely diagnosed Victorian condition involving weak semen and related symptoms] follows as a curse of the wicked act. Finally, these symptons resolve themselves into serious maladies such as epilepsy, hypochondria, hysteria, insanity, etc."

It is worth noting how similar many of these symptoms are to the symptoms of isolation as described by Donné ("pusillanimous," "melancholy," "effeminate," "irritable," etc.). The increasing life of urban isolation seems to have aided social anxiety in both ways, on one hand creating an audience rootless and gullible enough to swallow this pseudo-science and on the other directly fostering the loneliness in which hypochondria and other neuroses could flourish.

Regardless of its validity, this kind of advice on masturbation was common. Even Donné, the astute observer of isolation, feels obliged to comment on "the viscious habits to which it is no uncommon thing to see children addicted at a very early age" and proposes "microscopic examination of the [child's] urine [which] affords a means of arriving at the truth without allowing the child to be aware of it and without showing any distrust in him. . . . The urine of children addicted to the vice of which we speak contains, even before the age of puberty, particulate matters which observation enables us to discover when care is taken to procure it a short time after the moment that the child had abandoned himself to his baleful inclination." His book includes a plate illustrating the microscopic examination of urine. Verdi had several suggestions for preventing masturbation:

> "As soon as suspicion is induced by the foregoing symptoms, the parents ought to exert the strictest surveillance; they should never leave the child alone; it should not be allowed to retire to bed without sleeping."

The advice is comparable to a statement made by Dewees (1826): "Children should not be permitted to indulge in bed long after daylight, as the warmth, the accumulation of urine and faeces, and the exercise of the imagination, but too often lead to the precocious development of sexual instinct." Dewees did not offer as imaginative a collection of consequences from masturbation as those provided by Verdi; he still saw the problem primarily in physical rather than in moral terms.

Verdi further recommended that the child's reading should be supervised and "exciting" books proscribed; cold baths were some help in cooling off desire to practice the vice. Exercise if carried to exhaustion helped somewhat, and spicy food was forbidden. If all these remedies failed, Verdi proposed stronger measures:

> "If the habit has taken such hold as to be impossible to make the individual relinquish it, personal restraint may become necessary; his hands should be secure. . . . A grown person should sleep with the child when this vice is suspected.
>
> "The directors of asylums for the insane and for idiots could witness that we do not exaggerate when we call upon parents to use the utmost

vigilance, moral courage, and parental influence in detecting and dealing with this insidious vice; for it is capable of sapping the bodies, destroying the minds, and degrading the souls of their own dear children."

The history of the hostility to masturbation goes back to the early 1700s, but rarely had such exaggerated claims as Verdi's been made as to its ill effects.

While, on the one hand, Verdi opposed "forcing children beyond [their] intellectual or physical level," he was not shy about advising parents about their responsibility for moral training:

"Let no parent delude himself or attempt to screen his deficiency by putting forth the false argument of the child's perversity or natural depravity."

Life was, according to Verdi, divided into four stages. "Infancy, Adolescence, Virility, Dementia." During the first twelve or fourteen years, "infancy or childhood, is a period almost totally vegetative." In other words, the child was morally inert as he would have been physically if he had been swaddled. His behavior was a blank slate on which the parent was obliged to write his good conduct.

As early as the 1840s, in his Advice books (*Advice to a Wife, Advice to a Mother*), Pye Henry Chavasse recommended toilet training the child at an early age. At three months, the child was ready to be placed on the stool at a regular time to, as the old euphemism accurately expressed, do his duty. Verdi, however, raised this technique to the level of physical, and by extension moral, compulsion:

"As soon as the child can sit, put it to its chair every morning at the same hour, encouraging it to stool; and, if it be disinclined, a little stick of castile-soap may be introduced into the rectum for a few minutes, which will stimulate it to act."

The child's "duty" did not end with what he did on the potty. Duty was applied to all areas of his behavior. In Mrs. Barwell's *Infant Treatment*, alongside the advice that "every office for the child should be performed with love and care," is this moral admonition: "The first and most important truth to be impressed on mothers is *that the constitution of their offspring depends on natural consequences many of which are under their control.*" Among the areas to which this control should be applied was right- or left-handedness:

"Children are apt to accustom themselves to use the left hand more readily than the right and so become what is termed left-handed. Left-handedness is always a mark of careless nurture; for no species of imperfection is so easily guarded against. When the child begins to use a spoon or to handle any object, let care be taken to make it use the right hand chiefly and to accustom it to shake hands only by that hand. By these means it will soon learn that the right hand is the proper hand to employ, and in this respect will grow up faultless."

*　　*　　*

In the last quarter of the nineteenth century, pamphlets describing child care in simplified terms were distributed both by public health authorities and by babyfood manufacturers as a vehicle for advertising their products. Through these writings, the basics of child care were at last made available to the poor.

One of these pamphlets, issued by the Boston Board of Health in 1876, (*Rules for the Management of Infants and Children*) condenses the essentials into less than a dozen pages, managing somehow to avoid discussing the evils of masturbation, left-handedness and other fads and anxieties. Eight major points are made in the pamphlet, expressing the bare essentials of child care at that date:

(1) The child should be kept clean, bathed daily in warm water and changed as often as he becomes dirty.

(2) The child needs fresh air.

(3) Children's clothing should not be too tight [a final warning against swaddling?].

(4) Children need as much sleep as they want.

(5) The basic diet of the infant is milk, which should be given every two hours when he is small and gradually lengthened to every four hours. "All prepared varieties of so-called infant's food are to be avoided."

(6) Children are to be weaned by the ninth month.

(7) Children are to be vaccinated; children are not to be given cordials (opium); the doctor should be sent for when the child is ill.

(8) After a child reaches two years, "regularity of hours of sleeping and eating should be insisted on."

Pamphlets offered by babyfood manufacturers were similar to this and often virtually identical. The item numbered five, however, would be

altered, advising mothers that the particular formula sold by a given manu-
facturer was either an "aid" to the nursing mother or, in many cases, was
actually preferable to mother's milk. Testimonials would be included,
converting an objective pamphlet into a piece of advertising.

The increasing isolation of the family during the Victorian period
and afterwards not only made the family vulnerable to fads and peculiar
ideas in child care, it also had a positive effect. By breaking the cultural
link between generations, it became possible for new ideas in child care to
be more readily absorbed by society. There were few parents and grandparents around to say that the "old ways were best." No longer was the
baby seen to be an extension of the past, a new generation destined to
perpetuate an old culture. The baby had become a creature of the future,
destined to occupy a world his parents would not live to see.

> "Advertisements certainly have something to do with it. Our grand-
> mothers felt that they must nurse their babies or dire consequences
> would follow; and therefore they bent every effort towards that end;
> and so did all their relatives. But we, who are familiar with generations
> of Mellin's food babies; who see the Cannick baby fat and bursting on
> the cover of the package; who know, from posters and daily papers,
> just how happy peptonized milk makes the mother and child; we don't
> think it worth while to make such strenuous efforts to keep up a
> custom that often makes us very uncomfortable, spoils the fit of our
> dresses, and keeps us closely confined at home. Besides, we feel cow-
> like, and animal-like, and it is hard to keep from smelling milky."

This is from Marion Foster Washburn's *The Mother's Yearbook*
(1908), a month-by-month description of child care and child development
for the first year of life. Even so early in the twentieth century, in this
passage one can observe several of the characteristic themes of our times:
the influence of media (in this case print) flooding the family with advertisements and advice; the tendency to invalidate grandmother's ways of
child raising as inappropriate to the times; a mild aversion to things biological, squeamishness about the physical facts of life and a preference for
neat, mechanical, packaged answers. It was naturally in the interest of
formula manufacturers to play up the messy side of motherhood and to
brand grandmother's ways as old-fashioned. But Washburn's theme — the
new pro-synthetic bias — reflects the growing influence of industrial technology not only on commerce but on social style as well.

Washburn's protest is essentially retrogressive for the period. How
much her work is similar to that of nineteenth-century writers may be

noted in the following excerpt on the subject of baby massage. It is worth comparing to Harland on the same subject in her description of the baby's bath (Pages 89-90).

Massage For The Baby

"When he begins to tire of this [crawling], take him on your lap, and rub his little body all over, firmly and steadily, especially down his back. Knead the sweet flesh gently, and then slap it, also gently, with your cupped hand. This is massage for the baby and it will bring such a glow to his skin as will lead to a good night's sleep, and to firm, well-knit muscles, and to a good circulation. Besides, he will like it. And so will you. Nothing on earth is so delicious to the touch as the firm, fine flesh of a healthy baby! In these strokings and kneadings, something of your mother-love and magnetism passes over into the baby, and you are more closely bound to each other. Froebel says that the last consciousness of the baby who is going off to sleep, as also his first awakening, ought to be a consciousness of love. Touch is especially the love-sense, and we, who cannot yet make little children understand our words, can tell them, through our hands, how dear they are to us and how tenderly we care for them."

Crowing

"Very likely this will be the occasion of his first crowing — such a loud, triumphant shout of joy and of pleasure in being alive! When it first tears its way out of the little throat the baby himself is likely enough as surprised as we are about it, and show the whites of his eyes in astonishment. He tries to do it again, but he can't. At first this act, too, is involuntary, but, little by little, he learns to master it and then he crows away like a little rooster as he lies kicking and tossing in the sun."

This quote exemplifies the erotic tradition in child care. While such advice diminishes in the first third of this century, it is never entirely absent from the child-raising repertoire. Future trends, however, would emphasize impersonal scheduling, an objective view of early childhood development, frequently at the cost of sacrificing what is generally thought to be mother love.

PART THREE

Packaged Answers

(1900-1950)

"If a young mother were to ask me what I consider the keynote of successful baby training, I should say, without hesitation, regularity.

This means regularity in everything, eating sleeping, bathing, bowel habits, and exercise. . . .

"It is quite possible to train the baby to be an efficient little machine, and the more nearly perfect we make the running of this machine, the more wonderful will be the results achieved and the less trouble it will be for the mother."

MYRTLE ELDREN AND
HELEN LE CRON (1921)

CHAPTER 8

The Mechanical Baby

For the Young Mother, (1921) written by Murtle Eldren and Helen Le Cron, begins with a poem and is typical of child-care advice common in the early 1900s.

> "The clock is the Baby's truest friend
> As every Mother ought to know!
> From early dawn to evening's end,
> It points the way the day should go!
> 'Wake up!' it says at six o'clock,
> 'Wake up and have your morning meal!'
> And later, 'Time to bathe, (tick, tock!)'
> And 'Oh, how happy you will feel!'
> Then, 'Eat again,' then, 'Sleep,' then 'Take
> Your daily airing,' thus it goes —
> So mother ought, for Baby's sake,
> To take the clock's advice! It knows!"

The Value Of Regularity

"If a young mother were to ask me what I consider the keynote of successful baby training, I should say, without hesitation, regularity.

"This means regularity in everything, eating, sleeping, bathing, bowel

109

habits, and exercise. Each event in a baby's daily life should take place at exactly the same hour by the clock until the habit is established.

"It is quite possible to train the baby to be an efficient little machine, and the more nearly perfect we make the running of this machine, the more wonderful will be the results achieved and the less trouble it will be for the mother.

"The time to start this training is at birth. But one need not despair if the ideal is not accomplished immediately. It is best, though, to make out a schedule that you expect to carry out under all ordinary circumstances, and then follow it without deviation until the habits become automatic."

The image of the mechanical child can be traced back at least as far as Nelson in the 1750s. In earlier references, however, the mechanical child was held out metaphorically as an ideal type; much of the advice took into account the child's nature and humanity. It is only here, in the early twentieth century, that we find a conscious, systematic effort to actually turn the child into a biological machine.

There are references to scheduled feeding, both pro and con, as early as St. Marthe (1584), and there are descriptions of specific timetables in Hugh Smith. In his popular book *Letters to Married Ladies* (1767), Smith recommended feeding the child only "four or five times in the twenty-four hours." A first feeding was suggested at six or seven in the morning, a second after the mother's breakfast, a third "if she pleases" before lunch, a fourth at five or six in the evening and the last feeding "between ten and eleven, just before she goes to rest." The casualness of Smith's description suggests that the schedule is a convenience for the mother rather than a form of habit training.

By Victorian times, it was well appreciated that the intervals of feeding proposed by Smith, averaging about five hours, were too long For the newborn, a two- or two-and-a-half-hour schedule was more appropriate, which could be lengthened as the child grew older.

Towards the end of the 1800s, under the impetus of mass production of patent foods, chemical analysis of milk was begun with particular emphasis placed on the difference between cow's milk and mother's milk. Dr. Arthur Meigs (previously mentioned as a contributor to *Babyhood* magazine), working in Philadelphia, arrived at a set of percentages or ratios of the components of mother's milk: 4 units fat to 7 units sugar to 1 unit protein. To render cow's milk suitable for infants, it would be necessary to dilute it by half and to add a small amount of sugar. This attempt to duplicate the percentages of elements found in mother's milk came to be called "percentage feeding." It is still one method recommended for artificial feeding. Cheadle's *Artificial Feeding in Infants* (1892) describes the complications of standardization in these terms:

> "[Human] milk contains everything essential for the formation and nourishment of the child during the first months of life. . . . Human milk, therefore, must be taken as the type-food for an infant. . . as the standard of an infant's food when artificially made. The analyses of human milk show, however, considerable variation."

In 1873, Jacobi had written apropos of this problem that some women's milk contained too much casein (protein) and as a result, "We all know that sometimes an infant will thrive at the breast of one women while it will starve or fall ill at the breast of another." Some infants, in fact, can digest milk with 1.5 or 2 percent protein, while others cannot digest more than 1 percent.

In 1907, Thomas Rotch, reviewing the history of percentage feeding from Meigs on, commented that it had been learned that no one particular food was suitable for all infants or even for the same infant at different times, and as a result there was no value in the "old idea of the superiority of any one patent food." Nor was it possible to develop one synthetic food that would serve all infants equally well.

In spite of these difficulties, the impulse towards standardization spread from the factories to homes. Studies revealed that the richness of mothers' milk depended on the length of time between feedings. Despite the fact that these fluctuations had little or no effect on the child, mothers were encouraged to standardize their own milk. The first descriptions we find of rigid scheduling emphasize this aspect. The following account from Henry Chapin's *The Theory and Practice of Infant Feeding* (1902) is a good example:

> "The infant should not be allowed to occupy the bed of the mother at night, as this is a common cause of too frequent nursing. *Regularity of feeding is essential as the composition of the milk varies with unequal intervals between nursings*. The shorter the intervals, the richer the milk is in fat, so it is well each day to write down the hours at which nursings are to be given, as 5, 7, 9, 11 AM, 1, 3, 5, 7, 9 PM, etc."

The habit-training side of this scheduling process was well appreciated.

Five years before Chapin, Edmund Cautley, an English physician, writing on the same subject argues for regularity for the same reason, but adds that "with a little patience the child can be accustomed to being fed at fixed times and will wake up for its meals with the regularity of clockwork." The trend toward producing a mechanical baby was already evident. It was only a step to the introduction of morality into the scheduling process.

At the beginning of this century, the morality of the middle class was still tied to Victorian ideals, but technology was carrying the parents and children into another world. A time of optimism, everything seemed possible. If science could prevent disease, as Koch and Pasteur had shown, why couldn't it also prevent psychological disorder? And social disorder? Personal failure and poverty? If technology could guarantee consistency in manufactured goods, why couldn't it also guarantee the production of consistently wonderful children?

Enthusiasm for the application of technology to child care was expressed by Helen Campbell in the introduction to her book *Practical Motherhood* (1910):

"The field of child care is a wide one, for besides an acquaintance with the normal development of child life, we are beginning to realize that not only the dietary and the dress and all those hygenic principles involved in the maintenance of a perfect bodily health and growth, but also the 'opening mind of childhood' must be governed by definite and special knowledge on the part of those who have to deal with this interesting and fascinating undeveloped human material, and not left to chance instinct or affection or the old-fashioned rule-of-thumb methods of training. To Froebel, and those who have written on and explained his great philosophy to us, and to Darwin and later writers on evolution who have given us a scientific basis for the development of a child's mind, we owe the most fruitful seeds of the study of the psychology of the child and the correct training of its mind. And now that child literature is so voluminous, and that societies, comprising mothers, medical men and women, and teachers, which have for their object child study, have been added to other sociological associations in England and different parts of the world, one may, encouraged by the trend of modern thought, hope for a time in the not far distant future when the study of children and their care will find an important place in the *education* of every woman of every class; and when special training-schools for children's nurses are organized, not only in London but in all our big towns, on the lines of that attached to the Babies' Hospital in New York.

"The question of child care is an old one, yet it was never more new than today, I think, in the light of the clearer understanding of it we owe to the advance of science and to a more cultured womanhood. It is also by far the most important Woman's Question of the day, in that it must inevitably lie to a great extent at the root of those other much-discussed problems of Physical Degeneracy, Social Morality, and the National Welfare and Progress generally, for it is a well-known fact that the vast majority of children are born healthy, and that even delicate babies may often be reared into perfectly healthy adults; and in the hands of mothers lies the all-important task of the first education of the child, in the wider sense of the word."

The twentieth century was to be known, in its early years, as the Century of the Child, the title of a German work on social improvement by Ellen Key (in English, 1909). The epithet is not only an expression of the amount of attention focused on children and child study, but also a symbol of the high hopes parents had for reforming the world through their offspring.

Little was known about children in a scientific sense, but a good deal was known about production. Production demanded regularity, repetition and scheduling. All that seemed to be required of the family was that the parents submit to the same kind of systematization and discipline in the handling of their children as was routinely demanded of factory workers on a production line. Books of the time reflect the unanimity with which middle-class parents supported the new doctrines. It was schedule the child or spoil the child; no one was proposing that the child be spoiled. The new methodology appears in book after book, largely without argument.

The most popular blueprint for the construction of the mechanical child was a small book by Dr. Luther Emmett Holt entitled *The Care and Feeding of Children*, written in 1894 as a text for instructing nurses attending the Practical Training School for Nursery Maids (part of Babies' Hospital, mentioned by Helen Campbell). The second edition noted in the preface that the book had already received wider circulation. The third edition signaled this new readership in a change of dedication, from the one addressed in the first edition to Mrs. Robert Chapin (who had helped establish the school) to "The Young Mothers of America." Later editions were published through 1943 (after 1924, Holt's death, L.E. Holt, Jr., continued the series), more often expanded than revised.

The great popularity of Holt's work may be attributed to the highly detailed coverage he gives to the question of feeding and physical growth, and to the style in which the book is written. In 140 pages of the 1904 edition, 20 have to do with "care," (bathing, airing, etc.), 30 deal with miscellaneous problems, from playing with children to "bad habits" and 90 pages have to do with feeding. It is not, in fact, incorrect to regard Holt's work as basically a popularizaton of the research into feeding that had been done by Meigs and the other specialists.

Holt's book was certainly the most detailed dietary curriculum ever concocted. Each of the early stages of life was divided into a "period" with an entire series of formulas prescribed for the child. Here, for example, is the second series of formulas, for the "middle months," beginning at the third or fourth month and ending at the tenth or eleventh:

Second Series of Formulas – Middle Months

	I.	II.	III.	IV.	V.
7-per-cent milk	7 oz.	8 oz.	9 oz.	10 oz.	11 oz.
Milk sugar	1 "	1 "	1 "	¾ "	¾ "
Lime-water	1 "	1 "	1 "	1 "	1 "
Boiled water	12 "	11 "	10 "	5 "	3 "
Barley gruel	0 "	0 "	0 "	4 "	5 "
	20 oz.	20 oz.	20 oz.	20 oz.	20 oz.

"Since the sugar dissolves," Holt points out, "the total will be twenty ounces in each column." The parent was encouraged to make sure the child ate his full portion. As time went on, the quantities could be increased to "40 ounces, by using twice as much, exactly." The child would spend "a week or ten days" in Column I, "two weeks" in Column II and gradually move upwards to Column V where the "same formula may sometimes be continued for three or four months with no other change than an increase in quantity." The formula was to be modified according to Holt's directions for problems of digestion, constipation, etc.

Holt supplied parents with not only the formulas and methods of milk preparation (including the separation procedures necessary to derive 7 percent milk used in the formulas) but even backup data (such as the percentages of fat, protein and sugar these mixtures contained). This information (when standardized wholesome milk was not always available) was certainly important, yet, it was not necessarily adapted well to the individual child. The effect of Holt's book was to take over much of the mother's autonomy in handling her child and replace it with reliance on a book. This was, to some extent, progress: The formulas were often better than the slapdash preparations that preceded them. Nevertheless, it is hard to overlook the drawbacks in a work which encourages parents to rely more on fixed recipes than on the child's responses.

This tendency is evident in Holt's handling of crying. The problem is discussed in a careful, clinical question-and-answer "catechism". The tone of the work is professional and emotionally uninvolved – firm, positive and without ambiguity or doubts. Even its history, as a textbook for nurses, adds an aura of authority to the severely clinical advice *The Care and Feeding of Children* offers:

The Cry

"When is crying useful?
"In the newly born infant, the cry expands the lungs, and it is necessary that it should be repeated for a few minutes every day in order to keep them well expanded.

"How much crying is normal for a very young baby?
"From fifteen to thirty minutes a day is not too much.

"What is the nature of this cry?
"It is loud and strong. Infants get red in the face with it; in fact, it is a scream. This is necessary for health. It is the baby's exercise.

"When is a cry abnormal?
"When it is too long or too frequent. The abnormal cry is rarely strong, often it is a moaning or worrying cry, sometimes only a feeble whine.

"What are the causes of such crying?
"Pain, temper, hunger, illness, and habit.

"What is the cry of pain?
"It is usually strong and sharp, but not generally continuous. It is accompanied by contraction of the features, drawing up of the legs, and other symptoms of distress.

"What is the cry of hunger?
"It is usually a continuous, fretful cry, rarely strong and lusty.

"What is the cry of temper?
"It is loud and strong and accompanied by kicking or stiffening of the body, and is usually violent.

"What is the cry of illness?
"There is usually more of a fretfulness and moaning than real crying, although crying is excited by very slight causes.

"What is the cry of indulgence or from habit?
"This is often heard in very young infants, who cry to be rocked, to be carried about, sometimes for a light in the room, for a bottle to suck, or for the continuance of any other bad habit which has been acquired.

"How can we be sure that a child is crying to be indulged?
"If it stops immediately when it gets what it wants, and cries when it is withdrawn or withheld."

"Never give a child what it cries for," but instead, Holt advises, let it "cry out" and break the crying habit.

Pain, temper, hunger, illness, habit. Infants, it would appear, have hardly changed. Of course, in Holt's universe they do not cry because they need to be changed; presumably, they are all perfectly scheduled.

The adult reaction to the child has taken a new turn. The cry of the "child who has lain too long alone" in Metlinger — the cry of the child expressing his need for human contact — has with Holt become a cry for indulgence. It may be argued that Holt provided a list of excuses for nurses to offer mothers when children cry.

Since Holt opposed the use of opiates, and swaddling was no longer recommended, the nurse wishing to silence her charge was given the alternative of ignoring the baby.

In Holt, there is a growing isolation of child from parent. The baby is treated as an object. This attitude is almost a premonition of the behaviorist approach to psychology, where the animal is considered no more than a source of directionless activity until reinforcement is given or denied and its behavior is shaped.

Holt advocates the "suppository method" of toilet training which, he boldly suggests, may result in success within two months.

"How may a child be trained to be regular in the action of its bowels?
"By endeavouring to have them move at the exactly the same time every day.

"At what age may an infant be trained in this way?
"Usually by the second month if training is begun early.

"What is the best method of such training?
"A small chamber, about the size of a pint bowl, is placed between the nurse's knees, and upon this the infant is held, its back being against the nurse's chest and its body fully supported. This should be done twice a day, after the morning and afternoon feedings, and always at

the same hour. At first there may be necessary some local irritation, like that produced by tickling the anus or introducing just inside the rectum a small cone of oiled paper or a piece of soap, as a suggestion of the purpose for which the baby is placed upon the chamber; but in a surprisingly short time the position is all that is required. With most infants, after a few weeks the bowels will move as soon as the infant is placed on the chamber.

"What advantage has such training?
"It forms the habit of having the bowels move regularly at the same hours, which is a matter of great importance in infancy and makes regularity in childhood much easier. It also saves the nurse much trouble and labour."

On the subject of playing with the child, he remarks, "Babies under six months old should never be played with, and the less of it at any time the better." When asked *"What harm is done by playing with very young babies?"*, the response is a catch-all: "They are made nervous and irritable, sleep badly and suffer from indigestion and in many other respects." Apparently, unless a child was being washed or fed, or when a soap stick was being administered to regiment his bowels, the youngster was never to to touched. The aim was a desocialized child. The widespread acceptance of this book suggests that children at this period were being raised as automatons, to fill factories, not to own them.

Once Lister had demonstrated the relationship between antisepsis and contagion (1867), cleanliness became not only a social preoccupation but an obsession. By 1910, we can read (in Le Grand Kerr's *The Care and Training of Children*) that:

"Dirt is dangerous, not simply because it is earth, but because it is composed of excrement. To be clean is not merely an esthetic adornment, even though it be the result of fixt habit and training, it is a necessary sanitary measure. In a sense, to be clean is to be free from infectious disease, for germs multiply in filth. Personal cleanliness is far more important than public cleanliness, for without the former the latter is of little avail and fails in its purpose (which is to maintain health)."

In fact, good public sanitation can absorb the strain of a considerable amount of private filth, and plumbing lowers the mortality rate faster than soap.

The preoccupation with cleanliness and toilet training reflects a need to impose external order over internal impurity. The use of laxatives to nip filth in the bud can be viewed similarly. For many Americans in the early part of this century, spring house cleaning also involved a dose of castor oil. Enemas too were popular, not only for infants but for older children as well. A quotation from another book (Albert Bell's *Feeding, Diet and the General Care of Children*) suggests that the enema was not only a way to clean out the child physically but also had a punitive purpose:

> "A soapy enema, or a soap or glycerine suppository at intervals, is not so harmful as the constant use of drugs [laxatives] . A child who realizes that an enema will be given is not so likely to neglect other measures such as diet, water, going regularly to stool, etc. as he will be if anticipating only the less disagreeable, routine cathartic."

The passage suggests that bowel training is a means of enforcing a number of other kinds of social behavior. Regularity itself, in this context, seems to take on moral connotations. Constipation is seen as a way in which the child spites a mother rather than as a medical problem.

It was possible to go beyond enemas to irrigation. S. Josephine Baker's 1920 book, *Healthy Babies,* describes irrigation as a valuable treatment for use in "certain forms of bowel trouble or to remove poisonous or irritating matter from the bowels when the child has convulsions."

Method of Giving Irrigation

> "Place the baby on a table or bed which has been covered with rubber sheeting. The sheeting should extend over the side of the bed and be brought together so as to form a trough which reaches into a bowl placed on the floor at the side of the bed. The child should lie on his back, with legs flexed and buttocks extending over the edge of the bed or table. An ordinary fountain syringe should contain the solution being used. It is made of soap suds or a solution of a tablespoon of salt to a quart of water, at a temperature of 90 degrees Farenheit. The tube of the syringe should be connected with an ordinary soft rubber catheter. This may be done by using a glass medicine dropper which has one end inserted in the tube and the other in the end of the catheter. The latter should be greased with vaseline and the water from the bag allowed to flow through it. . . . "

Six or more inches of the tube are run up into the child, and the flow of water is used to hose out the child. This is a dangerous technique, not to be applied casually, certainly not on the vague indications of "certain forms of bowel trouble" offered by Baker (the vagueness of the diagnosis contrasts dramatically with the incredible detail of the procedure itself). The Baker book is illustrated not with pictures of mothers, for whom it was apparently intended, but with pictures of nurses demonstrating such techniques as the "Proper Method of Holding Baby." (Page 120)

Preventive surgery too became popular in the early twentieth century. Mary Read's *The Mothercraft Manual* (1916), like the Holt book, was used in training schools, The Mothercraft Centers.

"Adenoids and enlarged tonsils are abnormal growths of lymphatic tissue in the nose and throat that make breathing difficult and inefficient, and that become breeding places for germs. The infection that they harbor leads frequently to colds, earache, deafness, tonsillitis, diptheria, measles, scarlet fever. They obstruct the breathing and reduce the supply of oxygen, spoil the shape of the face, reduce the ability to think and by their discomfort produce irritability and nervousness. They greatly interfere with vitality. Adenoids should therefore be removed and tonsils treated, their removal being a last resort when they are diseased."

Tonsillectomy subsequently became something of a fad, and it is currently estimated that half a million unnecessary tonsillectomies are performed in the United States every year.

The mothers and physicians of the early 1900s did not stop at merely stripping the internal plumbing of biological obstructions. They extended their efforts to external surgery, most commonly to circumcision. The reasons offered for this operation (which was occasionally performed on girls as well as boys) differ from those given when the case for circumcision is argued today. From the contemporary point of view, one of the principal arguments for circumcision is that it eliminates the occurance of cervical cancer in the wives of circumcised men, a relationship publicized by Abraham Ravich in the early 1940s. At the beginning of this century, however, the primary reasons offered for circumcision were that it aided local cleanliness and that it prevented masturbation, masturbation being considered the result of unclean genitals.

Even apart from masturbation, there was a general feeling that the genitals were dirty. "Never let a child touch these parts," the *Mothercraft Manual* advised, and "see that [children's] hands are outside the bedcovers at night." "The need for circumcision can disturb sleep" and cause bed-wetting, *Mothercraft* advised. Other books went even further. One text,

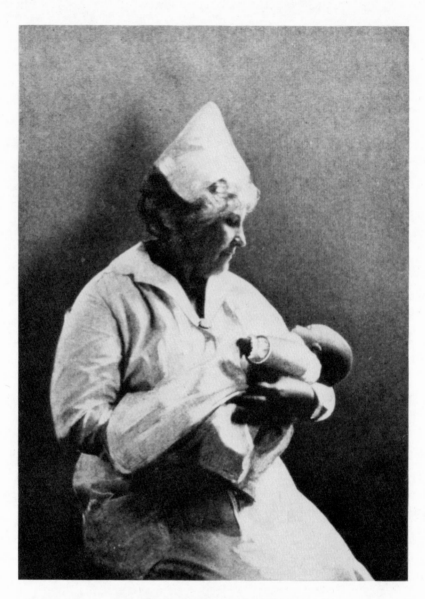

Proper Method of Holding Baby.
This Also Shows Card Board Cuff in Place.

Better Babies (1917) by Samuel Visanska asserted that circumcision could cure or prevent epilepsy (when the cause was uncertain), prolapse of the rectum and hernia, these problems presumably arising from the difficulty of passing urine with a foreskin intact. But advocacy went even beyond these exaggerated claims:

> "In the requirements set by the Contests for Better Babies the schedule requires that five marks be taken off candidates if the prepuce be abnormal (adherent), hence mothers entering babies in such contests would do well to remember that circumcision counts for the child's condition and failure to have the baby circumsized counts against his standing."

At this point the child has entered the final stage of production, the marketplace.

Infantile initiative in any area in which the mother was not specifically trying to train and encourage her child was viewed with suspicion. Alone, isolated in his crib, deprived of contact or companionship, the baby did have a few harmless ways of amusing himself and perhaps a few nervous tics as well. These innocuous baby occupations were soon branded "bad habits" and stopping them became a major enterprise. Nail-biting, thumb-sucking, masturbation were the three kinds of behavior that attracted the most attention, but even bed-wetting and head-banging often fell into this category.

Of all the bad habits thumb-sucking and masturbation were by far the most disturbing to parents. The amount of ingenuity devoted to stopping thumb-sucking is particularly noteworthy. A number of devices were marketed, ranging from stitching up the sleeves of the nightshirt to leather cuffs and aluminum mittens for covering the hands. Splints fastened to the child's elbow (one of Holt's suggestions) and linen elbow bandages stiffened with tongue depressors (proposed by Bell) prevented the child from bending his arm. Bad-tasting ointments for the fingers were also offered by Holt. Taping the baby's arm to his side was yet another approach to the problem.

A number of books contained patterns for making these devices. Baker includes a pattern for a "little cuff over the elbow... made of a roll of cardboard large enough to slip easily over the arm and about four or five inches long.

> "The edges of the cardboard may be fastened with adhesive plaster, and the roll pinned to the child's sleeve, just above the elbow. The use

of this cuff keeps the arm fairly stiff, but still allows a slight motion of the elbow joint. The child can play perfectly, but cannot put his hands in his mouth."

"The use of drugs," Baker comments, "or bitter substances. . . on the end of the thumb or fingers is not advised. While the drugs may make the child nauseated, that is generally their only effect, and their use seldom breaks up the habit."

American manufacturing was also able to get into the habit-breaking business and marketed aluminum mittens which, as Baker says, "have a broad cuff of muslin. These are placed over the baby's hands, and the cuffs pinned to the baby's sleeve." She praises the mits as "excellent" because the child "can thus move his hands freely, but cannot scratch his skin or get his fingers into his mouth." While Baker does not include a picture of these mittens, another book issued five years earlier, Richard M. Smith's *The Baby's First Two Years* (1915), not only contains such a photo but also includes another of "thigh spreaders," consisting of two straps connected by a bar to prevent the child from masturbating by rubbing the thighs together.

From the parents' point of view, thumb-sucking was not simply a neutral activity of a child in a crib, nor even something which might deform the teeth if carried on too long. Thumb-sucking was seen as a willful affront to the mother of a well-trained child, because it seemed to suggest that in spite of all the careful textbook care and attention the child was receiving, he was not getting something he needed from his mother. Thumb-sucking exposed parents to a painful truth about the urgency of individual needs.

In one sense, although swaddling was gone, its purpose, the control and shaping of children, remained. The devices for the prevention of thumb-sucking may be regarded as the inheritors of that long tradition of child control.*

Other traditions too were slow to die out, witness Holt:

"What can be done for children who take cold upon the slightest provocation?

They should be kept in cool rooms, especially when asleep. They

---

*As late as 1949, these methods of preventing thumb-sucking were apparently still in use. Dorothy Baruch, in *New Ways In Discipline* of that year, criticizes them and adds a reference to a "recent hideous device that fits the curve of the upper teeth, has rakelike prongs which protrude down into the mouth and close on the intruding thumb like a gopher trap, making the child withdraw it in pain!"

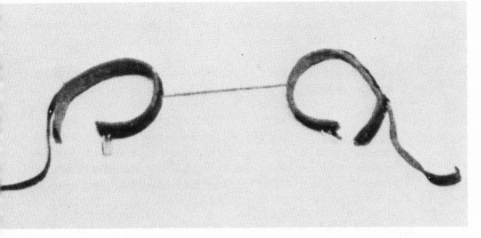

THIGH SPREADERS

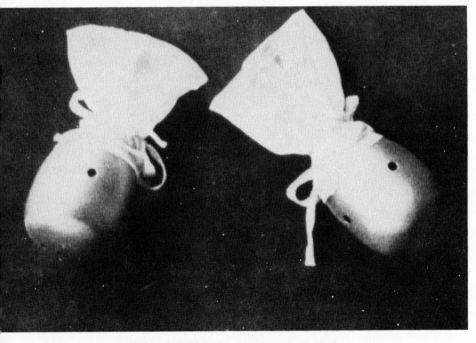

ALUMINUM MITTENS

should not wear such heavy clothing that they are in perspiration much of the time. Every morning the body, particularly the chest and back, should be sprayed with cold water (50° to 60° F.)."

Less ancient but equally strong beliefs on the subject of masturbation were repeated by Holt:

"What is masturbation?
It is the habit of rubbing the genital organs with the hands, with the clothing, against the bed, or rubbing the thighs together. Sometimes the child sits on the floor, closes its thighs tightly and rocks backwards and forwards. Many of these things are passed over lightly and regarded for months as simply a 'queer' trick of the child. . . . "

"How should such a child be treated?
Masturbation is the most injurious of all the bad habits and should be broken up just as early as possible. Children should especially be watched on going to sleep and on first waking. Punishment and mechanical restraints are of little avail except with infants, with older children they usually make matters worse. Some local cause of irritation is often present, which can be removed. Medical adivce should at once be sought."

This is from the 1904 edition. As medical and psychological knowledge increased, it became evident that the ill effects of masturbation had been exaggerated. The above passage, virtually all Holt had to say about the matter, was changed. In 1924, this included a first paragraph asking what masturbation led to. The answer included nervousness, lack of self-control, impairment of general health, lowered moral sense, and ominously, "sometimes to other sexual propensities." The second additional paragraph asked whether it led to feeble-mindedness; the answer was that there was "no evidence that this is the case."

By the 1920s it was known that masturbation did not cause insanity – Holt calls it an effect rather than a cause – yet even knowing this, the old warnings continued. Rather than focusing efforts on challenging old myths and superstitions, scientific research was directed to problems of methods, to techniques by which all child raising might be reduced to a standardized system.

The creation of a perfect child, however, also required bringing together the perfect parents. Darwin's discoveries, which had so upset the Victorians, had by the early twentieth century been assimilated into the popular culture. When a cousin of Darwin's, Francis Galton, developed a "science," eugenics, based on these ideas, the proposals seemed modern, progressive and had an element of moral and biological authority that was just the sort of thing to appeal to the child-care professionals.

Attention was devoted in many books to the two sides of eugenics, to the positive side, the "good stock" from which the child might be bred, and to the negative side, the list of "taints" that would or should preclude responsible parents from having children. The *Mothercraft Manual* provided a handy list of "genetic" defects:

"Some individuals should never become parents because they carry so serious a hereditary taint which some of their children would probably inherit and carry on. This includes individuals inflicted with the following:

"Neuropathic taint: feeblemindedness, idiocy, insanity, epilepsy, hysteria, chorea, sex perversion, alcoholism

"Syphilis

"Tuberculosis

"Deaf-mutism

"Otosclerosis (hardness of hearing due to rigid eardrum)

"Catarrhal deafness

"Retinitis (progressive degeneration of retina and atrophy of optic nerve, producing blindness)

"Albinism (absence of color in hair and eyes)

"Inherent lack of physical energy; pauperism."

It behooved parents not only to make sure that they carried none of these defects but also to get themselves in the best physical shape before breeding offspring.

"As soon as its far-reaching significance to themselves and to their children is generally perceived by parents and young people, men and women who genuinely love each other will voluntarily give and absolutely require a medical certificate before marriage. Before undertaking the responsibility of parenthood, both mother and father should put themselves into the best possible physical and spiritual condition, and if necessary go through a course of training as that of any aspirant for an athletic prize or of any priest for great spiritual work. The Vedas, the sacred books of the Hindoos, contained special prayers for those about to assume this creative work."

It would be wrong to assume that the primary focus of Mary Read's concern for genetic family purity is the improvement of society. The actual motivation appears to have been a concern for the survival and prosperity of the individual family line. Her view is Darwinian, and the family is seen as the functional unit of social and economic Darwinism, each family struggling as a unit for their survival in a competitive world. "On the average," Read writes, "four children to a family are required merely to maintain a constant population; families in which the average is less are in danger of extinction."

Read is writing for the middle class, a class concerned with the preservation and protection of their property. An excess of children may insure the continuity of the family name, but numerous offspring also dilute the inheritance — to say nothing of the costs of raising them. Birth control in this situation is a must:

> "Nature has provided one effective, safe, and ethical method of limiting the birth rate in the family, a method that is entirely in the control of the parents. This method is abstinence, except for the end to which nature has implanted the instinct — the creation of a new life. It is conducive to the welfare of the children. [And it] is in no wise harmful to the physical, mental, social, or spiritual well-being of men and women if they are both temperamentally adapted to each other. . . if they have learned to transmute this instinct and energy to other activities; and if their relationship and adjustments are normal and wholesome, not artificially stimulated."

This then is a part of our past, not simply a world of emotional self-control (or emotional passivity) built into the child through delivering "mothering, cuddling, fondling" at scheduled intervals regardless of the child's demands. The aim was to produce a pure, unspoiled, moral child, who would naturally develop into the perfect adult, normal, wholesome and not in need of artificial stimulation.

Purity was the goal — avoiding "adulterated [and] canned foods" was one method. Parents would "teach children never to use a public drinking cup or towel, and never to sit on a public toilet, even in a public school, without first laying a paper over it so they do not come in contact with the seat." They were advised to "cultivate a sense of modesty both in boys and girls from babyhood."

These theories and ideals could be modified in practice. There exists a highly interesting monograph by Anna G. Noyes published in 1913, entitled *How I Kept My Baby Well*, that shows us how this sometimes happened. It is a detailed, day-by-day study of the first twenty-five months of life of one child, Anna Noyes's son.* Noyes is a modern, college-educated woman, (superior according to the standard of the time) who comes (as does her husband) of "good stock". She says at the outset: "Dr. Holt's *Care and Feeding of Children* I kept at my right hand."

The book is almost entirely a series of charts and itemized descriptions of child behavior, nearly hour by hour, in which everything that one can imagine is measured: food consumption, feces texture, vomiting, feeding times, sleeping times and more. (Page 128)

The illustration is a summary chart. Elsewhere in Noyes's book, charts record other details of life, such as "disorder in the skin. . . grouped under six heads: 1, Rash; 2, Pimples; 3, Sore scalp; 4, Sore face; 5, Flesh rough (sore); 6, Sore about the anus." In the colums following these items were recorded the number of days each lasted. Naturally the basic indicators such as body weight are not overlooked.

On body weight Holt commented:

"Of what importance is the weight of the child?
"Nothing else tells us so accurately how well it is thriving."

This is, of course, the kind of oversimplified yardstick we might expect from a production-oriented society: more is better. But, in use, this approach to child progress measurement turned out to be the kind of connection to reality that tended to subvert the "moral" messages Holt had to offer. A child might, after all, suck his thumb, masturbate and wet his bed and yet gain weight, largely disproving at least some of the supposed ill-effects that might be attributed to these bad habits.

So it was with Noyes and her baby. She might write that "I began in the third month to accustom the baby to the use of the chamber," for bowel movements and urination, but on her chart it took approximately twenty months for the movements to finally stabilize at about a twenty-four-hour interval. This age conforms to contemporary expectations for the process, rather than the two months suggested by Holt as the time the baby could be trained.

Similarly, on thumb-sucking, in her summaries, Noyes records:

"At two years this habit was not yet broken. This is the Nemesis

---

*Noyes's was not the first of these day-by-day studies. Preyer had studied his own son, emphasizing observations on his mental development, and Millicent Shinn had published, in 1893, an extremely detailed account of her child's physical growth and mental competence, contrasting her child with Preyer's observations.

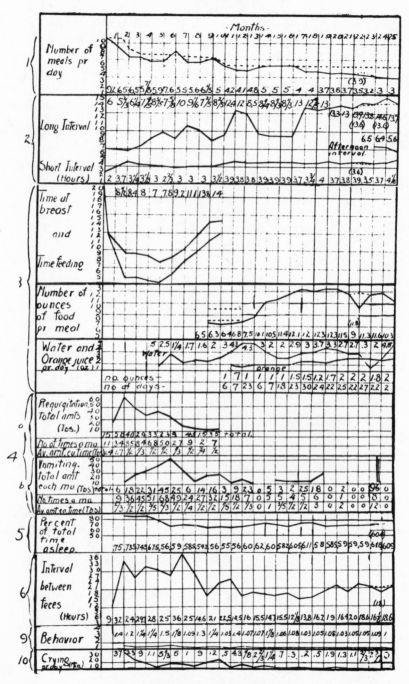

Summaries Tabulated.

following my failure to check an undesirable habit from the outset. It stole many hours from his sleep and from my time. I tried bitter quinine on the thumb, slapping the hand, pinching the finger, talking to him, holding his hand while he went to sleep, binding up his arm and hand, putting his hand in a round pasteboard roll, wrapping his thumbs with adhesive plaster, and so on, but he soon got over all the hurts inflicted and the bad taste in his mouth, and became most efficient in freeing this thumb from bondage. The habit has left no traces in the shape of the mouth or thumb, and the thumb was not in the mouth for a very long time (never when awake, and only for a few minutes as he dropped off to sleep)."

In her comments on the twenty-fifth month, she says:

"He has gone to sleep several times without the thumb in his mouth, and does not resent my taking it out after he has fallen asleep, so we are making progress there. He seems so reasonable about many things that I am hoping his sensibleness will help out in the breaking up of this habit. He is wearing drawers and going to be without a diaper. He asks now to go to the toilet, and can wait till he gets there."

When confronted by the reality of her own child's development, Noyes kept her own counsel, preferring to work out discrepancies between theory and observation by common sense and "inductive thinking" rather than by retreat to printed authority. She even manages to find authority for this in Holt himself and comments that "As Dr. Holt says, again and again, *conditions present are the best guide.*'" Noyes's own logic was excellent:

"Now, there is one thing that every doctor and nurse and mother with whom I have had the opportunity to discuss this matter admits at once, and that is *what will keep a baby well is the treatment for that baby*. Could anything be plainer than that? Our grandmothers knew it and practiced it before tables of averages were so much as dreamed of.

"And how is one to know when a baby is well? Any unprejudiced, normal person could, after a few moments for reflection, sum up the evidences of health in a baby: namely, pink cheeks; a clean, red tongue; soft, smooth skin, unbroken by pimples or roughness; long, peaceful naps; freedom from colds; agility of movement; the eye sparkling and the cornea blue white; a keen and regular appetite; all food thoroughly digested (as shown by a smooth and yellow feces);

steady growth, and a happy contented disposition. All these are readily admitted to be some of the evidences of good health in a baby.

"If these signs spell health, then the disappearance of them signifies that health is in danger. If the cheeks turn pale and the clear blue-white of the eye becomes yellowish, if the skin grows rough and blotched, and if bodily movements become listless, if the food is thrown up, and excreta are foul, and the weight is not increasing and the baby is irritable, all these changes must be noted, not necessarily with alarm, but frankly and to the full extent of their importance.

"And once the habit is established of noticing and admitting these little lapses, then must follow the search for the mischiefmaker.

"I believe that investigation should begin with the diet. If that is rightly managed, the cause of the trouble can usually be located at once and removed. And that is what I studied to do. If trouble so much as peeped out, I was after the cause of it. . . .

"Little by little [if all else, fresh air, clean water, proper and clean clothing, proved satisfactory] , I found where to look for evidences of wrong feeding. To begin with, I became very suspicious that throwing up was a sign of overfeeding. 'Everybody,' says that 'all babies vomit.' But why do they? I wondered. And so long as my baby continued to regurgitate, with my eye on the scale, watching his weight, I kept cutting down the quantity of food and increasing the intervals, until at one time he was one-sixth the *time* which Holt prescribes. But as the scales continued to rise and the baby kept well, I knew I was on the right track."

Noyes found that the "keynote in maintaining a baby's health will be found (after fresh air, pure water, and hygenic clothing have been secured) in *keeping the whole digestive tract in perfect order.*" And again, *"in the intestines was to be found a reliable guide in maintaining the baby's health.* Irregularities in excreta demanded a change in diet. . . . "

For a woman who was a self-proclaimed "novice in baby culture," Noyes had come an extraordinary way towards modern methods of child care. Her success is, naturally, reflected on the chart she offers of her baby's weight gain set off against the average offered by Holt. (Page 131)

The weight gain, general good health and sweet disposition recorded by Noyes, support the simple caution and care she suggests throughout the book. It is an outgrowth of the physical warmth of the relationship between Noyes and her child and of the security the baby seems to have felt. Throughout the book there are photos of mother and child and of father and child playing games, dandling, talking – doing all those physical

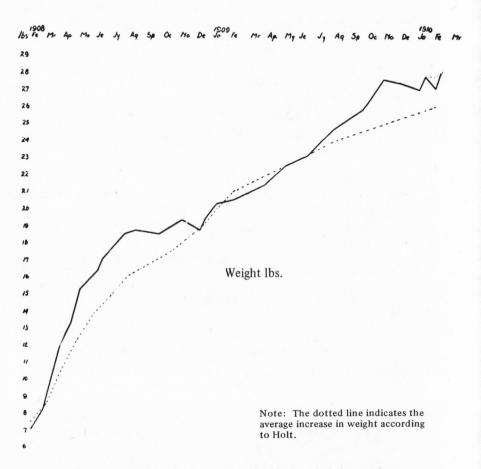

Weight lbs.

Note: The dotted line indicates the
average increase in weight according
to Holt.

Weaning, teething, and two winter colds retarded the weight.

things of which Holt advises "the less at any time the better."

In the conclusion, Noyes speaks of the apprehensions of her friends concerning her having a baby. Yet, she found, there was nothing as interesting as watching and participating in the process by which a small red little creature turns into a human being. For all her charts, averages and notions, Noyes falls squarely into the "erotic tradition" of child care along with Harland, Tuthill and others, who found that intelligence is a useful tool for raising a baby and need not preclude warmth and affection.

The results Noyes achieved come in part from her willingness to pay full and careful attention to her child, to, in her words, "keep the baby well so that he could not get sick." The lack of theory, the lack of morality in the abstract sense, was an asset and represents the best kind of scientific objectivity.

> "This (method). . . I should call the *common sense way of caring for a baby*, and it is, of course, the way in which mothers have already brought up their babies. But I cannot find one of them who has. . . any data to offer, in the shape of records, as to how the plan worked, even in one case.
>
> "And this is all I claim to have done. *I have a complete record of one baby who was kept well for two years by not being allowed to get sick*.
>
> "The thing to do next is to follow this record with the records of, say, fifty babies."

That was the direction the future would take.

In 1929, looking back at Holt's influence on child care, two of Holt's supporters, the psychologists Blatz and Bott, described what they believed to be his effect on history:

> "The publication of Dr. Holt's *Care and Feeding of Children* marked an epoch. It conveyed to the mothers of the generation to which it was addressed the idea of a positive regimen of right physical habits as essential to the child's health and well-being. Previous to this mothers had brought their children up by rule of thumb, the child's desires being the guage of the mother's behavior. Thus, if a baby cried he was fed, if he was fretful he was rocked or dandled, if he had colic he was walked the floor with, this being accepted as all in a day's work in bringing up a baby. All this Dr. Holt and his followers significantly changed. Instead of the baby's demands the routine laid down by the specialist prescribed the rule for the mother to follow. Regular times of feeding and hours of sleep, freedom from distraction, were all secured

for the child with startling results in his health and happiness.

"Besides demonstrating the importance of a good routine for health, such a system of training did more; it taught mothers to respect the welfare of the child and to make this their first consideration. . . . Once the importance of regularity and consistency in physical care was grasped, the old, careless practices stood condemned. We may hope to see an analogous respect for the *mental* integrity of the child as a result of improved methods of mental training."

The movement to regiment the child's mind was under way.

CHAPTER 9

The Psychologists' Child

World War I brought an end to the easy optimism that had viewed perfection of child and adult as simply a biological problem. Rather, in the face of the War, what seemed to be required was some sort of human *mental* engineering, some method of bringing destructive human emotions under social control, so that the facade of civilization might be patched together. Throughout the 1920s, we are confronted by this need which takes the form of a series of rapidly changing fashions in child care, all promoting various forms of physical and mental engineering. In prewar books, whatever the rigidities of biological scheduling, psychological differences between children were still dealt with in a relatively humane pragmatic fashion. In Mary Read's *The Mothercraft Manual*, for example, a book that advocated fixed feeding, sleeping and fondling schedules, discipline still varied according to the circumstance and child:

> "Discipline should be adapted to the child's temperament, to his stage of development, and to the particular offense. A sensitive, high strung, imaginative child must be dealt with gently though firmly, with special care that his self-respect, his confiding, his expressiveness are not weakened. A sturdy, matter-of-fact, phlegmatic realist usually needs more concrete, vigorous, physical form[s] of punishment to make him perceive the significance of events."

In contrast, the postwar psychology texts, while giving lip service to the child as an individual, proposed to eliminate the differences between children. A work by two well-known psychologists, William Blatz and Helen Bott — *Parents and the Pre-School Child* (1929) — expressed the prevailing view thirteen years after Read's *Mothercraft Manual*:

"If we were asked what was the keynote of a practical and common-sense parental attitude in respect to child training, we should sum the matter up in one word — *discipline*. By discipline we mean the reasonable regulation and supervision of the habits of a child throughout all stages of development and a consistent plan for having a child observe those rules that are laid down. Such simple rules as regular meal times, regular bed times, training in elemination, eating what is placed before him, wearing the clothes that are provided, observing certain proprieties of conduct — these. . . would probably suffice for the average home. Consistent adherence to a few simple rules without any deviation whatever will permit the child to learn to make adequate social adjustments."

This passage is reminiscent of the one quoted in Chapter 8 on "the value of regularity," but the emphasis has changed. In the Eldred-LeCron work, *For the Young Mother*, for all its versifying about how happy the baby will feel under the guidance of the friendly clock, the scheduled baby is still described in terms of "less work for mother." With Blatz and Bott, however, regularity is no longer simply a physical convenience; it is a means towards "adequate social adjustment."

The schedule, the key to moral as well as physical training, is proclaimed to be inherent in the child even before birth:

"What is the significance of habit for the organism? Why not allow each individual to be the arbiter of his own habit? The specious argument of following nature is here often advanced, specious because it is folly to assume that any creature can grow to maturity without establishing habits of a sort. Even in intra-uterine life certain habits have begun — for example, of alternating rhythms of quiet and activity — and these habits multiply from birth onward. The question is whether we are going to control the situation so that he is enabled to form habits that will be increasingly serviceable to him as he grows older. . . .

"One might enumerate some of the obvious advantages of good habits. They save time and energy. The first stages of habit formation are, as a rule, highly conscious — witness, for instance, the child learning to lace his boots or to write, etc. — but with practice the function drops to the level of automatic behavior and the attention is set free for other tasks. The person whose life does not fall into well-regulated habits is merely wasting conscious effort that might be set free for better uses. Life today is more complex than formerly, and it is the more important that our children learn to economize conscious

effort and reduce the excess of mental strain through proper organization of their lives.

"The social implications of habit are not always recognized, yet the
child with undesirable habits is, as Thom points out, largely incapa-
citated for social life. Many households are thrown into a daily
turmoil because children forget to wash their hands before each meal!
Punctuality would seem the essence of social consideration. Yet how
many excellent people have never acquired it. It is perhaps only fair to
point out that the social habits are acquired later and are harder to
establish as they must be built up on the basis of elementary bodily
habits. The responsibility for this must also rest with the parents."

The appeal is, as expected, to middle-class parents who place great value
on cleanliness and punctuality as expressions of good upbringing.

In the psychology of the 1920s, habit was not only a way of handling
training, it was also used as a system explaining other behavior. Neurotic
behavior, for example, was described as a bad habit — counterproductive
and inappropriate to the demands of society.

During this period, the child was seen as little more than a bundle of
reflexes and appetites which, while they could not be "eradicated" could
be "regulated and directed." As Blatz and Bott remark, "This process of
modifying the form [of the] original crude impulse is called conditioning."
The aim of conditioning was not to create individuals with real and flexible
responses to social situations but rather to promote reliable, efficient
reactions regardless of the circumstances. Awareness and consciousness
figured into this scheme only at the moment of learning; afterwards everything was to be automatic.

Blatz and Bott offer the classic experiment by Pavlov (where dogs
were trained to salivate at the sound of a bell) as one example of the conditioning process. They present a second example in which a rat "set to run
a maze [was] made to receive a slight electric current upon entering the
wrong passage. . .and in the future [learned] to avoid the passage where
the current is." "One shock," they note enthusiastically, "may be sufficient to set up a habit of avoidance which will last for the lifetime of the
individual."

"Punishment, with children, is one use of the method of shock in
order to establish avoidance responses. . .[but] as shock produces
emotional reactions. . . for the training of appetites, the building up of
positive responses is of greater significance."

"The parent-child relationship is felt to be the whole core of our problem," Blatz and Bott wrote. It was a problem seen not only in psychological terms but also in terms of the physical environment. They quote parents on the difficulties encountered:

"'Today houses and gardens are smaller. We live in congested quarters and children have little space in which to play.'

"'Children have to watch the traffic — this involves a severe nervous strain.'

"'More organizations work with children and their [i.e. children's] time is largely planned for and filled.'

"'Labor-saving devices have in a measure taken away woman's work and she must have something else to occupy her time.'

"'The general advance of medical science and psychology has made mothers discontented with old methods of doing things. They do not want to feed their babies in an up-to-date way and treat mental development in an old-fashioned way.'"

To reinforce this picture, consider the description of an infant's room by Roger Dennett in *The Healthy Baby* (1912 with editions through 1935):

"It seems to me that it takes a great deal of thought to ventilate the individual house or apartment properly. If the rooms are large and open into each other, one or two windows in the proper place will furnish fresh air for the whole house. If we are dealing with a small apartment, we must select one room where the windows may be opened top and bottom and from which the fresh air may circulate without causing too much breeze or draught. It is a well-known fact that open fireplaces are wonderfully good ventilators, but they are now considered a luxury, I am sorry to say. At any cost, keep the air good night and day.

"The temperature of living rooms should be 65° to 70° F. A thermometer should hang in the rooms that are most frequented by the children, and should be placed at the height of their heads. Overheating is the commonest error in the city. In the country perhaps the most usual mistake is draughty rooms, floors, and cold halls. On the other hand airtight rooms in which the same air is breathed over and over again without once changing is a common occurrence.

"The sleeping room should have one or more windows wide open top and bottom throughout the year. The bed should be as far away from the windows as possible and in a corner out of direct draught. If this is not possible, a blanket may be pinned around the crib, so that the winter winds will not blow directly upon the baby."

The world Dennett describes is that of the city dweller, cramped into small apartments, crowded into tiny houses on narrow lots; yet rural America was hardly better. "It is my observation," Dennett remarks, "that city children get more fresh air than country children during the first and second years." The city child gets his airing on a regular basis because he is "carefully brought up," whereas the country child is relatively neglected. The energy of modern society flowed increasingly towards urban centers.

Social pressures for conformity increased during the 1920s. In Ada Hart Arlitt's *The Child from One to Six* (1930), not only physical but also mental training hinged on regularity. Your child, Arlitt writes, "will never know that there are laws that govern the universe unless he knows that there are laws that govern the home." She adds, quoting Blatz and Bott, "It was formerly believed that mother love was the simple and safe basis for the problems of training; it is now known that a much more adequate guide is the kitchen timepiece. . . . Blatz and Bott state that it was not unusual to find a fifteen- to twenty-minute variation in the time for meals when the family insisted that their schedule for eating was absolutely regular. Such irregularities should not be present."

The purpose of all the regularity, according to Arlitt was "willed obedience," that is, child control. This extended even to punishment:

"While punishments themselves are not equally effective for different children, there are certain considerations in giving punishments which do apply in every family. The first of these is that punishment should be resorted to infrequently. . . . If punishments are administered too frequently, they, like medicine, lose all their force. The child who is constantly punished, soon learns to take punishment as a matter of course. In some cases, he enjoys it. . . .

"Another thing to keep in mind is that punishment must not be excessive. If the punishment is excessive, it may be so exciting and intense that it makes the child repeat the act. . . .

"Cut down the number of times that one speaks to the child. Speak only when necessary then expect to be obeyed."

The family is now no longer simply isolated from its community by urbanization and from its tradition by industrialization and science, its members have finally reached the "modern" situation, isolated from one another. Is it any wonder that under these circumstances children may, as Arlitt suggests, learn to enjoy punishment, since that is the only way in which their parents physically relate to them?

To solve the problems of family breakdown, professional and institutional help and Habit Clinics were established in several cities, including Boston, New York and Baltimore. The director of the Boston clinic, Douglas A. Thom, previously mentioned in the quote from Blatz and Bott, recorded the neurotic "failures of adaptation" that he saw in his office. His book, *Everyday Problems of the Everyday Child* (1927), recounts the problems of "a parent [who] lost his wife from an infectious disease, which he felt might well have been prevented, when his little boy was about five years of age."

"From that time on, he built the latter's life around this particular emotional experience. The child was forbidden to go out and mingle with other children and was kept away from every person and situation that might possibly lead to physical illness. . . . At the age of ten, the boy has no idea how to play with other children and lives in horror of acquiring some dire illness that will result in death. . . .

"There is nothing more pathetic than the child who has the misfortune to inherit parents who refuse to allow him to grow up; who deny to him opportunities to develop a personality from the mental characteristics with which he was originally endowed; who entertain certain preconceived ideas as to just what he should do and what he should think, and who resent any deviation that nature may bring about in his development. How many parents dominate the thoughts and actions of their children because they glory in the fact that 'My child just can't get along without me!' During pre-school years, they attempt to keep their children in that infantile state where they may feed them, lie down with them at nap time, respond to their midnight calls, and wait upon them to the point where the child is simply vegetating. A little later they march their children back and forth from school, protect and sympathize with them in their conflicts with the teacher, fight their battles with other children, and receive them with open arms when they meet fear and failure in the outside world.

"If these children are permitted to have companions at all, it is the parent who does the selecting. Their companions must be well-mannered, clean, neither rough and active; nor must the intellectual and cultural setting of the family background be ignored. Such unhappy children must conform to parental ideas of race, color and religion. Above all, they must not be 'tough' nor belong to the 'dreadful gang around the corner,' in all probability consisting merely of a lot of dirty-faced, healthy boys who are too busy with the real problems of life to get either into a bathtub or into any real trouble. . . .

"Over-solicitousness on the part of parents. . .often produces the selfish, self-centered, clinging vine type of child."

Worth noting in this passage is the description of middle- or upper-middle-class life. Not since Donné in the mid 1800s had the life of wealthy children been portrayed in these terms, isolated from the rough interaction with children their own age and (going beyond Donné) forming a neurotic bond with their fellow prisoners of the household, their mothers. The world, in the intervening sixty-odd years, has grown richer and the middle class has expanded. Once only the few could afford this kind of neurotic upbringing. With the aid of science and industry, a great number of upper-middle-class families could now achieve the same results.

As parents sought to raise their children according to the charts given in books, the investment of time and labor soon encouraged living vicariously through the child. Thom comments on parents becoming emotionally upset if the child's behavior did not meet their expectations:

"Appetite is looked upon by many laymen as an index of the individual's well-being. . . . Many mothers have been made anxious by the attempts to standardize the height and weight of children, much the fashion during these past few years. . . .

"All these factors [height, weight, appetite, etc.] should be looked upon by parents in a common sense way. Mental and physical health cannot be obtained for the child if every violation. . . of the feeding regimen arouses an emotional reaction on the part of the parents."

Some of Thom's comments are incisive: "Whether children are obedient or disobedient depends to a great extend upon the standards and requirements of the enviroment and the attitude of those in authority." Yet the underlying superficiality of a psychology in which virtually all behavior is seen as a form of habit ultimately damages his work. His analysis of jealousy as "usually the result of selfishness, which means faulty training" is clearly oversimplified.

"The child should be taught to share his toys and playthings, his candy, books and pennies with other children. In games, he must learn to strive for the good of the group and not for personal achievement. If defeated, he must learn to acknowledge superior skill on the part of others with a smile. . . . Unselfish conduct should be rewarded by commendation and occasionally by some reward of a material nature. There is certainly no disadvantage in the child's learning from experience that unselfishness is a paying proposition."

Another book, *Your Nervous Child*, published the same year as Thom's, approached the problem of neurotic behavior from the psychiatric point of view. Written by a German physician, Dr. Erwin Wexberg associated with the Adler Institute, it lists the symptoms of "nervousness" – apparently the principal psychological disorder of the 1920s – as well as its supposed psychological roots. The range of symptoms is startling; the book includes lengthy descriptions of each of the following conditions: children who won't eat their food, who won't chew solid food, who vomit, who tyranize their parents with eccentric demands or with constipation, who wet their beds after they are two years old, who have nightmares, who are cowardly or anxious, who hate school and throw fits when faced with it, who suck their thumbs, nose-pick or ear-pick, masturbate, lie, grimace or are stubborn.

Cases discussed range from the pitifully sick stuttering child to the little devil Wexberg describes who won't eat unless Grandma puts on a certain hat. The cause, according to Wexberg, of all these defects is a lack of self-esteem and courage. He describes masturbation, for example, in these terms:

"The child who regards the acquisition of pleasure from his body as the only consolation in a hostile world learns that he is spiritually and physically lost if he does not give up this source of gratification. If this discovery were made by a normal, healthy, courageous child, he would not find it too difficult to resign his harmful habit in favor of a more harmless one, as for instance candy-eating. But here we have to do with children whose deficient courage and self-confidence are the very causes of their bad habit."

In the Victorian scheme, the person who masturbated lost courage and self-confidence; according to Wexberg, the child who has no self-confidence masturbates.

There were several ways to cure nervousness. Strengthening the child physically was one of them. "Courage must be learned and practiced and the opportunities are plenty in life if the educator looks for them," Wexberg writes. Athletics was one way: "Jumping, running, and especially swimming are not only good for the body but help the progress of the soul." Work was another. Wexberg preferred his undiluted: "The clever trick of. . . uniting play with work side-tracks the issue more than it solves it. For sooner or later the child will have to learn what it is to work."

Love, too, had its place in Wexberg's scheme of rehabilitation:

"Love is the positive force that is capable of winning the child for humanity. We do not mean by this the sensual tenderness with which mothers burden their children only too often. We mean the indestructible well-wishing of the educator that the child feels even when there is no exchange of tenderness."

The parent-child relationship is to be modeled on the teacher-pupil relationship.

"Punishments in the usual sense are not necessary. It will always be sufficient to take care that the actions of a child have their natural and necessary consequences. These consequences should result from the nature of the deed, and not seem to come from the educator, and will fulfill the purpose of punishment but without having the evil effects thereof."

If a child breaks something, according to Wexberg, he must pay for it or be deprived of something he would otherwise get. If he hits the parent, the parent should let the child know that it hurt.

Wexberg's ideas were influenced by the ideas of the German psychologist Wilhelm Preyer and the educational reformer Friedrich Froebel. Preyer's book *The Mind of the Child* (German 1882, English 1893), too, was concerned with the "weakness of the child's will" and how it might be strengthened through the "development of voluntary inhibitions, upon which most depends in the formation of character."

"Exercises in being obedient cannot begin too early, and I have, during an almost daily observation of six years, discovered no harm will come from an early, consistent guiding of the germinating will, provided only this guiding be done with the greatest mildness and justice, as if the infant had already an insight into the benefits of obedience. By assuming insight in the child, insight will be earlier awakened than by training; and by giving a true and reasonable ground for every command, as soon as the understanding begins, and by avoiding all groundless *prohibitions*, obedience is made decidedly more easy."

The oversimplification of Wexberg's emphasis on self-control and courage — the last line of his book reads: "The goal is Courage!" — or the superficiality of the American psychologists' focus on habit both seem to express the same fear about the child: the fear that the child is somehow beyond the capacity of parents to handle.

The child is never described as a complete human being, but always as something else: a machine, a pupil, anything to avoid admitting the human relationship between parent and child.

Into the emptiness of these relationships, increasingly through the 1920s, came fads and fashions. The belief in cold baths was largely gone, but an enthusiasm for cold air (hinted at in the selection from Dennett) and its benefits was asserted by some writers in almost the same terms, i.e., hardening the child to ward off diseases. Dr. Philip Lovell — the *Editor of the Most Widely Read Health Column in the World, "Care of the Body" Department of the Los Angeles Times*, as the title page of his book *The Health of the Child* (1926) reads — had a menagerie of faddish ideas. It is from Lovell, known as a "Drugless Practitioner," that we learn that in the mid-twenties (a dozen years after the Harrison Narcotic Act limited the availability of opiates) mothers were still beseeching doctors for those infant tranquilizers. Lovell also mentions "a mysterious substance known as vitamins" that can prevent rickets and cure other diseases.

Lovell believed in nature and natural things as healing remedies and demonstrated hostility to the technology of modern medicine. "There is no finer external healing agent than the sun. It is infinitely superior to medicine, ointments and lotions."

The Ultra-Violet Rays are the Life Rays

"Experiment and investigation have shown that the various rays, visible and invisible, have certain powers of healing or destruction. The rays that concern us most in the process of healing are the ones known as ultra-violet.

"These are invisible rays and may be used either to the detriment or for the blessing of man. It is these rays which create sunburn. It is these rays which give the life properties to living cells. They activate, stimulate and energize the living tissue and furnish it with a vital something without which life could not be maintained. . . . These rays also have a penetrating power. It is assumed they reach the bloodstream directly through the layers of the skin.

"It is then that their most important action takes place. The blood literally takes on a new baptism of life and passes through all the vessels with fresh vigor and vim."

The cleansing of the system assumed great importance in Lovell's vision of health:

A Clean Bowel Implies Clean Blood

"We also know that the source of nutrition comes from the intestinal system. Hence, if we keep the source clean and untainted, the innumerable blood vessels must contain relatively clean, pure blood."

Roughage is suggested as a cleanser for the intestinal tract, and regularity is, of course, essential. Not only does internal uncleanliness lead to impure bodily fluids, it may also lead to dangerous habits:

"Internal uncleanliness, especially the pressure of a bowel loaded with wastes, and of a rectum filled with undischarged fecal substance, will induce masturbative habits. . . .

"Of course, here the solution is to 'clean house.' Remove the debris from the rectum and the pressure which, in turn, induces masturbation, will be relieved. Constipation must be overcome by natural methods only. . . .

[Lovell then talks about irritation from smegma in the uncircumsized male.] "Even though it may be astonishing to many mothers, circumcision is often recommendable for girls as well as boys, especially when they have what is known in medical parlance as a 'hooded clitoris.'

"As in the boy, chronic constipation will also induce masturbation in the girl. This, primarily, because of a blood stream that is filled with food products which heat and stimulate the blood stream unnaturally, and which consequently arouse the sex passions."

Lovell advises fresh air and light bedclothes and warns against "the habit of remaining in bed after awakening."

"He should be compelled to get out of bed the moment he awakens. Do not let him linger in its cozy warmth. . . . [the] entire problem of masturbation is largely an individual one of training. . . . Fast company, loose literature, salacious moving pictures, and suggestive magazines — these form an almost irresistible combination."

How seriously Lovell took this matter of masturbation is suggested by his mention of circumcision. Like most "nature" doctors, Lovell opposed circumcision, which he described as almost "universal." "There is no necessity for a mother to be stampeded into this operation for her child. . . . There is no reason why it cannot be postponed for several months. . . . Far too many babies who, to all appearances, seem to need it shortly after birth, have been found not to need it after several months have elapsed." A true observation but a bad suggestion: After several months the operation becomes substantially more complicated and, if we are to believe the psychiatrists, traumatic as well.

Although Lovell favored vitamins, he nevertheless was against the "fraud of inoculation," quoting a Dr. Hadwen writing for the magazine *Truth*, who describes it as "'the latest medical craze.'"

"'It is the panacea for every ill. It will prevent disease in the case of typhoid and tetanus, but it will not cure. It will cure in the case of tuberculosis and boils, but it will not prevent. And it will prevent as well as cure in the case of diptheria, cholera, plague, and a few other diseases. This is the claim.

"'When a patient is inoculated against a certain aliment and does not subsequently contract it, the inoculation gets the credit. If, after inoculation, a mild attack supervenes, it is the inoculation which saved the patient from a severe one. . . .

"'When, however, death itself claims the subject of inoculation, we are informed that there must have been something wrong with the prophylactic, or that the patient was inoculated too soon or too late, or in an unskilled manner. . . .

"'Nothing must be said against inoculation. It is the fashion of the hour, and resembles the image which Nebuchadnezzar set up; for everyone must bow down to it and worship, or the fiery furnace awaits him.'"

The psychological counterpart of Lovell in faddishness, though not in attitude, was John B. Watson. Far from believing in nature, Watson sided with other psychologists holding the child was a malleable creature, but went far beyond them in suggesting the degree to which a child might be molded. "Give me a dozen healthy infants," he had said, "well-formed, and my own specified world to bring them up in and I'll guarantee to take any one at random and train him to become any type of specialist I might select — into a doctor, lawyer, artist, merchant-chief, and yes, even into beggar-man and thief, regardless of his talents, penchants, tendencies, abilities, vocations and race of ancestors."

This was a wonderful promise for any man to make, seemingly more akin to advertising than to science. Watson, who had started his career as a reputable psychologist of the behaviorist school (that is, of the school that studies only the external behavior of animals without speculating on the mental state that produces it), had in 1920 given up his post at Johns Hopkins to enter advertising, which taught him to sell a product by simplifying, by hedging on flaws and packaging an idea attractively. The product he marketed in 1928 was child psychology; the book he created as packaging was *Psychological Care of Infant and Child*.

It is possible to place the lowest ebb of parent-child relations somewhere in the remote past, such as when children were swaddled into rigid bundles, or later, when infants were abandoned in the streets or brought up under the severity of Puritanism. Yet, for the most part, these practices arose either from ignorance, social necessity or from a naive enthusiasm for new methods. With Watson's book the nadir in child-care advice was reached.

Critic Grace Adams wrote in 1934:

"Thousands of American parents rushed to hear this great man's lectures and to buy his books, for this Dr. Watson, it seemed to them, not only confirmed the popular belief that any male child could become the President of these United States, but he knew the formula by which every separate father could groom his favorite son for the high office."

Psychological Care was, in its way, a brilliant book. Smoothly written, convincing and apparently logical, it offers many insights into the mind of the times. Even the dedication is cleverly contrived:

Dedicated To The First Mother Who Brings Up A Happy Child

This boldly contradicts the common notion that childhood is a happy time and instead brings it closer to the truth — a time of difficulty and incomprehension, of frequent fear and unhappiness in a world of giant adults. The dedication also suggests that there has never before been a happy child who, by his happiness confirms, the mother's own humanity. The phrase bluntly advertises that if you are the singular mother who achieves the goal all mothers strive for, then this book is dedicated to *you*!

Watson begins:

"Ever since my first glimpse of Dr. Holt's *The Care and Feeding of Children*, I hoped some day to be able to write a book on the psychological care of the infant. I believed then that psychological care was just as necessary as physiological care. Today I believe that it is in some ways more important. Healthy babies do grow up under the most varied forms of feeding and bodily care. They can be stunted by poor food and ill health and then in a few days of proper regimen be made to pick up their weight and bodily strength.

"But once a child's character has been spoiled by bad handling which can be done in a few days, who can say that the damage is ever repaired?"

This view of psychological damage is similar to the Puritan idea of sin and damnation: one false step dooms you forever.

After drawing the above comparison of his work with Holt, Watson compares Holt to the Bible, sanctifying himself by analogy with Holt's success: "The 28 editions of his [Holt's] work abundantly prove [its value] ." The marketplace is here again the arbiter of truth.

The world Watson portrays is dangerous to the psychology of infants. The fault is not within the infant but with parents who ignorantly made the child what he has become. Grandmother had fourteen children and raised ten, Watson asserts, but many had rickets, bad teeth and undernourished bodies. This has been changed by modern science. Now there are three kinds of mothers: the mothers who trust to nature, the mothers who dote on their children and have faith in love and the "modern mother" who searches for new "psychological facts." Yet even in the search for facts, there are hazards. *"No one today knows enough to raise a baby."* Watson proclaims boldly. "Will you believe the almost astounding truth that *no well trained man or woman has ever watched the complete and daily development of a single child from birth to its third year?"*

At the time Watson wrote these words, Dr. Arnold Gesell's clinic had been studying the child for approximately seventeen years, and there were, of course, Noyes's study, Shinn's, Preyer's and others. In 1900, Stuart Rowe published a book on the methods and criteria for objective child study. Yet Watson would probably argue that, in his terms, since these early studies were not conducted by behaviorists, the investigators were not "well trained."

Watson's arguments are not generally legalistic. Rather, he displays a feeling for fact that is geared more to effect than to context. At one point, describing progress and, by extension, himself, he says that we are witnessing a social Renaissance more important than "the scientific Renaissance which began with Bacon in the fifteenth century." (Bacon's work was done in the seventeenth.) As closely as one can make out, the elaborate theory that Watson was to spin on child raising rested, at bottom, on less than a handful of facts. One fact, for example, that Watson finds significant is that children instinctively fear only two things: loud noises and loss of support. Watson, in his early years at Johns Hopkins, did some of his best work in the area of fear, conditioning and extinguishing fear reactions in babies. He discovered that if a baby is exposed to a rabbit, for example, the child show no fear. But if a child is exposed to a rabbit and a loud noise at the same time, the child learns to fear the rabbit. This led him towards a false hope that all other responses might be as easily conditioned:

> "The behaviorists believe that there is nothing within to develop [that is, there is no mind]. If you start with a healthy body, the right number of fingers and toes, eyes, and a few elementary movements that are present at birth, you do not need anything else in the way of raw material to make a man, be that a man of genius, a cultured gentleman, a rowdy or a thug."

"Children are made not born," he asserts in a kind of perverse existentialism. This is science in the service of egalitarian ideals and has a certain rhetorial power regardless of its inaccuracies.

Watson mentions another significant discovery made by psychologists:

> "The one situation which from birth will call out the response of rage [in the infant] is interference with the infant's activity. Holding the head, legs or trunk gently but firmly will almost invariably call it out. Other objects come to call it out [only] through conditioning." *

The basic emotions of fear and rage are, according to Watson a human's only natural endowments — other than his physical equipment. Although John Dewey believed that the basis of education was a child's desire to

---

*It may be suggested that the "rage" reaction Watson notes is not rage at all. Instead, the child's cries when he is held "firmly" might be calls for help, such as a baby animal might make if it found itself trapped. Carrying this idea further, this reaction to being rendered immobile suggests that the passivity associated with swaddled babies is similar to the self-hypnotic passivity with which trapped animals await death when they discover that struggle is useless.

learn (a structure which has since been assimilated into psychology as a "competence drive"), the idea that the child had drives "which allow [him] to develop from within" was dangerous nonsense in Watson's view.

> "This [theory] is really a doctrine of mystery. It teaches us that there are hidden springs of activity, hidden possibilities of unfolding within the child which must be waited for until they appear and then be fostered and tended. I think this doctrine has done serious harm. He [John Dewey] has made us lose our opportunity to implant and encourage a real eagerness for vocations at an early age."

A system such as Dewey's could not guarantee results, at least not such results as those promised by Watsonian psychology:

> "A happy child — a child who never cries unless actually stuck with a pin, figuratively speaking — who loses himself in work and play — who quickly learns to overcome the small difficulties in his environment without running to mother, father, nurse or other adults — who soon builds up a wealth of habits that tides him over dark and rainy days — who puts on such habits of politeness and neatness and cleanliness that adults are willing to be around him at least part of the day; a child who is willing to be around adults without fighting incessantly for notice — who eats what is set before him and asks no questions for conscience sake — who sleeps and rests when he is put to bed for sleep and rest — who puts away two year old habits when the third year has to be faced — who passes into adolesence so well equipped that adolescense is just a stretch of fertile years — and who finally enters manhood so bulwarked with stable work and emotional habits that no adversity can quite overcome him."

This is hardly a real child at all; his happiness seems beside the point. Except for the peculiar effectiveness of Watson's style and his paucity of facts, these assertions are little more extreme than those made by many psychologists during the twenties. Yet Watson goes beyond even the most mechanistic psychologists of his time by suggesting that the child — this happy child that he is urging mothers to be the first on their block to create — must under no circumstances be given love.

> "Only one thing will bring out a love response in the child — stroking and touching its skin, lips, sex organs, and the like. It doesn't matter who strokes it. It will 'love' the stroker. This is the clay out of which

all love — maternal, paternal, wifely or husbandly — is made. Hard to believe? But true. A certain amount of affectional response is socially necessary but few parents realize how easily they can overtrain their children in this direction. It may tear the heartstrings a bit, this thought of stopping the tender outward demonstration of your love for your children or of their love for you. But if you are convinced that this is best for the child, aren't you willing to stifle a few pangs? Mothers just don't know how, when they kiss their children and pick them up and rock them, caress them and jiggle them upon their knee, that they are slowly building up a human being totally unable to cope with the world it must later live in."

Watson then describes explicitly how love corrupts the child.

"The child sees the mother's face as she pets it. Soon the *mere sight of the mother's face* calls out the love response. A touch of the skin is no longer necessary to call it out. A conditioned reaction has been formed. Even if she puts the child in the dark, the *sound* of her voice as she croons soon comes to call out a love response. This is the psychological explanation of the child's joyous reaction to the sound of the mother's voice. So with her footsteps, the sight of the mother's clothes, of her photograph. All too soon the child is shot through with these love reactions. In addition the child gets honeycombed with love responses for the nurse, for the father, and for any other constant attendant who fondles it. Love reactions soon dominate the child. It requires no instinct, no 'intelligence,' no 'reasoning,' on the child's part for such responses to grow up."

The consequences of such an upbringing, according to Watson, included hypochondria — invalidism, he calls it — and "nest habits" where the child deals with every problem in life by running home to mother. In the end, he predicts, nest habits lead to a destroyed marriage, even to insanity and suicide. In Watson's work love itself took on the opprobrium and symptoms that had formerly been attributed to masturbation.

It is now understood that close physical contact between parent and child gives the child the confidence that enables him to deal with the world and that the lack of these things forces the child into hypochondria and other devices to gain the parent's attention. Watson's role was, however, to rationalize the hostility to physical contact prevalent in his time.

Isolation of child from parent in Watson's system approaches psychopathology. The child is to be left alone. "Let the child overcome difficulties

almost from the moment of birth," he proposes in a tone reminiscent of
Rousseau. "If your heart is [too] tender and you must watch the child,"
he suggests that you use a peephole from an adjacent room or a periscope
over the fence in the yard. When one *has to* communicate with the child,
there is a way:

> "There is a sensible way of treating children. Treat them as though
> they were young adults. Dress them, bathe them with care and circum-
> spection. Let your behavior always be objective and kindly firm. Never
> hug and kiss them, never let them sit in your lap. If you must, kiss
> them once on the forehead when they say good night. Shake hands
> with them in the morning. Give them a pat on the head if they have
> made an extraordinarily good job of a difficult task. Try it out. In a
> week's time, you will find out how easy it is to be perfectly objective
> with your child and at the same time kindly. You will be utterly
> ashamed of the mawkish, sentimental way you have been handling it."

With their "love reactions" extinguished, it would be highly unsuitable
for children to manifest hate reactions. Watson's plan for removing the
child's temper involves similar aloofness on the part of the parents. "The
child for the first year must be handled very gently. Some nurses and
mothers develop a marvelous technique and deftness and softness of touch."
They don't, he adds, linger over, coddle or shush the child. Watson recommends that mothers learn these techniques from the practice of infant
nurses in hospitals.

In a sense, this is Watson's true aim — the institutional child. At one
point in the book he muses sadly over the difficulties of doing away with
the family:

> "It is a serious question in my mind whether there should be individual
> homes for children — or even whether children should know their own
> parents. There are undoubtedly much more scientific ways of bringing
> up children which will probably mean finer and happier children. . . .
> [But] the social pressures to have a child, to own a child, to be known
> in the community as a woman with a legitimate child [make this
> impossible]."

It is a rare moment of caution when Watson says that collective methods
will "probably" make a happier child. Later writers were much bolder.

Failing the institutionalization of all children under the guidance of
psychologists, Watson was proposing the introduction of institutional

methods and attitudes into the home. It is "easy to recognize the economic value of [a] system [which gives] the mother more time for household chores, gossiping, bridge, shopping." His aim is also to raise a maleable child who will fit into society, whatever the future has to hold, a "problem-solving child" free of the "fixed molds our parents imposed on us" and, more specifically, "a child as free as possible of sensitivities to people and one who, almost from birth, is relatively independent of the family situation."

Since the end of the Second World War, the public has seen the work on institutional children by René Spitz as well as studies of the effects of isolation on young primates by Harry Harlow — both of which show the real consequences of the methods Watson proposes. Long before these investigations, the withdrawn, unhappy lives of children in orphanages and other institutions had been noted. Watson ignored this evidence. He was interested in marketing a product, not in what happened to the product once you got it home.

Watson's ideas were not permitted to slip into the culture without comment or criticism from his fellow psychologists. Even before Watson's book was published, while Watson was trying his ideas on the lecture circuit, he had been engaged in a debate with the English psychologist William McDougall, a confrontation that took place on February 5, 1924, at the Psychological Club in Washington, D.C.

The specifics of the debate are unimportant. Watson presented positions approximately identical to the statements on instinct and conditioning he was later to include in *Psychological Care*. MacDougall argued for the insufficiency of that system to explain anything of any complexity in human behavior. Each man distorted the other's position slightly to score points and, after the debate, when a vote was taken among the professionals to see who had won, Watson lost by a small majority. In the afterword to the published text of the debate, *The Battle of Behaviorism* (1928/29), MacDougall commented on the score with a statement that is outrageously sexist as well as ominous:

"When account is taken of the amusing fact that the considerable number of women students from the university voted almost unanimously for Dr. Watson and his Behaviorism, the vote may be regarded as an overwhelming verdict of sober good sense against him from a representative American gathering. Yet it is the success of his appeal among young students that is the disturbing fact for those who hope much from the splendid developments of American universities now going on so rapidly. . . .

"In America the tide of Behaviorism seems to flow increasingly. The press acclaims Dr. Watson's recent volume [*Behaviorism*, 1925] in the most flattering terms. The leading daily says: 'Perhaps this is the most important book ever written; and another asserts 'It marks an epoch in the intellectual history of man.' In England, on the other hand, the press is content to note that here is a system which claims 'to revolutionize ethics, religion, psychoanalysis — in fact all the mental and moral sciences.' It might have gone further and noted that it claims, not merely to revolutionize, but to abolish all these august things."

Watson's concepts continued to have influence beyond the twenties. The idea that you "shouldn't play with your baby" is still occasionally voiced. It may be said, however, that the end of the twenties did mark the beginning of change. There was less speculation among writers and greater concentration on the necessity of understanding what was, in fact, the reality of the child. The place to begin was with measurements and observations, not with theories.

CHAPTER 10

The Normal Child

Observation, measurement, recording, analysis, the serious work of studying real children as they grow and learn, had by 1930 been underway for more than a quarter-century. In 1905, Binet and Simon published studies on intelligence which, a few years later, were to result in the concept of the IQ. Jean Piaget, who had studied with them, in 1921 went to work at the Institute Jean Jacques Rousseau in Paris and began systematically examining the stages of awareness leading to adult consciousness. In Vienna, Charlotte Buhler watched the daily progress of infants through the glass wall of a nursery, and in New Haven Dr. Arnold Gesell recorded it on film.

It was the facts gathered by these patient researchers that gave the child an irrefutable claim to his own biological, innate process of development, setting limits on what parents or theoreticians might reasonably demand of him. It was in these dry bones of fact that the course of modern child raising was set.

Dr. Arnold Gesell had begun work as a psychologist with an interest in the problems of the abnormal child. He soon became aware of the lack of factual information concerning *normal* children, the kind of information that was necessary to give his studies of the exceptions meaning. In 1911, he founded the Yale Clinic of Child Development (originally the Yale Psycho-Clinic) and it was this institution that he gradually turned towards the scientific examination of child development. Starting intensively in 1919, he began a series of experiments that was to result in 1925 in the publication of his first major work on child development: *The Mental Growth of the Pre-School Child: A Psychological Outline of Normal Development from Birth to the Sixth Year, Including a System of Development Diagnosis*. As the subtitle suggests, the book was primarily an academic work not intended for popular consumption. Gesell's style lacked the seductive smoothness that had made Watson so popular. Sentences like "Our data were secured by means of repeated developmental examinations of individual infants," posed a substantial hurdle to the general public. As a result, the book, which might have provided a means for eliminating many speculative theories in circulation, had only a limited audience.

Much of the book dealt with methodology and specific case-by-case results. Children's behavior was examined and fitted into four categories, which were in turn subdivided into specific "performances" (Buhler's word):

"Motor

Postural control
Locomotion
Prehension [grabbing and holding on]
Drawing and Hand Control

"Language

Vocabulary
Word comprehension
Conversation
Reproduction [ability to repeat things said]

"Adaptive Behavior

Eye-hand coordination
Imitation
Recovery of objects
Comprehension
Discriminative performance
Apperception and completion
Number concept

"Personal and Social Behavior

Reactions to persons
Personal habits
Initiative and independence
Play response
Acquired information"

For each of these items, tests were devised, ranging from puzzles that a child at one of the nine ages — 4 months, 6, 9, 12, 18; 2 years, 3, 4 and 5 — could solve to other forms of examination and description of how a child at various ages manipulates objects he is given.

The book is detailed; the generalities on which a parent might try to base his or her own handling of a child are few. Nevertheless, near the end of the book, Gesell includes a section called "Normative Summaries" describing in eight pages what sort of behavior one might expect from the child at the nine different ages. It was only a short section of the book, yet it may be said that these eight pages formed the basis of all the popular works that Gesell subsequently produced on child raising. In fact, *Infant and Child in the Culture of Today, The first Five Years, The Child from Five to Ten, Youth: The Years from Ten to Sixteen* — all the basic Gesell texts for parents — are in large part an expansion of the material presented in this brief part of the early book.

Gesell's interest was in the use of the normal to define the abnormal. At the end of his introduction to the summaries, he comments: "Diagnosis and prognosis alike depend upon the considered use of normative criteria. The following normative summaries, in a measure, are abridged developmental schedules. They may therefore be utilized as cues for preliminary clinical orientation, and even for rough, approximate classification in cases of retardation."

"Four Months

"Motor Characteristics

Prefers to lie on back
Tries to raise self, lifting head and shoulders
Can roll from side to back (or back to side)
Holds head erect when carried
Lifts head when prone
Pushes with feet against floor when held

"Language

Coos
Smiles
Laughs aloud
Makes several vocalizations

"Adaptive Behavior

Notices large objects
May notice spoon on table
Hands react to table

"Personal-Social Behavior
Shows selective interest in animated face
Makes anticipatory postural adjustment on being lifted
Not much affected by strange persons, new scenes or solicitude
Turns head to voice
Plays with hands"

Through the nine lists, the reader watches the progress of the child until, at age five, he can lace his shoes and put on his hat and coat unassisted.

But the true impact of Gesell's summaries is the impact of fact on myth: In one short item in the category of *Personal-Social Behavior* at 18 months, he notes: "Bowel control practically established." After all the texts advocating or promising "toilet training from birth" if not before, we now can look at page 381 of Gesell and know that the normal child is unlikely to achieve bowel control before a year and a half.

By 1930, Gesell was ready to write a "popular" book on child raising, based on the results of this new understanding. The book was *The Guidance of Mental Growth in Infant and Child*, a title either consciously or unconsciously reminiscent of Watson's book of two years earlier. The book is a mixture of history, science, fact and old-fashioned moralizing of the kind we might expect from far less knowledgeable writers. "What are the mental health characteristics of the normal child?" Gesell asks, and then replies:

"1. *Wholesome habits of eating, of sleeping, of relaxation, and of elimination:* These are often regarded as 'purely physical' matters. Actually they are of basic psychological importance. They are ways of living; they require proper organization of the nervous system. The child who is not well-trained in these everyday habits has not learned even the first letters of the alphabet of nervous or mental health.

"2. *Wholesome habits of feeling:* Here again we deal with the organization of the nervous system. Mental hygiene is much concerned with the organization of emotional life. Happily, the feelings respond to training. It is quite wrong to think that temper tantrums, morbid fears, timidity, jealousy, sensitiveness, suspiciousness, and other unhealthly mental states are beyond training.

"The thoroughly normal child has positive emotional habituations which make for good nature, for sociability, for self-control, and even for a measure of sympathy and cooperativeness. Consistent training and a favorable home environment will bring him under the spell of socialized good will. . . .

"3. *Healthy attitudes of action:* Self-reliance is a cardinal virtue in the code of mental health. Growing up in the psychological sense means attaining sufficient stamina to meet the demands of life squarely on one's own resources. It is a steady process of detachment, first from the apron strings, later from the home itself. . . . "

It is no wonder that an acute observer, Grace Adams, commented apropos of this new morality based on normality, "The American craze for standardization has given us, among thousands of other standardized objects, the standardized child." (*Your Child Is Normal,* 1934 — well ahead of its time.)

To the end of his life, Frances Ilg, Gesell's coworker, reported that Gesell believed that "mind manifests itself" in behavior, that behavior is significant because it represents the way in which we think. Whether true or false, it was essentially a moralistic idea. If the child was abnormal, was the child also bad?

This was a question not easily answered. The weight of science stood behind the statistical concept of normal as good. Yet, while a child (or adult, for that matter) may be good simply by virtue of his not being bad, to be normal implies conformity to a fixed list of behaviors that science has drawn from group studies. Good can encompass a whole range and variety of types and behaviors but, theoretically, only one type of child can be "thoroughly normal." The normal child is a mathematical abstraction that does not exist.

To judge by the considerable amount of space Gesell devoted in his later books to the defense of the individual against the statistical average, the relationship of good to normal was a problem he found troubling. He felt that his works were being misused by parents who constantly compared their children to his behavioral tables, just as earlier parents had weighed their infants against the curve in Holt. There can be no mistaking Gesell's sympathy for the individual and his "self-reliance," no matter how atypical such an individual may be.

In 1934, Gesell published *The Atlas of Infant Behavior,* a two-volume study of the behavior of children engaged in various activities: sleep, bath, feeding, mastering motility, postures, portraits and social interactions. The book is documented with thousands of photographs arranged in sequences of approximately a dozen pictures with commentary below.

One excerpt from it will give an example of its character (the letters in parentheses refer to the photos and are included here to give some idea of the integration of text and photos). This is after the baby's bath:

"The mother rubs the baby's body with oil. The baby is socially responsive. She pushes her feet against the mother, waves her arms, and smiles pleasantly at the mother (a-c). As the mother dresses the baby, she [baby] plays with a stocking, fingering it and waving it (d-g). When dressing is complete, the mother lifts the baby to the standing position. She looks about pleasantly [photo shows baby smiling] but slumps when mother releases her left hand. The mother straightens the baby's posture, then releases both of the baby's hands (h), holding her own arms wide to catch the baby if she should fall. The baby responds to the situation playfully. She reaches for the mother's hands as she falls forward. The mother holds her securely. Confidently, the baby takes two steps forward (i, j), then sinks upon her left knee (k). This is the first walking experience for the baby."

A triumphant moment, the first steps, beautifully, simply and dramatically recorded. Gesell here falls within the erotic tradition with Tuthill, Harland, Washburn and Noyes. The degree of finely detailed observation necessitated by the preparation of this vast project seems to have had a good effect on Gesell, bringing him closer to the moment-to-moment reality of the child's world.

Four years later, Gesell's analytic methods had extended beyond the child to cover the family situation as well, as recorded in a later academically oriented work, *The Psychology of Early Growth* (1938), largely an expansion of the 1925 study.

Another book, however, written in the 1920s, may be said to sum up the emotions that stirred Gesell as he watched his little subjects gradually grow and develop competence. In *Infancy and Human Growth* (1928), a text on mental and physical growth, Gesell moves towards an almost mystical synthesis of the meanings of growth and life, similar to the special meaning that the Chinese find in the concept of change. As exemplified by the I Ching, change was not merely movement within a neutral framework but was rather a process of evolution, an adaptation of internal and external forces which contained the moral implication that virtue resulted from moving with the natural processes of the universe.

In Gesell, while his language is less poetic, the magical meaning of growth is the same. "Growth is a word to conjure with," he remarks in his introduction:

"The mind grows. . . .
"Growth is one of the most fundamental manifestations of human

life. It may well be called a function, and as such constitutes a subject for systematic inquiry even in the elusive sphere of mind. Particularly true is this for the period of human infancy, when the drama of development proceeds with such swift and varied action. Is the movement of the drama lawful and ordered?"

Gesell spent much of his life pursuing the "elusive" mind through the study of growth. It was, in a sense, the attempt to reconcile the observable world of the behaviorists with the invisible world of the psychiatrists. In 1945, he wrote (with Amatruda) a book on *The Embryology of Behavior: The Beginnings of the Human Mind*, attempting to trace the mind to its roots in pre-natal biology and post-natal experience. By then, however, child study had taken a different direction.

*   *   *

With the collapse of business in 1929, it was no longer possible to preach efficiency, productivity and social success as absolute virtues. For two years, 1925 and 1926, the best seller on the nonfiction lists was a strange book, *The Man Nobody Knows*, which purported to prove that Jesus was the greatest business executive who ever lived, who "picked up twelve men from the bottom ranks of business and forged them into an organization that conquered the world." By 1930, to call a man a businessman was no longer a compliment.

In the twenties, psychologists promised the world, if parents would only follow their advice; by the mid-thirties, the emphasis was rapidly moving towards the "natural" way of raising children. The popularity of natural childbirth, too, dates from this period.

Grace Adams's *Your Child Is Normal* — already quoted on the subject of Watson and on the "standardized child" — was one of the most acerbic and intelligent books to reassert the values of the natural home.

"The young child's mind according to the mature thought of the biologists is a more mysterious and intricate phenomenon than its pancreas or thyroid or any other organ within its body. And the means by which it can be affected and modified are too subtle and various to admit of any universal formula. Particularly, there seem to be a few special mental traits that cannot be altered even by the most painstaking methods of conditioning."

The example of an unconditionable trait Adams gives is handedness, right or left. She says, "Not so many years ago there was a distinct educational vogue for ambidexterity," conceived by "some clever theorist" who thought it would make fuller use of the brain.

The progressive writers of the thirties stressed the *failures* of conditioning rather than such successes as it had, or might have achieved. "Parents," Adams says, "need less of the theories generalized from the memories of neurotic grown people and more facts based on competent observation of actual, normal children." On the subject of corporal punishment, she adds, "The parent's most urgent and pertinent question is: does it really, truly and effectively correct a child's young faults?

> "The advocates of corporal punishment have a smug, affirmative answer neatly formed into the proverb: 'The burnt child shuns the fire.' . . . The child, they say, should learn through unrelenting repetition that a thwack upon its tender backsides is as natural a retribution for disobedience as a sore smarting finger is for trying to clutch too closely at a flame.
>
> "But does a burnt child always shun the fire? . . .
>
> "When Bubi Scupin was one year and five months old his mother warned him not to touch the stove because it was hot and would hurt him. And Bubi went straightaway and placed his tiny hand upon the outlawed stove door. The fire burnt him and, according to the proverb, he should henceforth and forever have avoided it. . . .
>
> "His mother was, of course, well pleased with how easily he had been taught his lesson. But no sooner had she turned her eyes and her thoughts from the child than another cry of anguish smote her ears. Bubi's experimental fingers had just reached out and clutched the hot stove door a second time."

Adams gives several other examples and then comments:

> "Physical pain, unless it is severe, often repeated and entangled with unpleasant and dangerous emotions, is not of itself sufficient to cause an inquisitive child to avoid its sources. . . . To make a real deterrent, a punishment must make an impression not only upon the child's young flesh but on its steadily developing mind.
>
> "Children do, however, respond at a very tender age to the voices and facial expressions of adults. And psychologists who are aware of this fact have discovered that the child's mind is far more sensitive to disapproving tones and stern countenances than its body is to indiscrimi-

nate raps and taps. A firm but even-tempered reproof was generally the most effective form of discipline the Sterns [another "example" family] used with their children. For small misdeeds their mother did not even have to scold them. She needed only to look reproachfully at them for a minute and they would become contrite and assure her, many times with tears in their eyes, that they would be good again if only she would promise not to look so sad."

In examining this passage, it is not important to ask whether or not the advice it contained is practical or accurate. The slant it conveys demonstrates the change in attitude that has come about since the rigid theoretical disciplines and conditioning advocated in the 1920s. If, underlying the earlier systems, we can sense a lack of faith in the parents' own instincts it is apparent that, by the 1930s, these attitudes had altered. With society in flux and the economy collapsed, there was a reemergence of reliance on the basic emotional interaction of parent and child.

On discipline, Adams reflects an earlier American idea evident from Hitchcock through Twain: household order is dependent on the mutual respect of the members. The individualism of the 1920s was yielding to the collective "We Do Our Part" ethic of the Depression decade.

Yet parents were not ready to entirely forsake the comfort scheduling offered them and, almost to the end of the thirties, books recommending it continued to appear. Frederic Bartlett's *Infants and Children* (1932) is fairly typical. The older reasons for scheduling offered by Holt, Blatz and Bott and others had been, to some extent, undercut by the collapse of efficiency as a social aim in child care, but the schedules were still offered along with a variety of explanations as to their virtues. Bartlett says, at one point, that "it is far better to spend your time [toilet] training the baby than to spend it washing diapers," and at another, "I am taking it for granted that you will train your baby from early infancy to have a regular bowel movement every day. . . . Lack of such training will often result in constipation." He recommends an enema "in many difficult situations" ranging from constipation to diarrhea to colic.

Bartlett approves of the soapstick as one means of conditioning the baby to use the chamber on cue, beginning at one or two months, but cautions that it not be used more than four days in a row so that they baby does not become "dependent on it and [unable] to have a movement without it." Rather, he suggests, as a standard procedure it is better simply to sit the child on the bowl and "the power of suggestion may be used by the mother's grunting to indicate to the baby what is expected of him." Taken together, these suggestions form an image of child raising aims in the thirties — the hope was that the child would still end up as regular as clockwork — but the tendency was towards less mechanical methods to achieve that goal.

On masturbation, Bartlett is also fairly typical of his time. By the 1930s it was admitted that masturbation did no harm and, when it was "excessive," it was probably the result of anxiety rather than an indication of impending insanity. There was no organic reason to deny a child his pleasures but, since it still made parents uncomfortable, it was to be discouraged. Bartlett includes the advice that it is unwise to get excited over masturbation or punish the child, instead suggesting that the child be taken to the physician for a friendly chat. He includes the friendly chat in his book:

> "Don't let what I am going to say worry you. I know that you have been handling your sex organs frequently. This is called masturbation. You do it because you are getting pleasure out of it. You may do a lot of other things for pleasure, such as eating a lot of candy. Eating a lot of candy is not good for your health, nor is handling yourself good for your health. I am not going to scold you or punish you for it. I don't think it is a good thing to do, anymore than I think it is good for you to bite your nails or suck your fingers. The trouble is that if you handle yourself too frequently, you are apt to become nervous. Also you oftentimes are unhappy about it. You wish you had not done it after you have done it. I want you to understand that there is nothing bad in doing it. In fact, it is more natural for a growing boy to have masturbated than it is for him not to have masturbated.
>
> "The way to stop doing it is, when you feel that you want to handle yourself, to make yourself do something else, such as going outdoors or getting a toy to play with. You may not be able to do this every time at the start but keep trying."

Boys and girls, Bartlett notes, sometimes masturbate together, which is also natural and should be discouraged. "As the child grows older and enters puberty, the habit, in almost all instances, is practiced infrequently or dropped." More to the point, the habit becomes concealed and, from the parents' standpoint, invisible.

If threats of madness and physical restraint were not utilized to stop masturbation, guilt could still be mobilized for that purpose, even while admitting its irrationality. The passage by Bartlett expresses the transition between the two worlds: on one hand, the knowledge that there was nothing wrong, and on the other, the feeling that masturbation should be stopped anyway.

It may be said that an amalgam of the two dominant themes of the 1930s (the increasing knowledge of the facts of growth and behavior, and the reaffirmation of nature and the natural human relations within the family structure) produced the most influential book of the decade, *Babies Are Human Beings* (1938) by Dr. C. Anderson Aldrich and his wife Mary M. Aldrich. The roots of the revolution in child raising that today is commonly attributed to Dr. Spock are to be found in this book. The books that followed the Aldriches' are in most respects contemporary.

The avowed aim of the Aldriches in writing *Babies Are Human Beings* was not so ambitious as its effect might suggest. The book was intended to take the work of Gesell and the other anthropometricians and render it into simple form for consumption by the general public. Such texts consisted largely of statistics and close descriptions of the behavior of children confronted by puzzles or other objects along with descriptions of various kinds of interactions with adults. Conclusions were generally omitted or limited to describing what sorts of behavior a parent might expect from a child at a given age. In popularizing this material, the Aldrichs went beyond a simple statement of the facts into the implications of the facts:

> "In the early years of childhood, physical and mental functions are so merged that they cannot be considered separately. Since this is so, there can be no mental hygiene as sharply distinguished from physical hygiene. Considerate physical care is good mental hygiene in infancy. To give a baby all the warmth, comfort and cuddling that he seems to need; to meet his wishes in the matter of satisfying and appropriate food, to adjust our habit-training to his individual rhythms; and to see that he has an opportunity to exercise each new accomplishment as it emerges; these are the beginnings of a forward-looking program in mental hygiene.
>
> "Every human being, as he grows into childhood, must inevitably be hampered and opposed by the restrictions of his environment, and the best we can hope for is to modify somewhat the urgency of this conflict. The degree to which we are considerate of our baby's early needs, however, may be the measure of his later ability to feel secure in a world of change and to adapt himself to the necessities of circumstance."

The understanding that the child develops according to his own schedule has led to the conclusion that the child is the best guide to his own needs, the contemporary view. The Aldriches no longer regard the baby as some kind of alien creature who requires special training, manipulation and shaping before he will become a human being. He is seen as human from birth. The Aldriches' book, coming at the end of the 1930s, as the world slipped from Depression into war, also gave parents a promise, the promise of the "secure" child in a "world of change."

The Aldriches based theoretical conclusions on physical evidence. For example, considering the proper time to wean a child, measurements by researchers gave new force to the arguments against too early weaning:

> "[The baby's] lower jaw is relatively small and retracted at birth, a perfectly proportioned arrangement for sucking from the nipple. In order to fit nature's scheme for his later eating habits, however, the lower jaw begins at once to grow at a much faster rate than that of any other bone of the face, so that by the time the teeth erupt and the baby is ready to chew we find that it has come forward to meet the upper jaw accurately, in the best possible position for mastication."

The authority of the child by which he makes demands on us is his own physical reality, the evolution of his natural reflexes, responses and body functions into their necessary form.

The Aldrichs were, however, not simply bio-mechanists. They were aware of the differences between children. Some children, they explain, are quiet and others are "sparklers" and full of energy. Like many writers of artistic sensibility, they give a slight edge to the energetic child and devote some space to arguing that lively children be allowed their heads. "From the growth standpoint, obedience is not a virtue. We grow by experience and interpretation, not by submission. . . . "True training in any habit implies that the brain take over its control." The vocabulary of "habit training" is still present, but its meaning is reversed. Whereas Blatz and Bott argued *against* the conscious part of habitual activities, saying that consciousness should be reserved for higher activities, in the Aldriches, consciousness itself is essential in training a human being.

In practical terms, their proposals regarding the "brain tak[ing] over" in the training of habits were easier to state than to apply. The conflict between what the Aldriches believed and the desire to give mothers and fathers what they wanted in a trained child finally erupted on the subject of toilet training.

They start with a discussion of how dependent the world seems to have become on laxatives, tracing the difficulty to the use of the soap stick and other forms of artificial stimulation in toilet training. "This situation is the most arresting proof that our management of elimination functions has failed to get satisfactory results." This analysis of the problem is followed with a detailed and accurate description of the way in which the colon prepares itself for evacuation. In brief, the walls of the colon squeeze the waste towards the rectum in a spontaneous "mass movement" at the biologically appropriate time. When, they explain, we train the child to respond to soap sticks, suppositories and laxatives rather than this natural process, the child becomes dependent on them:

> "It is unhygenic to ignore the mass movement as an initiating force in the rhythm of evacuations, for when we ignore a natural force long enough it tends to disappear entirely from our list of assets. This is what actually happens to most constipated adults. The internal stimulas has either disappeared entirely or has been disregarded so long that it cannot be recognized as the automatic call to the toilet."

Faced with these facts, we might expect that the Aldriches would recommend that toilet training be put off, as it now generally is, until the child can control his own response to these internal signals. The pressure to find some method of delivering a toilet-trained child to the parents was, however, irresistable. Since the child could not be trained early enough, the authors resorted to the other alternative, training the mother, although the process is still disguised as cognitive development for the child:

> "The developmental formula for true training is simple and efficient. After a few weeks, automatic evacuations gradually become less frequent so that only one or two occur daily. Their time and number vary in different children but the tendency for them to come at definite periods in each day is steadily more pronounced. As soon as it is possible to discover the exact moment at which the mass movement takes place, it is reasonable to put the baby on a chamber or toilet seat and relieve his mother of the irksome task of diaper-washing. When he is placed on the toilet seat at *his* right time, his brain naturally develops the necessary association between the mass movement, the toilet seat and his own, satisfying effort. Our cooperation in this growth process is merely to observe the baby's own rhythm, in selecting the times of day for a bowel movement. Such synchrony leads to training at a reasonably early date and does not subtract from the baby's innate capabilities. When this is done, real, permanent training becomes a fact and his future health is protected, even though the period of diaper-washing may be prolonged for a few weeks."

When watching or holding a child on the potty waiting for him to do his duty was too passive for many impatient mothers, and since soap sticks were out, other books attempted to find alternative methods that would produce the same results without severely damaging the child's psychology. *Home Guidance for Young Children* (1938) by Grace Langdon describes another method that was widely recommended at this time:

> "Usually all that is necessary to bring about a movement is a gentle massage of the abdomen at a regular time until the habit is established, but *only* until it is established. The use of enemas, suppositories, and soap sticks, is ill advised unless upon the recommendation and under the direction of a physician. Their use may bring about the desired movement but if continued may so accustom the baby to them that he grows to enjoy the feeling, depends on them and cannot have a movement without them. Far better to use a natural means, leaving any artificial stimulation for emergencies."

Even with this technique, Langdon admits that "it will be many, many weeks before the baby has learned" to use the chamber.

One interesting aside to the massage method of toilet training comes from Gavin Maxwell's *Ring of Bright Water* (1960), a book not about raising children but about bringing up otters. At one point, an infant otter is in distress because she cannot have a bowel movement. She is finally relieved when the family dog licks her belly, a "necessary maternal service" for many "very young animals" it is explained. Whether or not the analogy with humans is valid may be worth investigating.

One measure of the effect of the Aldriches' work may be seen in a subsequent book published by Gesell (then and afterwards in partnership with Dr. Frances L. Ilg), *Infant and Child in the Culture of Today* (1943). From the standpoint of practical, usable advice, this was Gesell's most accessible work to that time. When parents claim to be raising their children according to Gesell, this (or its companion works that follow the child to the age of sixteen) is the book they generally have in mind.

The largest part of the book, as has been mentioned, was an expansion of the eight pages of "normative summaries" from the 1925 work, *Mental Growth*. Unlike the earlier work, however, here the descriptions of the normal child are taken to their logical consequences.

In *Infant and Child*, each age group not only includes a "behavioral profile," which is derived from the summaries given in the earlier book, but also contains a description of the child's "behavior day" at each age level, what a typical day with a child of a certain age is likely to include. At four weeks old, for example, after the infant is fed and changed, the behavior day description includes the following:

"The baby is put back into the bassinet. He sleeps for a period of from two to five hours and wakes up as before for the prime purpose of feeding again. We call this a sleep period rather than a nap. A nap is a restricted and well-demarcated interval of sleep immediately preceded or followed by an equally well-defined period of wakefulness. But at four weeks the baby's day resolves itself into five or six zones of sleep; each terminating typically with a hunger cry. The baby has not yet learned to wake up for more advanced reasons. He does not nap. His capacity for wakefulness is very immature.

"In the late afternoon (typically between four and six o'clock), however, he has a wider margin for perceptual and pre-social behavior. This, therefore, is an optimal time, though not the conventional one, for his daily bath. Where he might show resistance in the morning, he now enjoys the experience of immersion in the tepid water. His eyes open wider; his general body activity may abate. He often gives tokens of pleasurable response to the sound of the voice and to the handling which gives him a feeling of tactility, and to being tucked in when he is dressed and restored to the bassinet for another sleep period.

"Whether the infant cries because he is awake, or whether he is awake because he cries poses a philosophical problem. The four-week-old infant is maturing his capacity to wake up and extend his area of sense perception. Hunger is the chief cause of his crying, but this cries are beginning to differentiate and there are distinctive features in the cries associated with the various kinds of discomfort.

"He frets or cries when his alimentary tract and his eliminative organs are not functioning smoothly. He basks with contentment when his physiological wellbeing is at least temporarily achieved. In these brief periods, he has a margin for more advanced perceptual adjustments. He may give absorbed attention to his sense of wellbeing. He likes to gaze in the direction of his accustomed tonic-neck-reflex attitude and sometimes his fretfulness subsides if he is given an opportunity to fixate his restless eyes on some large and not too bright pattern.

"Needless to say, these evidences of perceptual and pre-social interest are slight and fugitive. Some children do not show them at all until the age of 6 or 8 weeks. At times this early crying seems to be quite without reason; almost as if it were crying for its own sake. But the very fact that the baby quiets recurrently to slight environmental changes suggests that he is entitled to some of these changes. The handling should be restricted to his actual needs. He is not ready for social stimulation. At this age no two behavior days are likely to be identical. Some are stormier than others. Excess storminess may mean that the appropriate adjustments between the organism and the environment have not been attained. All of which suggests that it is well to be alert to such signals as the baby is able to give during the course of his behavior day."

In keeping with their belief in the individuality of babies, Gesell and Ilg add the comment that the behavior day "is not set up as a model, but as a suggestive example." At the end of each chapter, they add more details with specific suggestions offered in brackets, for example: "If crying is associated with wet or soiled diapers, changing will quiet the infant. This cause of crying is to be differentiated from hunger crying."

Parents are encouraged, particularly during the first few months, to keep a "Behavior Day Chart" of the child's activities. It "serves to smooth the transition from hospital to home. The chart helps the mother to a fuller understanding of the child because it both symbolizes and directs her growing insight into the baby's individuality" and his growth.

This, then, is the parent as a scientist, observing, measuring and recording as a means of seeking insight into the child. There is none of the reliance on instinct and emotion that was to become popular a few years later, none of Spock's "you know more than you think you do." In *Infant and Child*, the parent knows nothing unless it is explained.

Infant and Child is a book that favors the individual child. The introduction exposes the individual as the mainstay of democracy — this being written in the midst of war — and the book vigorously supports "self-demand" as the technique of scheduling. The charts and schedules follow the baby's behavior rather than lead it. Yet with the charts offered, one of which shows the baby gradually consolidating his sleeping and waking periods from six of each, at four weeks, to three of each at fifty-two weeks, it is hard to entirely resist the temptation to urge the baby along, if for no other reason than to simplify the bookkeeping or to realize the progress that the charts lead one to expect.

Whatever the consequences of their commitment to scientific specificity, Gesell and Ilg are sincere in their belief in the child not as a creature ascending a mechanically regular stepladder of charts but as a dynamic being. The strength of their belief in this vision may be sensed in even this short passage on the first stage of infant awareness:

"When one thinks how neatly the baby's skin separates him from the impinging universe, one might infer that this dermatological envelope would make a most effective container for a well-defined personality! As a matter of fact this surface so bristles with sensitive receptors that

BEHAVIOR-DAY CHART

NAME — — — — — — 12 AGE WT 12 DATE — — — — — 1 2 3 4 5 6 7 8 9 10 11 12 BIRTH DATE — — — — — BIRTH WEIGHT — — — 12 11 10 COMMENT

4 WEEK ZONE

DATE		COMMENT
7-29	3 WKS 3 DAYS	On formula. Total intake 20.75 oz. x 7 feedings. When wet - cries, changed, quiets
7-30	4	21 oz x 6; likes water, 2-4 oz per day.
7-31	5	17 oz x 5; took orange juice (O.J.) from spoon.
8-1	6	14.5 oz x 5.
8-2	4 WKS 8 LBS	15.5 oz x 6. Smiles twice in response to talking (not sen point)
8-3	1	15.5 oz x 5. Not an avid baby; very slow after takes 2 oz. Seldom finishes bottle.
8-4	2	17.5 oz x 5. Body straightening out. Can't progress forward in crib as previously.

16 WEEK ZONE

DATE		COMMENT
10-22	15 WKS 3 DAYS	23.5 x 3 Pre-creeping motions of legs in play pen.
10-23	4	22.5 x 3 (1 split bottle) Much clasping of hands together.
10-24	5	24 x 3 Tries to turn over from back to stomach. Succeeds once.
10-25	6	24 x 3 Bats & pulls at dangling toy.
10-26	16 WKS 13 LBS	23 x 3 (1 split)
10-27	1	21.5 x 3 No demand for attention
10-28	2	20 x 3 Several days in succession tries to turn from back to stomach, then ceases

28 WEEK ZONE

DATE		COMMENT
1-14	27 WKS 3 DAYS	22.5 x 3 Tries to make me clap hands when I sing Pat-a-cake.
1-15	4	23 x 3 Cold continues. Nose still running a little.
1-16	5	22.5 x 3 Call at friend's house. Say, esp. with 2 year old child
1-17	6	22.5 x 3 Passion to stand up, past week. Can't quite pull self up alone.
1-18	28 WKS 16 LBS 10 OZ	23 x 3 Pulls self up in big crib.
1-19	1	23 x 3 Train trip to grandmother's. Good all the way.
1-20	2	20.5 x 3 Uncertain but no tears; soon friendly. Increased sleep & night waking

Fig. 17. Excerpts from an actual chart showing the recordings for 4th, 16th and 28th weeks.

Code

▨ = asleep
☐ = awake
x = crying
V = vomiting
OJ = orange juice
B = bath
8 = 8 ounces
BM = bowel movement

— = feeding
aw = awakened
wa = water
cr = carriage

it serves also to merge him with the cosmos in which he is immersed. It takes time, it takes complicated developments of the central nervous system, it takes the distance senses of sight and hearing to disengage him from the context to which he is so closely united."

The principle effect of Gesell — when used as recommended, following baby's progress rather than forcing it — seems to have been to calm parents by assuring them that their children were progressing normally. Nevertheless, the tendency to match one's child against given norms cannot be denied; Gesell's charts can represent one more hindrance to parents dealing with the immediate and individual needs of each child. In spite of possibilities of misinterpretation, Gesell's work has had lasting value by contributing to parental trust in the natural processes of birth and child rearing and in lessening the impact of prior rigid child-raising theories.

CHAPTER 11

The Child of Democracy

"'A Hitler-Jugend grown into manhood, upright, well-groomed, slender, fair, but all alike — skulls with no eyes, no glance-moving corpses, a people who has lost its soul.'*

"That seems a far cry from anything that we could imagine as a future for our children who are of preschool age now at our entrance into the World War. But something comparable to it can happen to any generation of children who are biased to thinking in war terms during the most plastic years of their youth. . . .

"Right now we are close to the problem of what to do to mitigate the immediate fear of small children in the midst of war tensions and experiences. . . .

"If psychology has taught us one thing it is that the way the child lives in these early years determines to a great extent the kind of adult he will be. While we are making a world safe for democracy we must preserve in children readiness for democracy — these are the people in whose hands the new world order will be molded.

"The war may go on for some time. This is their one childhood; we must do all that is possible to let them grow and stretch to the very limit of all the opportunities under the changing circumstances."　　·

*This is from an article by Annette Kolb, the German author, in "Decision."

The Second World War introduced a deep polarization into the theories of child care, elevating child raising from a problem in hygiene or psychology to a political struggle; *our* system had to be defended against *theirs.* It was no longer enough to assert, as the Aldriches had a few years earlier, that *Babies Are Human Beings.* C. Madeleine Dixon's book, from which the above quote is taken, expresses the new problem and a new anxiety. Her book was called *Keep Them Human.* It was written in 1942.

The image of the Germans as soulless, authoritarians forced writers to defend democracy by extending its principles to home management. Dorothy Baruch's *You, Your Children, and War*, also written in 1942, contained similar advice:

Democracy Needed

"We are fighting to preserve the democratic way of life. And yet, as an inevitable by-product of war, there has come into our existence the tightening of authoritarian reins. No longer does individual liberty function as freely as in pre-war days. We may not use as much gasoline as we desire, nor as much sugar, or wool, or rubber. We may not charge what prices we wish to our customers. We may not exert the right to choose whether or not to enlist in the armed forces. We may soon be deprived of choosing whether to go to work or not, as have the people of England where labor is conscripted. More and more, our cherished freedoms are being tabled.

"As a result, our children see in the world about them no very true picture of democratic living. They see, instead, a kind of autocracy in action. And yet, if they are to live democratically, they should know what constitutes democarcy. They should *like* what constitutes democracy. They should have a warm, familiar, expansive feeling about democracy and sure knowledge of the principles on which it rests. . . .

"To our children, democracy must not be something you-speak-of-but-do-not-live-by. . . .

"*The first essential to democracy is free participation.* Self-chosen participation. Not the forced participation of the Nazis. Not participation because of being led in lock-step to feed machines or work in mines. People in a democracy must *want* to participate. Children growing up in a democracy must learn that participation can be satisfying and good."

The absolute authority of parents over children, a major theme in child care-books since the beginning of this history, became suspect in the face of the Nazi example of authoritarianism. In 1943, writing the introduction to *Infant and Child*, Gesell and Ilg made this feeling specific. Describing the family as an institution of the transmission of culture, the "most fundamental unit of culture. . .throughout the long history of man," they present the family not as had been done in the past as a miniature state but as a social group:

> "The spirit and organization of the family. . .reflect the historic culture. A totalitarian 'Kultur' subordinates the family completely to the state, fosters autocratic parent-child relationships, favors despotic discipline, and relaxes the tradition of monogamy. It is not concerned with the individual as a person. A democratic culture, on the contrary, affirms the dignity of the individual person. It exhalts the status of the family as a social group, favors reciprocity in parent-child reltionships, and encourages humane discipline of the child through guidance and understanding.
>
> "In a very profound way the democratic ideal is also bound up with the spirit of liberty. Liberty is the life principle of democracy, in the home as well as in the community. . . . "

For much of our history, we had advocated precisely the kind of "autocratic parent-child relationships" that are here condemned.

For writers most sympathetic to democratic and individualized methods of child raising, the Nazis represented everything undesirable. For more mechanistically inclined authors, on the other hand, the Nazi ideal represented, on a functional level at least, the realization of many of their theories. William Blatz, whose work with Helen Bott we have already examined, expressed this ambiguity clearly in his *Understanding the Young Child*, published in London in 1944:

> "Hitler, having a narrow view of social life, was able, in a short time, through teaching to build up his kind of society. It is often asked why we, in the democracies, do not follow his plan. It seemed so effective. Learning is a fundamental process in all human beings. The German children learn in exactly the same way as the English or French children. Training methods vary, but the secret of Hitler's success is not altogether in the way he taught, but in *what* he taught. There were no ambiguities: 'you must be obedient, truthful to me alone, loyal to me alone, industrious and *unquestioning*.' One can see that there were no doubts or confusions; anyone who felt doubts was liquidated. Granted

the premise that Hitler was always right, the system is not only logical it is satisfying. Thus an apparently astonishing success was attained. Why can't we do that in a democracy? We could, but it would not be a democracy.

"Fascism is static, democracy is dynamic. In a democracy the individual is free to act without the threat of physical violence. But obviously he hasn't unlimited choice. Abnormal behavior, as judged by the community, is followed, after due process of law, by restriction of liberties, ostracism, denial of citizenship. It is readily understood how much more difficult it is to *learn* to fit into a democracy and also how difficult it is to teach such a project. . . . "

The allure of fascism is certainly evident here; even the Nazi belief in automatic behavior and habit — the lack, as Blatz says, of ambiguity — when brought to fruition in the hands of a Hitler are seen as failures of ends rather than of means.

Wartime anxieties and the methods of protecting children from them occupied much of the mid-war psychologists' time. It was generally agreed that the best way to handle this problem was to express the fears openly rather than to deny or repress them behind a facade of bravery. Not only was this seen as an intrinsically healthy approach, it was seen in its political implications as a step in the direction of preventing the consequences of repression. In Baruch's *You, Your Children, and War* (1942), a book largely concerned with these problems, repressed hostility was, for example, seen as leading to war. "Hostility well off the chest does not make children more warlike. It makes for peace."

"TO BE SOUGHT [in Child Raising]

"1. We want our children to handle their hostilities realistically and squarely, straightforwardly and directly, not by subterfuge.

"2. We will not make our children ashamed when they evidence hostility towards us.

"3. We will help children to bring out their hostile feelings so that the strength of them beomes diluted.

"4. We will help our children to accept their feelings for what they are without needing to be torn by the guilt which makes people bury feelings from knowledge.

"5. We will want to remember that war sanctions the expression of hatred. War talk and war play are frequently the child's way of getting hostility off his chest.

"6. We will want to remember that causes of hostility are lessened as our children achieve basic satisfactions.

"7. When children are hostile we will help them to realize that we know how they feel, and that we have at times, felt similarly."

The influence of the Freudian vision that war arises out of frustration is evident here, but what is also apparent is that the war has given the idea new meaning and a new urgency.

One effect of this openness about feelings of hostility and anxiety was the molding of the family into a closer emotional unit. In a sense, fear equalized them. Both parents and children could, after all, be equally afraid, but through this openness they could share their fear rather than keep it bottled inside. More particularly, with so many husbands of child-raising age away at the front or otherwise involving their energies in wartime production, the War appears to have brought about a closer bonding of mother and child. *Your First Baby*, written in 1943 by Louise Cripps Glemser, expresses this situation clearly:

"We are living in a world at war. We do not know what horrors the future may hold. There may be insufficiency of the right food for our children; they may be bombed. Today, it is an act of faith to have a child. But the urge to procreate is primitive. Through wars, revolutions, earthquakes, women still go on producing children. They will inherit the world we have made for them. The courage, the ability, the humanity with which they approach their tasks as grown men and women depend now on their mothers.

"And whatever the shape of the world to come, by giving the best to your baby — not material things alone, but your love, your supporting, your intelligence — you will have equipped him with the inestimable blessings of good health, kindliness and courage with which to enter life. That will be the greatest contribution you could possibly make to the new, peaceful society of our dreams."

There is a parallel between the absent husbands of the war years and the Victorian husbands working twelve and sixteen hours a day in the offices and mills. In both cases, the wife is isolated with the child and the child becomes the focus of much of the emotional attention that would otherwise find an outlet through the husband. The similarity of some of the writings of this time to Harland's and to other writers of the erotic tradition is evident throughout the period.

The work that many of the forties writers referred to for authority was the humane book *Babies Are Human Beings*. Glemser mentions her debt to the Aldriches in her introduction. Aldrich himself wrote the introduction to what was certainly the best of the wartime books, Dr. Dorothy V. Whipple's *Our American Babies* (1944). Aldrich says of the book that Whipple has taken his description of "what" happens in child development and added the essential "*how* to 'get it across' so that child care will really work."

Whipple brought a real warmth to the subject and a personal honesty that, as explicitly as Glemser's, reflected the new openness and closeness of the time. In her introduction, she tells of how she had been trained at Johns Hopkins, spiritual home of Watson and the behaviorists:

> "I was taught, as was the rest of my medical generation, that early conditioning of the infant was essential. Regularity is the keynote of infant care. Babies were put on a schedule from birth. . . . We were assured that crying did no harm; that it was in fact good exercise. Unnecessary handling of a baby was frowned upon and kissing was looked upon only as a means of conveying germs. . . .
>
> "With this background of training I entered upon my own work with children. But first I had a baby of my own. . . . I soon found out that it made a lot of difference to me whose baby was crying. I had been able to go away with equanimity from some other mother's screaming child, with the knowledge that a skilled nurse would see that he is lacking nothing; but to go away from my own crying baby, and stay within earshot for another hour or more before the clock said I could give him the milk I knew he wanted, that, I confess, I found to be a different matter."

"Soon," she adds, "I found myself modifying the tenets of my teaching. . . and whenever I had occasion to guide a mother I told her how I felt; usually she too picked up her baby when he cried, fed him when he was hungry, and did not feel ashamed to rock him, sing to him, love him demonstratively."

There was still some uncertainty in her approach, reflected in a pamphlet published in 1942, the United States Department of Labor Children's Bureau publication *Infant Care*. One of the least expensive and most popular sources of child-care information, *Infant Care* had been in circulation since 1914, revised once in 1929 and again in 1938. By 1942, less than four years later, it was out of date. Whipple, working with an author of the 1938 edition, Marian Crane, was asked to rewrite the pamphlet.

On many major points, the 1942 edition of *Infant Care* resembles the later Whipple book. While the overall attitude reflects the new feeling of warmth, what Aldrich speaks of as her "attitude of respect and tolerance for the development of the child," there is still a certain lack of authority, a tendency to mix the old advice with the new ideas she wishes to put across. For example, this is the passage on crying from *Infant Care*:

Crying

"When the baby cries it is a signal that something needs to be done. He may need to be turned over, to have his diaper changed, to be given a drink of water, or to have some companionship.

"Frequently the small amount of attention that goes with satisfying his wants will give him all the companionship he needs, and he will become peaceful. Sometimes, however, a baby will continue to cry. It is true that short periods of crying will not harm a young baby and that crying is good exercise if it does not last too long. If the crying lasts for more than 15 minutes, however, after the baby has apparently been made comfortable, he probably needs further attention.

"If it is near his feeding time the mother may pick him up, hold him, and sing to him a little until it is the time for feeding.

"If it is not near the feeding time it is possible that the baby may need a little extra food; if so, he should have it.

"If the little baby frequently wakes and cries when it is not his feeding time, he is probably not getting enough food or the right kind of food, or he is not being fed at the right intervals, or something else is the matter. The doctor should be consulted.

"It should be remembered that if a baby cries for no apparent reason he may be sick. If you suspect that he is sick, take his temperature."

Feeding, interpreting Gesell, is scheduled in *Infant Care* according to a rhythm from the baby. "It is possible," the pamphlet says, "to find for each baby some time interval that suits his needs, and it is therefore neither desirable nor necessary to force him into any schedule merely because that schedule has been found good for some other baby."

By way of contrast, compare the passage on crying from *Our American Babies*, two years later.

Crying

"Did you ever stop to think how much louder a baby can cry than the young of any other animal?

"Young kittens and puppies whimper a little, a calf or a baby goat can give a pathetic little bleat, baby lions and tigers — so the zoo keeper tells me — have a soft whimper; but not a single newborn animal I know about can rouse the neighbors with a lusty yell as can a baby when he has been only a few weeks in this world.

"A baby can cry, but he cannot do much about taking care of his wants. The young of most other species can pull themselves around, can hunt around for that meal their stomachs tell them they need; but the baby just lies in one place and yells for someone to come and make him comfortable.

"A baby's ability to cry is nature's way of seeing that his needs are taken care of. It is up to us adults to keep in step with nature and heed his cry. A baby does not cry for nothing; he cries because he is uncomfortable. It is up to us to find out why and fix it.

"Sometimes a baby cries for a perfectly obvious reason. He may be hungry or cold or wet or stuck with a pin, and then what to do is clear. But sometimes a baby cries, and for the life of us we cannot see that anything is the matter. He seems warm; he is dry; he has just finished a meal; he does not seem to have a pain; he is not sick. There does not seem to be any reason at all for the screaming, and yet the natural instinct of his mother tells her what to do. She holds him and rocks him a little, maybe she sings to him and whispers to him all those sweet nothings that mothers and babies understand. And that is what he wanted. He is quiet and peaceful immediately; his crying brought him what he was crying for — his mother's loving attention.

"And let that be a lesson to us. Babies do not cry for nothing. They cry because of some need. You will never spoil a baby by attending to his needs. A baby needs food and warmth; but he also needs love and all the little baby things that go with his mother's demonstration of her love. A baby who gets plenty of this kind of attention will not cry for more. It is the baby who never has enough who is always crying for more. *He* is the spoiled baby."

At approximately the same time, that Dorothy Whipple was at work on *Infant Care*, she discovered the Aldriches: "One day a year or so ago," she writes in the introduction to her book (dated 1943), "I was handed a book and asked to review it. It was the Aldriches' book, *Babies Are Human Beings.* I read it; then I read it again. I wanted to shout. Here was what I had been struggling with. Here it was, all written down." *Our American Babies* certainly, in some measure, represents in its attitudes the support for her convictions that she found in reading the Aldriches' work.

The opening chapter of *Our American Babies,* entitled "A Baby in Wartime — A Victory Baby," talks about the effects of war on child care in psychological terms.

> "Whatever affects the baby's parents affects him; he lives and grows by means of them. If the father goes away to war or a war job mother must be both parents to her baby. It is not easy for a young wife to give up her husband. Not only does she miss his companionship, but she is worried about his safety. Her worry may make her tense and nervous, she may drop everything when the evening paper comes; perhaps she cannot keep her mind on her task as she watches for the postman; maybe she has a radio on for the evening news while she feeds her baby. . . .
>
> "No one can ask a woman not to be worried when she knows the man she loves is in a danger zone; but if she realizes that her baby needs her more than ever when there is no father coming home at night, she will find a way to give wholeheartedly to that baby what he needs — her loving care."

This is only a fraction of the chapter, which goes on to detail the shortages of laundry service, gasoline and rubber.

Some hardships were a blessing in disguise, Whipple points out. While "the War Production Board agreed that there was no good substitute for rubber nipples and therefore granted priorities for their manufacture," it was necessary to replace rubber pants with "oiled silk or other waterproof material. These materials are not as waterproof as rubber but for that very reason they are better for the baby!"

Other sections of the book include valuable advice on budgeting the expense of a baby from conception through the first year. Such material is generally omitted from contemporary books on child care — perhaps, in this time of inflation, it would make them out-of-date too rapidly. Looking at the 1944 costs gives one a jolt.

Medical care for the mother:
    Doctor's bill $ 50.00

Hospital: ten days in a semi-private room at $5 per day	50.00
Delivery room fees	10.00
Anaesthetic fee	10.00
Board for baby, ten days at $1.50 per day	15.00
Laboratory fees and special medicines	5.00
Nurse: Special nurses for twenty-four hours (2 nurses for twelve hours each at $8)	16.00

Medical care for the baby:

During first year: twelve visits	36.00
Croup kettle	1.98

Total medical cost — $193.98

This is the record of a real family. The husband, "principal of an elementary school. . . makes $2500 a year." The itemization includes all the other expenses, cribs, clothing, etc. Even the necessity of larger housing ("Moved to suburbs, increased rent $5 per month") is included. The middle-class flight to the country (or its surburban approximation) to raise children was already established before the end of the war brought a flood of new families.

During the war, when a wife as well as a husband might be engaged in defense work, older brothers or sisters were expected to play a role in caring for the younger members of the family. There were even books intended for high-school students aimed directly at this problem. Where older children were not available, nurses might be employed. Whipple comments:

"If you have a nurse select her with care. She will be a significant person to your baby. Her health, her personality and temperament, her training are all-important. A nurse must be healthy, and this fortunately is usually the easiest thing to check up. She should be examined by a doctor before you employ her, and must, of course, be free from infectious disease.

"The kind of person the nurse is cannot always be determined so easily. A woman who is happy, whose life is satisfactory to herself, is most apt to make a good nurse. She will become fond of your baby. She will love him as any normal woman loves a baby whom she is with constantly; and her genuine affection will prompt her to do the little things that make the baby feel happy and secure.

"A woman who is unhappy, who is emotionally starved, is apt to pour forth so much pent-up emotion on the baby that she smothers him with her love. She wants to do so much for him that she does not allow him the independence his maturing mind and body needs.

"There are some women to whom a baby makes no appeal. Such a woman may, if she is conscientious, take good physical care of your baby; but she will do it with a frigid austerity that does not give the baby a sense of friendly companionship. . . . "

It is, in sum, advice that would have been familiar to Guillemeau three and a quarter centuries earlier.

In addition to raising wartime children with the assistance of siblings or nurses, the nursery school came into vogue. As Dixon writes in *Keep Them Human*:

"The nursery school is not any one person's brightly thought up idea. It is the result of many laboratories using the best that education has to offer in terms of trained people and tried equipment and experimental attitude that is thoroughly scientific. For twenty years nuclei all over the country have been using these laboratory methods based on what we have learned through psychology and the social sciences. They have come to almost identical conclusions regarding methods. We would be silly not to take advantage of their findings, now in times of particular stress."

The methods of the nursery school were also available for use in the home:

"The stronger our ability to use the nursery school method of getting the child to watch the other fellow and his rights, along with assertion on his own rights – this alike with contemporaries and grown-ups – the better we meet his immediate need and the better we prepare him [to be] an all-round grown-up who knows what he wants but will not take it at the unfair expense of another, but who will stand strong, and sure of getting what is his right to have."

It cannot be said that the nursery school, with its touch of democratic collectivization, or the uses of brothers and sisters while the mother was at work, or, for that matter, even the use of nurses, diminished the war-strengthened bond between mother and child. In some ways, even these influences served to reinforce and romanticize this bond. It is, after all, a

lot easier to deal with a small child in a humane way when one only sees
the child for a few hours each day.

"What shall I do about discipline?" is the first thing a helper asks
the departing mother in Dixon's book. If "the mother cannot say, Do not
bother about disciplines, leave that to me," she can at least leave behind a
routine for the child, and a list of the "usual and unusual responses of the
child to that routine."

> " The very first thing to be aware of and the last thing and all the way
> in between is that the child must be, assured of the fact that whereas
> rules exist and must be met, they will be balanced with times of
> deciding for himself — times of choice."

She goes on to be explicit about how the routine is to be applied:

> "Routine for little children should be much slower than with grown-
> ups. This does not mean needless lagging and loitering, but it does
> mean that dressing, eating, getting ready to go outdoors become full
> of tensions if they are speeded up to grown-up standards, and children
> are thwarted if they cannot produce results quickly and become balky
> and refuse to try. Compare his speed in accomplishments and his
> ability to do things with other children and then expect results half
> way between the more able and the less able children."

There is again an interpretation of Gesell, the sense of the child's biological
time versus the accelerated social time adults live by. Dixon's further
comments remind one of Gesell as well:

> "The more that can be done objectively, the better. This does not
> mean that a grown-up will be an automaton. Oh no, not so long as she
> is working with a real child. Even at best she will find herself getting
> mad and showing resentment. But if she keeps a chart she may be
> prodded to keep tabs on her own ability to listen and to try to find
> out why Johnny does this and that which is annoying. Charts help a
> person to look at behavior as something that can be partially met with
> wiser planning.
>
> "*Charts* are fine for reference. . . . We look on the chart and see
> at five o'clock a drink of water is in order or a story or a quiet game. . .
> but if Jimmy is deep in a play interest. . . we don't yank him away for
> a drink of water. We say, Here Mr. Busman, perhaps you'd like a cup
> of coffee. We learn to sell our wares, learn to sell our program. . . .

"The best discipline means that you say Don't just as few times a day as possible; jot down the number of times you say Don't, or Hurry, and then see if you could go on without them. Substitute confidence for don'ts. . . . Rather than, "Don't move the furniture," say "It would be all right to move those two chairs so that you would have more room." Watch the difference in the child's face when you stop saying Don't and Hurry. He is more relaxed. And there is the secret of a manageable child, a relaxed child. Then he can begin to get hold of his own interests, and an interested child is good to be with."

Dixon was willing to balance discipline or rules with free time for the child to follow his own inclinations. In fact, the tendency of the times was away from rules entirely. When a problem of conflict arose between the parent and child, it was explained away. Behavior, in this scheme, tended to become neither good nor bad but "problem," demanding solution rather than retribution. Punishment was out.

In Glemser's *Your First Baby*, the question of discipline is reduced to a single page:

"The question of punishment must be considered, for some parents do mete out punishment even to babies.

"You act, of course, in the interest of the child himself, doing it for his own good. But seriously consider your attitude in this. Are you going to make your child do what you think he should do, just because he is afraid of you? It is the easiest method of dealing with him, and you do not have to think it out at all. But use the rod and you are sure to spoil the child. Spankings should be omitted from your training of him, or at least be few. On the other hand, don't 'reason' with a little child. You might as well talk gibberish most of the time. If your son or daughter has tantrums — and they will not have many if you have dealt sympathetically with them — then a little kicking and rolling on the floor by themselves will soon cure them. But you must expect a healthy, spirited child to put up a good fight to get something he particularly wants. Be sure, first of all, that there is a good reason why he cannot have it, and then try to direct him by giving him something else that is an equal treat. On the whole, children are very amiable, reasonable creatures if properly handled."

Even in a book composed of short pieces on each aspect of child raising, this is brief coverage of an old problem. The tendency in the early forties was to ignore the subject of discipline. Typical solutions to the problem of behavior were to distract or ignore the child. "When he does things you do not want repeated," Whipple writes, pay no attention. "Ignore undesirable behavior; there is nothing so dull as being ignored." The following is all she has to say about "Scoldings and Punishment."

"There is no such thing as a bad baby. No baby — certainly no baby under two — needs punishment.

"Babies may be annoying and troublesome, true enough, but they are not bad. Badness is willful wrongdoing. Babies are not born with a sense of right and wrong. A baby does anything and everything he can. He has the whole world to learn about.

"He needs a place where he can experiment and explore, where no one says: 'Don't touch that' or 'Come away from there.'

"Eventually a baby gains enough experience so that he does not need to finger everything he sees; and at the same time he observes grownups closely enough to begin to copy the way they act. In the long run, it is much better that a baby should give up his annoying behavior because he has outgrown it than because he has been punished until he is afraid to touch the interesting and fascinating things about him."

Whipple's section on "The Habits We Do Not Want" continues the theme. The child is either to be distracted or not to be interfered with and should be given or allowed to do what he wants if it is at all possible. If the child sucks his thumb, "let the baby stay at the breast a little longer" or give him "something that will keep his hands busy." If he still sucks his thumb after weaning, or, last resort, if he is older, tell him, "Daddy doesn't suck his thumb; you want to grow up to be a big man like daddy."

"Playing with the Genitals" brings out the advice: "Let your young baby discover and play with his genitals. As he gets older, see that he has plenty of interesting toys to occupy him so that he does not fall back on his genitals out of boredom; and in addition be sure that your baby has all the love and attention he requires, and does not need to comfort himself with his own body. . . . Never punish. . .it only makes matters worse."

If one can judge a time from its books, the 1940s during the War and in the years immediately afterwards may be described as the most permissive time in child care. The Second World War, in child care as in so many other things, drove a wedge between the past and the future. Regardless of the protests against "permissiveness," it is unlikely we will be able to return to morals of either the nineteenth century with its certainties of good and evil or the early twentieth and the search for scientific certaintly in schedules and routines.

Whipple's book (however superbly written and however valid its advice) disappeared from print and is now hard to obtain. People did not want to be reminded of a war, the lessons of which were increasingly elusive. Post-war books assimilated Whipple's ideas but contained a new approach to child care. Then appeared the most popular book written in this field: *The Common Sense Book of Baby and Child Care* by Dr. Benjamin Spock.

CHAPTER 12

"Common-Sense" Child Care

If the First World War had helped to spread the message of psychology among the general public, the Second had a similar impact on the acceptance of psychiatry. In 1924, in the Watson-MacDougall debate, the British psychologist had mentioned his hopes that psychology would play a role in avoiding future conflicts:

> "At the present time in all parts of the world men and women of good will and public spirit are seeking and striving to find some way to prevent the outbreak of a new world war. But if the mechanical psychology [behaviorism in the Watsonian sense] is true. . . all of us may just as well. . . eat, drink, and be merry, for our thinking, our plans, our League of Nations, our disarmament treaties. . . all alike are perfectly futile."

On the level of logical debate, MacDougall's statement was faulty – the behaviorists did offer the possibility of changing man so profoundly that the elimination of war seemed a simple matter. But World War Two exposed the superficiality of mechanistic psychology's idea of what it took to achieve human perfection. Its theories were not only insufficient to describe social behavior, they were also obviously incapable of controlling it.

As Anna Freud wrote: "It needed nearly fifty years of psychoanalytic research. . . and the added impact of two world wars to break down an age-old prejudice and make the adult world realize that children, no less than the adults themselves, are dominated by their sexual impulses and aggressive strivings." Post-war children were to be psychoanalyzed as deeply as their parents.

Your Child Makes Sense (1949) by Edith Buxbaum, with an introduction by Anna Freud (from which these quotations are taken), was one of the books that dealt most explicitly with the psychiatric approach to child care. Written for use in the home, it is an attempt to interpret the insights of psychiatry for practical application. Anna Freud adds:

> "In the course of the patient and laborious exploration of many adult patients the fact gradually emerged that the content of a child's first years is different from what the adult world had imagined it to be: that childhood is not a period of undisturbed growth and development, lived in an atmosphere of happy, care-free unconcern. On the contrary: from birth onwards, children feel the pressure of urgent body needs and powerful instinctive urges (such as hunger, sex, aggression) which clamor for satisfaction. Soon afterwards, the child encounters the demands for restraint, and the prohibitions on unlimited wish-ful-fillment, which come from the parents whose task it is to turn their children from unrestrained, greedy and cruel little savages into well-behaved, socially adapted, civilized beings. It is difficult for the help-less young child to bear the painful tensions of his frustrated wishes; it is equally difficult for him to oppose his parents on whose love and care he depends for the necessities of his very existence. There is a constant clash between the claims made by the inner world of the child (his instinctive wishes) and those of the external world (represented by the parents). There are further and equally distressing clashes between the various instinctive urges, which are only too often incompatible with each other. Children love and hate the same persons all in one breath; they want to eat things and have them, destroy them and preserve them, etc. The manner in which the individual child manages to solve these unavoidable external and internal conflicts decides, not only his future mental health and illness, but equally the formation of his character, his usefulness as a citizen and his success in love and married life."

The psychoanalytic vision of the human mind was one that the age was prepared to accept. Conflict was seen as unavoidable, yet it could still be resolved to the advantage of the child if it were properly understood, honestly faced, accepted and properly managed. Analysis and the conclusions derived from it still held out the hope of producing a useful, healthy citizen, a "success in love and married life."

On the subject of the common practice of separating the baby from his mother in the hospital, Buxbaum comments:

"Psychologically the enforced hospital separation is all wrong. The mother had had her baby very close within her for the better part of a year. She is looking forward to seeing, feeling, smelling, hearing, and holding it as well as feeding it and changing its diapers. . . .

"The baby. . . needs his mother from the start. He needs as little change in his environment and handling as possible. Instead of three or four different nurses handling him each day the mother can take care of him except for bathing the first day or two. . . . The baby in turn gets used to just one person handling him, gets used to the feel of her hands, her particular smell, the tone of her voice. Baby and mother can come to know each other and may become quite good friends by the time they leave for home. This is a good start towards general emotional health for the baby and cements his relationship with his mother."*

The advice is old but the reference point, the child's emotional health, is relatively new. Prior to the 1930s, the relationship between parent and child was based on the child adapting to the desires and timetable of the adult. The difference between writers was in their visions of how far or fast the child could be brought in this direction. With Gesell and Aldrich, it was gradually understood that there were physical and mental processes going on in the child that could not be altered regardless of the parents' desires and that these limited how parents could shape children. With the psychiatric approach, and the acceptance of a logical process of personality development, limitations were extended still further. *"Should we cater to the child?"* is one question Buxbaum asks. "The question is how to do it without disturbing him."

"We tend to think, 'mother knows best what's good for the child' — actually, the healthy baby knows even better. Instinctively, he fights for his right to grow and develop; only the sickly baby, the physically or emotionally disturbed one, gives up easily. . . . The young child

*The first chapter of *Your Baby Makes Sense*, "Physical Development & Care," from which this quote is taken, was written by Florence L. Swanson, M.D.

may, when frightened [by punishment], give up an activity altogether instead of just that part in which he was restrained. In this instance, the child gives up more than the adult asked for. He may refuse to eat at all after he was punished for using his hands; he may not be able to paint for fear of getting dirty; he may be afraid of washing and bathing when he has been scolded for splashing. He may become timid and afraid to try anything new. The child may be equally discouraged in his attempts at imitating adults and children in their actions and attitudes. Since imitation is not only a way of learning but also a factor in his character development an important avenue for his growth can be blocked by discouraging imitation."

In the parent-child relationship under this new scheme, the child, by virtue of his physical, mental and psychological right to develop, is the dominant figure. A mother might be seething with rage at the child but afraid to take action for fear of the consequences when the child grows up, a situation on which Spock was to comment incisively in the 1957 revision of his book.

Unfortunately, misinterpreting these theories, the tendency was all too often to avoid frustrating the child at whatever cost in frustration to the parent. Every part of child training held the threat of potential damage: "Bowel training," Buxbaum advises, "has much more potentiality for emotional trauma than bladder training." In reviewing the rigid methods of the past, she adds "'Forcing' defecation [with suppositories, etc.] at certain times of the day may be just one more coercive and emotionally highly charged experience in the child's daily living. . . . If the child is constipated the mother should consider the psychological aspects of her treatment very carefully." How many mothers possessed the training and experience to give these matters the balanced psychological consideration recommended? Instead of simplifying the relationship between mother and child, this vision of the child's emotional fragility encouraged the mother to be more anxious rather than less. Even though the book recommended handling toilet training in a "gentle and matter-of-fact manner," the implication of this approach and the effect of the book was to leave the mother torn, on one side wanting to move the child out of the diaper-changing stage and on the other apprehensive about doing permanent damage to the child's psyche.

Some other books of the same period, took a less dogmatic and lighter view of the likelihood of damage. The intelligently written *Stop Annoying Your Children* (1947) by W.W. Bauer balances an awareness of the child's emotional sensitivity with an equal astuteness about the child's emotional resilience. And, too, the author is not unaware of his book's likely impact in the home. "The kids are going to love this book, the parents aren't," Bauer says at the outset.

> "Being a good parent means working at it. Too many parents are spending too much time on their own careers or on social obligations or on their own pleasures to be really good parents. We are accustomed to think of bad parents as those who get hauled into court for neglecting their children. We recall tales of young mothers who park the baby in the crib, lock up the house and make the rounds of the cocktail lounges. We think of fathers who come home drunk and beat their children. These are truly bad parents but they are the extremes and exceptions. Often, despite their vices they love and understand their children better than do 'good' people!. . .
>
> "When children are annoyed, it is likely to be more often by people who consider themselves good parents and who are good parents in the sense that they commit no outrageous depredations upon the welfare of their children. . . ."

Such parents are too earnest, too humorless: "They try too hard," "Too much science," Bauer comments, "can ruin childhood as easily as too little." There is no use trying to be perfect; we are only to do our best:

> "There can be no question that in spite of our best efforts we will annoy our children from time to time. Yet there is no necessity for making these occasions needlessly frequent. There is no need to be stupid about the relationships between parents and children. It is up to us as parents to make an effort. We are the ones who are experienced. Upon us falls the burden of blame if there is a failure."

On "who is the boss," Bauer points out that "excessive repression is as bad as untrammeled self-expression. . . . Children definitely need to know who's boss."

Bauer suggests that two questions children ask offer the parents insight into child's deepest needs.

> "The first of these questions is "Daddy, do you love me?' This cannot be taken for granted. Children need and should have a regular show of affection from both their parents. This should mean more than an absent-minded kiss in the morning and at night. Genuine evidence of affection includes a willingness to make many small sacrifices. Few

parents will be found wanting when it comes to larger sacrifices. Let a child fall sick and Mother gives up her sleep and her social life and perhaps even a quart of her blood to save the life of the child. Father will spend everything he can lay his hands on and mortgage all the rest to save the life of the child, to say nothing of standing ready to face fire or flood if necessary.

"These are not the true tests of good parent-child relationships. Much less conspicuous, much less heroic and much more difficult is the daily necessity for postponing the reading of the evening paper until youngsters have had a chance to tell what happened in school that day. Less spectacular and more important is the willingness to accept small and inconsequential confidences in order to keep the way open for the important communications that may come later. Mother may have to wrench herself from a fascinating committee in order to be at home when the children arrive from school. . . . "

Regarding the second question, "Did you miss me?" Bauer comments:

"Next to the necessity of being loved is the necessity for being needed. An individual of character cannot be content merely to be loved. To be loved and useless is an unsatisfying kind of life. Every individual needs to feel that what he is doing is of value to the community as a whole."

Bauer suggests that children be allowed to help around the house even if, as he points out, this ends up making more work for the parents.

In his observations and suggestions, Bauer's descriptions of the proper family relationships evoke an image of the post-war world of the 1940s, a time covered in Sloan Wilson's novel *The Man in the Grey Flannel Suit*. Returning veterans sought security and stability, *normalcy*, a reassertion of the supremacy of family life and values. In Wilson's book, the hero, Tom Rath, characteristically turns down a job that might lead him to become the head of a broadcasting network: "I've been through one war. Maybe another one's coming. If one is, I want to be able to look back and figure I spent the time between the wars with my family, the way it should have been spent."

The late forties were a more conservative time than the war years. Bauer, Spock, Baruch and other writers of the period were again willing to discuss discipline. Yet, though the word had returned, the implication had changed. It was pointed out — by Dorothy Baruch in her *New Ways in Discipline* (1949) — that discipline did not originally mean to punish but to make disciples, to educate. In accordance with this vision, the use of parental authority, while still regarded as necessary, was tempered. The new insights, or more accurately the newly accepted insights of psychiatry, did not permit a return to the old severities. Harsh punishment had become emotionally unacceptable. It tended to undermine the picture of family harmony that was the chief ambition of the time.

When conflicts arose, for all the child's need to "know who's boss," the proper parental response was to understand why the child had done something, or, alternatively, to examine his or her own response for reacting so strongly to the child's behavior. Only then, if all else failed, was punishment permitted; the object was to "make the punishment fit the crime." In one of Bauer's examples, if the child is late for lunch, the parent should understand that children have no sense of time. If the parent still feels the need to punish the child to get across the need for promptness, he should let the child go without the meal he has missed.

In dealing with what earlier writers had called bad habits, psychiatric theory was utilized. Bedwetting was "essentially a symptom of insecurity and a protest against an intolerable life situation," according to Bauer. Masturbation was similarly described as "the indirect expression of revolt against unacceptable conditions of living." Persistent crying, when it is not due "to conditions which are readily recognizable, such as physical discomfort, digestive disturbances, colic or other pains, or evidences of acute illness. . . may be due to the insistence by overconscientious parents on a wrong schedule for the child. . . . Remember," Bauer writes, "what Dr. Aldrich said about babies — they do not come wired to alarm clocks."

> "Many a baby cries because he does not have enough love and affection. He cries in protest. Such a need should be easy to supply; just a little bit of judicious attention will solve his problem. Another baby cries because he is spoiled. He requires the opposite treatment — some wholesome letting alone. . . .
>
> "Persistent crying may be due to causes which lie deeper than merely too much attention or too little. One of the gravest situations which can arise in a family is what psychologists call rejection of an unwanted child by its parents. This seldom takes the simple form occasionally reported in the press — leaving the baby on a doorstep or giving it up by adoption. Most normal parents, recognizing that they are prejudiced against an unwanted child, recoil from the idea because it makes them feel guilty. They know that it is wrong to reject a child which was in no way responsible for its own arrival. Sometimes such rejecting parents, in order to spare their own sense of guilt, become overindulgent toward a child as a subconscious way to prove that they are not doing

the wicked thing which they fear, that is, mistreating, it.

"Many children are accused of sulking. A child does not naturally sulk. Children are fundamentally happy unless they have been in discouraging contact with adults. If a child shows a tendency to be moody, irritable, pouty and unpredictable, the chances are that he is being annoyed by his elders."

The perceptions are psychiatric but the "unavoidable" conflict between parent and child described by Anna Freud is seen as largely the parent's fault. Such conflict is to be eliminated if possible. In a character-istically American way, psychiatric problems have been brought to the surface where they can be handled directly. Even the terms Bauer uses reflect this process. The child is not "disturbed" or "upset" by his parents, he is annoyed; rather than being "neurotic" or "nervous" his symptoms — moody, irritable, etc. — are described as the problems themselves.

Using this simplified approach, parents were encouraged to identify with the child, rather than concern themselves with how well the child satisfied their own demands. As a result, new insights continually arose. One "seldom mentioned problem" that Bauer raises is the "problem of the excessively good child."

"Many a foolish parent boasts because his child never gives him any trouble. Instead of boasting, he should be worried. Children ought to give trouble. It is normal for them to break out in unexpected places. They should be trying something new, and it is to be expected that a percentage of their experiments will get them into difficulties. They ought to be annoying their parents, their teachers and the grown-up world in general. The only way children learn is by trying — and trying is so much better than observing, even if more hazardous.

"When the child is too passive. . . [he] is likely to be giving up the struggle against circumstances."

One treatment proposed for such a problem is to put the child with more active playmates, but sometimes psychiatric help may be necessary. The child Bauer hopes for is Gesell's dynamic child, Aldrich's sparkler, a growing creature testing the limits of his mind, body and society, trying to learn how much he can get through the use of his hands and his mouth. It is a process that, hopefully, is never over in life and a feeling that parents can share.

*   *   *

It is from our understanding of the post-war years and of the philosophies of child raising at that time that we can best understand both the content and the success of Spock's *Baby and Child Care*. The overwhelming popularity of the Spock book is not simply a matter of his book being different or better than other books. It is a matter of fit, in the evolutionary sense. Spock's book, like Holt's, and like the work of other popular writers of each period, fit the emotional and practical needs of its time.

For the most part, this book quotes the original edition of *Baby and Child Care*, in preparation from 1943 to 1946 (when it was first published). Subsequent editions in 1957, 1968, and 1976 represent a certain retrenchment and movement towards conservatism.

To anyone who has looked at later Spock editions, the 1946 book comes as a surprise. Lean and often witty, it is a book of strong opinions carefully concealed behind a frequent repetition of the idea that everything is or will be all right if the mother only follows her best instincts. It begins with the statement, "You know more than you think you do," and continues:

"Soon you're going to have a baby. Maybe you have him already. You're happy and excited, but if you haven't had much experience, you wonder whether you are going to know how to do a good job. Lately you have been listening more carefully to your friends and relatives when they talk about bringing up a child. You've begun to read articles by experts in the magazines and newspapers. After the baby is born, the doctors and nurses will begin to give you instructions too. Sometimes it sounds like a very serious business. . . .

"Don't take too seriously all that the neighbors say. Don't be overawed by what the experts say. Don't be afraid to trust your own common sense. Bringing up a child won't be a complicated job if you take it easy, trust your own instincts, and follow the directions your doctor gives you. We know for a fact that the natural loving care that kindly parents give their children is a hundred times more valuable than their knowing how to pin a diaper on just right or how to make up a formula expertly. . . .

"It may surprise you to hear that the more people have studied different methods of bringing up children, the more they have come to the conclusion that what good mothers and fathers instinctively feel like doing for their children is usually best, after all. Furthermore, all parents do their best job when they have a natural easy confidence in themselves. Better to make a few mistakes from being natural than to do everything letter-perfect out of a feeling of worry."

This excerpt is, in large measure, typical of the approach of the book as a whole, moving slowly, reassuringly, repetitiously. The emphasis is on comforting or tranquilizing the anxieties of parents. In its approach and style it recognizes how anxious new parents are.

The War's end had brought with it a baby boom and a substantial demographic movement. People were moving from the country and city to the newly laid out suburbs. There were thousands of young families living side by side remote from parental guidance. Like their parents, and their parents before them, the post-war generation was determined to do a better job on their children than their own parents had. Spock's book appealed to young parents, alone and insecure, needing advice and comfort, eager to accept a book that asserted the primacy of love and family closeness in raising children.

A second element of the book's success was its comprehensiveness. Virtually every problem, whether real or in the parent's mind, was dealt with in a consistent thorough way. For all its statements about reliance on instinct, the book is as chock full of specific information as a dictionary.

The index to the work was assembled by Spock himself, and in it he realized an opportunity that had largely been overlooked in child-care books. Here, for example, is Whipple's index coverage of baby's crying:

> "Crying, baby's.
> before feeding time
> in pain
> when restrained'

By contrast, here is Spock's:

> "Crying,
> attention
> from bubble
> from colic
> from ear pain
> on going to bed
> from hunger
> in indigestion
> irritable
> the irritable baby
> some causes in infancy
> from spoiling
> from wetness
> when mother leaves the one-year-old"

Spock had perceived that when something unusual happens, mothers turn to the index first. If a mother had turned to the page indicated under the heading "attention", she would have found ready to comfort her: "His cry is there to call you. The uneasy feeling you have when you hear him cry, is meant to be part of your nature, too. A little gentle rocking may actually be good for him." Additional comments advised the reader to check other sections of the book and referred her to *Babies Are Human Beings* by the Aldriches. "Meanwhile," the section concludes, "be natural and comfortable, and enjoy your baby."

Spock possesses a gift that few other doctors, and even fewer psychiatrists claim: the ability to return the abstractions of psychology and psychiatry to their sources in behavior. He is able to offer the public insights without jargon. At one point, in explaining that the baby isn't "frail," he mentions a point to which Watson had given much attention and which Whipple had classified under a separate heading: crying "when restrained." Spock disposes of the subject in one sentence: "If he gets his head tangled in anything he has a strong instinct to struggle and yell."

The psychiatric perspective on child care was a deeply held position that Spock wanted to communicate to the world. As early as 1938, in collaboration with Dr. Mable Huschka, he had written an article entitled "The Psychological Aspects of Pediatric Practice." It pointed out that strict training can lead children to become submissive or rebellious, anxious and neurotically self-destructive and advocated the "natural and sound pattern" of letting the child find his own patterns of eating and toilet training. At least as far as eating is concerned, this is not as permissive as it sounds. Spock's concern, in 1946, was that the mother not try to force too much food or a prearranged schedule on the child. He nevertheless still advocated "working towards a regular schedule" set up with the cooperation of the baby as the Gesell book indicated. On the subject of pure "demand" feeding, Spock comments:

"Some doctors and parents have been trying the experiment lately of going back to nature — never waking the baby, but feeding him whenever he seems hungry. . . .

"If more and more babies come to be fed this way, and if it works out well, it may possibly become, in the future, one of the 'regular' ways to feed babies. . . .

"One trouble with the 'demand' schedule, in these days when the regular schedule has been so much the custom, is that it may leave an inexperienced mother feeling uncertain. She wonders how she will know when her baby is hungry. . . . The demand schedule may be more difficult also for the mother who herself has to keep a strict schedule because of a job, or meals for her husband and older children, or because she wants to nurse the baby at times when a jealous older child is most apt to be busy outside the house.

"I don't myself think it's very important whether a baby is fed purely according to his own demand or whether the mother is working towards a regular schedule — just as long as she is willing to be flexible and adjust to the baby's needs and happiness."

This balanced approach in which Spock seems genuinely in doubt about the virtues of one system over another is the exception. Generally, behind his constant it's-all-right, Spock has definite opinions, some of the strongest of which crystalize around the subject of psychiatry. On the effect of jealousy, he comments:

"Do your best to avoid jealousy. Jealousy is a strong emotion, even in grownups, but it is particularly disturbing to the young child before the age of five. Such traits as selfishness, unfriendliness, self-consciousness can often be traced back to a bitter jealousy created in the small child by the arrival of a baby brother or sister. Jealousy is one of the facts of life and it can't be completely prevented in family life. A little jealousy that is gradually conquered may be constructive. It teaches the individual how to get along in the world outside the family. But the burning jealousy of the small child may do real harm to his personality. To prevent it or minimize it is worth a lot of effort."

The best means of preventing it include preparing the child for the new arrival and cushioning the shock by making sure the child is out of the house when the baby comes home. When he returns, his mother can devote her full attention to him. Subsequently, the child should be encouraged to deal with his feelings openly, but his parents should not let him extend that openness to attacking the baby.

In dealing with a problem such as jealousy that he considers psychologically dangerous, Spock is undisguisedly direct. There is no repetition of the advice that a mother can rely on her instincts here.

"When the child attacks the baby, a mother's natural impulse is to shame him. This doesn't work out well for two reasons. He dislikes the baby because he's afraid that his mother is going to love her instead of him. When she threatens not to love him any more, it makes him feel more worried and cruel inside. Shaming also may make him bottle up his feeling of jealousy. Suppressed jealousy will do more harm to his spirit and last longer than if it came out in the open."

Spock's handling of this kind of problem is oriented towards the reality of the situation. He confines himself to what is happening in the home rather than discussing the psychodynamics of ego and ego threat. The consequence of this method is to make even the extreme "burning jealousy" seem natural and appropriate within the framework of family life. Spock normalizes the situation.

In attempting to de-emotionalize family difficulties so that they can be handled objectively as problems rather than in terms of good and bad (the terms in which the mother "shames" the child), Spock calls his wit into play. It is hard to get upset about even the most violent of children's jealous acts when they are described in the following terms:

"Jealousy takes many forms. If a child picks up a large block and swats the baby with it, the mother knows well enough that it's jealousy. But another child is more polite. He admires the baby for a couple of days without enthusiasm and then says, 'Now take her back to the hospital.' . . . "

There is another element in the success of *Baby and Child Care* that is worth mentioning. When Spock's book came out, simultaneously in hardback as *The Common Sense Book of Baby and Child Care* and in paper as *The Pocket Book of Baby and Child Care,* the latter selling for 25¢, there was not another book that competed with it in terms of completeness, price and appeal to its audience. The paperback outsold the hardcover (at $3) by 90 to 1; it is primarily through this medium that Spock reached and continues to reach his widest audience.

In subsequent revisions of his book, Spocks views on discipline changed. In the 1946 edition, the accent had been on being "firm and friendly" but, with regard to corporal punishment, Spock had commented that "people who have specialized in child care feel that it is seldom required. . . . I disagree with the grim or irritable parent who seriously believes that punishment is a good regular method of controlling a child."

By 1957, while he was still inclined against punishment, Spock had removed these fairly stern injunctions against it. As a consequence, a few statements (such as: "I'm not advocating spanking, but I think it is less poisonous than lengthy disapproval, because it clears the air, for parent and child.") which were in the earlier edition stand out in relief. He added this comment:

"A great majority of good parents feel that they have to punish once in a while. On the other hand, a few parents find that they can success- fully manage their children without ever having to punish. A lot depends on how the parents were brought up. If they were punished occasionally for good cause, they naturally expect to have to punish in similar situations. And if they were kept in line by positive guidance alone, they find that they can do the same with their children."

Thus, a 1946 parent looks into the book and sees that if he or she punishes, he belongs to a grim minority that is out of touch with expert thought. A 1957 or later parent finds that he or she has some support from Spock if, with good cause, it is occasionally necessary to punish the child.

Some of the humor is reduced in later editions. The tendency is to be more specific. On the subject of biting, Spock argues against the approach of the bitten parent biting back, saying that it is better to be a "friendly boss" than to descend "to his age level with bites, slaps, or shouts. . . . The only thing you need to do is to keep from getting bitten again, by drawing back when he gets that gleam in his eye." That is 1946; in 1957 he has appended a less playful terminal to that last sentence: ". . . that gleam in his eye, showing him clearly that you don't like it and won't let it happen."

In part these changes have occurred, as Spock points out in his intro- duction to the 1957 edition, in reaction to the times:

"When I was writing the first edition, between 1943 and 1946, the attitude of a majority of people towards infant feeding, toilet training, and general child management was still fairly strict and inflexible. However, the need for greater understanding of children and for flexi- bility in their care had been made clear by educators, psychoanalysts, and pediatricians, and I was trying to encourage this. Since then a great change in attitude has occurred, and nowadays there seems to be more chance of a conscientious parent's getting into trouble with permis- siveness than with strictness. So I have tried to give a more balanced view."

Balanced or not, this is only part of the story. Historically, what people have sought in child-raising books is not balance but the reaffirmation of their ideas and sensibilities; the 1950s were certainly a more conservative time than the 1940s.

During the fifties, too, the emphasis in child-care books gradually changed. As *Baby and Child Care* moved into its present position as the standard reference work, its domination of the market tended to discourage other books on the physical care of children. Competing texts now often emphasize psychological subtleties of the parent-child relationship. Currently, there seems to be a sense that the problems of the family stem, at least in part, from a lack of self-awareness or self-respect, a lack of confidence as well as a lack of knowledge that makes parents either unaware of or incapable of rationally dealing with the needs of their offspring.

Recently, a concensus has formed around the idea that the problems of child raising are, in fact, the problems of raising adults, of creating people fit to be parents.

PART FOUR

Parent Training
(child-care trends since 1950)

"Children's energy to organize the world is awesome. The role of the adult in this process is. . . to offer the child the resources he will need to accomplish this task."

JEFFREY EISEN (1975)

CHAPTER 13

The Family Child

"The Langleys wanted to buy a new home. The whole family spent an evening trying to decide what sort of things they wanted in a house: the architectural design, the size, the kind of building material, and so on. Mr. Langley talked with them about the family finances and how much they would be able to spend for a home. Then every Sunday afternoon for two months they looked at houses for sale and decided what they thought about each, until finally the family choice was made. But when the Williamses decided to move they said nothing to their eleven-year-old Trixie until all the plans were made. For years afterward Trixie felt that she was a pawn in the hands of her parents. . . . She felt her feelings and ideas were so unimportant as to deserve no consideration, that she herself was an unworthy person, else they would have consulted her or confided in her. . . . She had no opportunity to see the process of making a wise choice. . . . "

By the 1950s, parental ambition had changed. From the promise a quarter century earlier of two chickens in every pot, the family looked forward to two cars in each garage. Togetherness was a model of ideal family life, promising serenity, peace, life placid as the front lawn. It was a condition to be consciously fabricated. Christine Beasley's *Democracy in the Home* (1954), from which the above quote is taken, was one of many books offering a methodology for togetherness. Beasley's chapter on "Group Morale and Family Fun" is typical of the times:

"Since it is adults largely who plan, direct, and guide both their own
and their children's lives, and since we are prone to lose sight of the
fact that our own needs and those of our children are not always the
same, family life has been, for the most part, adult-centered. During
the past few decades, however, families have been urged to 'make the
home a child-centered home!' and as a result many parents have come
to neglect their own needs in the attempt to fulfill all those of their
children."

Family-centered Home Living

"Today the pendulum is approaching a happy mid-point between the
two extremes. . . . Families are growing to understand that neither the
child nor the adult has the greater rights, that no individual. . . is more
important than another in the family, that sometimes the group is as
important as the individual.

"The need to belong to a group is an underlying part of human
nature. . . . We are social beings. Belonging to a family that has developed a high degree of group spirit is one of the best ways of fulfilling
our need for love and status.

"The family may be the most basic and the most natural unit for
group functioning, but our modern way of life is so removed from the
natural order that families sometimes are little more than a biological
unit. Society has taken over many of the original functions of the
home: education, religious training, recreation, socialization, and. . .
the various agencies that have been assigned these responsibilities
require so much of our time and energy that often little of us is left
for family life. Family-centeredness is not automatic; there must be a
deliberate effort to create and maintain a group spirit if it is to be
realized."

The family no longer relies on love to provide a sense of cohesiveness.
Rather, they build a "group spirit" through a series of conscientiously
shared activities:

"It would seem needless to say that a 'we' attitude grows from 'we'
activities. The idea is so simple that it is often overlooked in the
complexity of everyday life. Things which the individual automatically
does in the course of living may, with design, become those things he
does *with* family members. Everybody works, plans, plays, relaxes,
grows and feels. He often needs a measure of aloneness for these, but
more often they call for a cooperative or shared experience."

Each of these matters — working together, playing together, relaxing together, creating together, feeling together, and maintaining ties when the
members of the group are separated — is given separate consideration.
Regarding "feeling together," for example, Beasley offers such suggestions
as the sharing of family jokes, the common sharing of crises and common
religious experience.

What is most evident in these comments is their self-consciousness.
It is not as if a close family naturally shares experience and keeps in touch
when they are separated; rather it is necessary to imitate a real family by
doing these things. There is a sense that the family is a lost, forgotten institution that it is necessary to rebuild. It is a vision of great emptiness at the
heart of modern life.

The same feeling of emptiness pervades Beasley's description of the
house which she presents as "a symbol of family life."

"It is at home, in the location of our house, that we can put down
roots and feel that we belong. We can belong to the family when 'our'
common roof shelters us, we can belong to the community if our
house marks a place in it for us. We can belong to the soil, and the
people, and the institutions. . . .

"The symbolism of a house goes far beyond signifying merely the
existence of a biological unit. . . [It should offer security] a measure of
protection against the vicissitudes of nature. . . . It makes us feel much
more secure than we actually are. Perhaps the feeling is as important
as the reality. Somehow a house — our house — seems so solid and
permanent. It is part of our link with the past and the future; we are a
part of its continuity."

A house may offer status: "Our house has social value. It represents
us to the community." It can be a symbol of authority: "'Whose house is
it anyway?'" asks one of Beasley's parents. "'It's not your house, it's *our*
house,'" the child answers. It was a setting for family life: self-expression,
privacy, companionship, balanced living, growth and change are all measured, expressed and encouraged by the house.

The resurgence of feeling about the home seems to coincide closely
with the disappearance of its traditional meaning. What, after all, were
these highly symbolic homes that Beasley praises but more or less identical
tract homes, whose tenants had neither roots in the land, nor continuity
in time, nor attachment to community? The description of the home, like
the description of the equally synthetic techniques for family closeness,

represents not a picture of reality, but an ideal pursued by the middle-class families of the fifties.

Within this symbolic house, this conscientiously close family was encouraged to make decisions democratically. A family council was proposed, and it was assigned a specific place and time to meet with shared leadership. Compromise and consensus were the goals, Beasley's book deals with the problems of achieving agreement in a family setting:

"The highest type of agreement known by some groups is that of majority rule. But this method tends to emphasize rather than minimize differences. You are forced to take an all-or-none position concerning an idea. Your vote may mean choosing the least of several evils. The minority group tends to feel hostile; the winning side is apt to feel superior or guilty. . . .

"The only truly effective method of resolving differences is that of unanimous free-will agreement. Consensus means that everybody gets what he wants without sacrificing anything. In many cases it means that a new idea — one in nobody's mind at the beginning of the discussion — is found."

Like the house and the tenants, unanimity was an ideal and idealized image of family unity, a democratic discussion ending with perfect agreement.

The same hope of achieving a peaceful resolution of differences permeates the section on discipline:

"The best test for any sort of discipline is whether it accomplishes what you are after without having other serious effects. Spanking and whipping will cause a child to stop whatever his behavior is at the moment, and it may even prevent his doing it again in your presence, but it is not a very effective teacher of self-discipline. Rewards may result in a repetition of the behavior that earned them but the child learns to be good for the sake of the reward rather than as an expression of his own goodness. To receive a reward or to avoid punishment is not a well-founded reason for conformity, nor does it lead to habits of conformity. . . .

"There is one type of reward that is legitimate in good discipline: overt and appropriate signs of approval and appreciation. A child wants more than anything else to be accepted and loved, and he is willing to do anything in order to get this approval. Little unexpected rewards which grow out of his good behavior represent the most positive technique available to parents."

Discipline, the expression of the child's goodness, it represented by that popular 1950s word, conformity. Differences are glossed over and the agreement or submission is achieved through the use of group or parental approval. No unresolvable feeling was allowed to intrude upon the dream.

In contrast to Beasley's book, Elinor G. Smith's *The Complete Book of Absolutely Perfect Baby and Child Care* (1957) has the ring of real life. The book is humorous, but underneath the jokes it is serious, accurate and to the point. Even in its humor, the book is revealing, suggesting that the anxiety over child care had finally reached a plateau and that some parents had, at this point, learned to feel confident enough to laugh at familiar problems rather than to worry about them.

The book is short and may be regarded as a commentary on child care rather than as an instructive manual. Near the start, Smith says bluntly "The one absolute essential in keeping and attempting to raise a baby is a copy of Dr. Spock's *Baby and Child Care*. Do not attempt any baby keeping at all until you have this book in your possession as it is *against the rules*."

Smith's comments are wide ranging. Describing how Gesell's developmental norms were being interpreted literally by some parents, Smith says:

"A crises sometimes arises during the early months when you discover that Gesell's babies all hold up their right hand and look at it. Yours hasn't done this yet. The important thing is not to mention this awful fact to your relatives and neighbors. Should any of them bring up the subject, remember the RULE. [The definition of the RULE will follow] . Meanwhile, call the pediatrician, never mind what time it is. However, he's often unsympathetic. Here you are with this new baby that has something terrible the matter with it, and the pediatrician *doesn't care*."

Of course, when Smith's child is finally taken to see the doctor, he immediately holds up his right hand and looks at it. He had been doing it for weeks, it turns out. The only trouble was that "he only did it while he was alone."

Similarly, she is especially acute on the pressures and anxieties that lead mothers to compete with other mothers with children the same age. Here she offers the RULE mentioned earlier:

"[This is] the primary rule of baby raising which is the solution to. . . all subsequent problems. . . . [It] must be followed faithfully, and practiced regularly, and you should make it a habit to repeat it to yourself ten times a day. It is the *Golden Rule* of raising babies. LIE. Lie to your mother, lie to your sisters, aunts, and above all to all the other mothers you meet on the street. When a newer mother asks you for help, tell her you never had the least trouble. . . . "

It is a mark of progress that this subject, the competitiveness and pressure of mothers on each other for social conformity, is finally brought into the open. For most of this history, it has lingered at the edges of the descriptions of child care, hinted at but rarely mentioned directly.* By opening this subject, Smith's book goes far beyond many of the more serious texts on child care.

Another aspect of the reality of home life exposed by Smith's book is the notion that children are always wonderful company for adults:

"The fact is that children are abysmally ignorant and their vocabularies are distinctly limited. It is far better for them to go outdoors and get some fresh air until their command of English improves. . . . There is nothing more maddening than to have some illiterate little child keep asking silly questions like, 'What's transcendental?' 'What's syzygy?' 'What were the Peloponnesian Wars?' 'Who was Anaximander?' 'What's a prefrontal lobotomy?' Such children are simply not ready for association with adult human company. Get them a swing, and send them outside to swing on it."

The notion that the ideal child is a healthy, happy, energetic, friendly extrovert is also given some gentle scrutiny. "I myself have always had a sickly ingoing personality," Smith writes, pointing out that her husband and child are the same. Which would you rather have, she asks, a child who drags all his friends over to the house making a nuisance of himself and a headache for you or a nice "ingoing" child who is perfectly happy to curl up with a book? "What this country needs is more introverted children."

Smith's comments on persuading children to work around the house also have the ring of experience:

"Every child should take his share of the family's work around the house. In this way he learns to share responsibilities with other members of the family unit, and to understand that to have a place in a

---

*Note this statement from a 1942 work, *How To Raise Your Baby* by Dr. Allen Roy Defoe, the physician who delivered the Dionne quintuplets: "I don't suppose that anything gives a mother more pleasure than to be able to announce to other mothers that she has taught her baby to control bowel movement."

social unit imposes obligations as well as conferring benefits. . . .

"There are many such jobs that even the smallest child can do, such as emptying waste baskets and ash trays, watering plants, feeding pets. . . . Any child can certainly help with setting the table and clearing away, as well as washing and drying dishes.

"That is, they *can* — the only trouble is, they *won't*. Which is just as well, because if they *do* you wish they *didn't*."

The trouble, Elinor Smith explains, is that you must "never send a boy to do a boy's job," he won't find it interesting. Children would rather "paint and paper the whole house, take over the driving. . . . pave the whole drive-way with concrete all by themselves."

At the end of her book, discussing "The Advantages of Having Children over Hamsters or Kittens," she talks of the real joy of being an adult in a characteristically direct and unromantic way.

"Children around the house are a constant reminder of your own great and unexpected good luck in having finally, yourself, grown up. Daily you will be reminded how really marvelous it is. . . that you no longer have to practice piano lessons. . . .

"You can make them stay home with a sitter while you go off to any movie you like, and nobody will decide that it's 'not suitable' or 'not good for you.' . . .

"Nobody is going to scold you anymore if you spill things or drop things or lose things, but *you* can scold the children. They're children."

The pleasures of adult autonomy and authority, having someone look up to you, almost compensate for the amount of responsibility you must assume in the role of parent. Smith writes not of a mythical family but of a house with parents and kids, living together, getting into each other's hair and touched with odd moments of affection and satisfaction.

CHAPTER 14

Communicating with Children

The movement towards family unity and the glossing over of individual differences was the leitmotif of family life in the 1950s. The next decade put its faith in the problem-solving virtues of communication. Reading the books of the sixties, we sense that many if not most of the difficulties that arise in the household arise from the inability of parents and children to understand one another.

One book that expresses this belief is the very popular guide to parent-child interaction, *Between Parent and Child* (1965) by Dr. Haim Ginott:

> "Children often resist dialogues with parents. They resent being preached at, talked at, and criticized. They feel that parents talk too much. Says eight-year-old David to his mother, 'When I ask you a small question, why do you give me such a long answer?' To his friends he confides, 'I don't tell mother anything. If I start in with her, I have no time left to play.'"

The works of the 1960s concentrate on the outward expression of the failure to communicate rather than on its causes. The question is made one of skill, and the implicit promise is that if a parent acquires that skill the child will be able to communicate with the parent as openly and honestly as he does with his friends.

212

The techniques Ginott employs are "non-directional" therapy methods. Judgment is withheld and evaluation of the significance of a statement postponed. When a child relates an event, the emphasis is not on talking about the event itself but on probing the child's feelings about it. Ginott mentions the story of a young girl whose "friend was pushed off the sidewalk into a rain-filled gutter." Rather than evaluate the event, saying for example what a mess it must have made, or judging it (asserting how bad the boys were to push her friend) or moralizing and blaming the child (telling her to stay away from those boys) or lecturing her on self-defense, the parent is encouraged to probe the child's feelings:

"That must have upset you.
"You were angry at the boys who did it.
"You are still mad at them. . . .
"You are afraid that they may do it to you, too?"

Each statement if framed as a positive assertion so that the child is not put on the defensive. If the child had instead been asked a question such as "Are you upset?" the usual tendency would be to deny it. A question puts one in the position of having to supply an answer which may be judged by the questioner. When an assent, a *yes*, is all that is needed, the child sides with the parent's interpretation of the problem; they are both on the same side.

Not only does a question save the child's "face," it saves the parent as well. If a parent asks, "Are you upset?" another common response other than denial or agreement is: "Of course I'm upset, can't you see that?" The clear implication is that the parent is stupid. Using the passive form for the first question (*it upset you* rather than *you are upset*), the problem becomes less emotionally charged.

The order of questioning is also important. The most general statement is put first: "That must have upset you." Subsequent statements are made more and more specific until, finally, the child's real feeling is reached: "You are afraid . . . ." At that point, apparently the parent's voice signals a question and the subject is opened for the child's comment: "Let them try, I'll drag them with me. That would make a splash."

It is worth examining the picture of family life presented by this technique. Although Ginott describes the parents as loving their children, there seems to be little empathy between them. To understand the child, they must look for clues:

"Children give us clues. Their feelings come through in a word and in tone, in gesture and in posture . . . .

"Our inner motto is: Let me understand. Let me show what I understand. Let me show in words that do not automatically criticize or condemn."

The relationship between parent and child is developed on this level, the level of "understanding" and "words." It is primarily a verbal relationship. When the right feeling is named, the child's problem is resolved. There is little sense of the child's need for physical reassurance, warmth and contact.

When the subject of love is raised by Ginott, it is seen either as the child's response to verbal communication (the child loves the parent when the parent understands) or it is in some way connected to a problem. Of the entries on love in the index, all seven lead us to just three subjects: discipline, jealousy and sex. On discipline, for example, Ginott writes:

"The cornerstone of the new approach to discipline is the distinction between wishes and acts. We set limits on acts; we do not restrict wishes. . . .
"The modern approach helps the child with both his feelings and his conduct. The parents allow the child. . . to speak out about what he feels, but limit and [re] direct undesirable acts."

In the excerpt below — on masturbation— even Ginott's language changes. The vocabulary suddenly blossoms into a series of social abstractions that would do justice to any nineteenth-century critic of the practice:

"Self-gratification may make the child less accessible to the influence of parents and peers. When he takes this short cut to satisfaction he does not have to depend on pleasing anyone but himself . . . .
"Persistent masturbation may become a too ready consolation for mishaps and failures and a too easy substitute for efforts and accomplishments.
"Children's entry into civilization hinges on their willingness to delay or give up immediate gratification for the more lasting satisfaction of parental and (later) social approval."

Parents are encouraged to "exert a mild pressure against self-indulgence," as excessive pressure will backfire.

On other sexual matters, Ginott is also quite restrictive. He declares that children's sex games should be flatly forbidden or they will "burden the child with guilt" without satisfying his needs. Apparently, it is the games themselves rather than the parents' attitude that burdens the child with guilt. On the use of dirty words, Ginott upholds the parents' right to forbid them in the home.

A less judgmental analysis than Ginott's of the communication gap between parents and children is contained in *P.E.T. Parent Effectiveness Training* (1970) by Thomas Gordon. The book is an outgrowth of the work in P.E.T. schools for parents, a textbook, systematic and logical, making few stylistic concessions to the casual reader.

The Gordon book offers a deeper structural analysis of the parent-child conflict than Ginott. It does so at the expense of most psychiatric problems, yet it does not oversimplify the difficulties. Gordon says bluntly that there is "no gimmick or quick road to effective parenthood; the. . . method [proposed here] requires a basic change in the attitude of most parents towards their children."

Gordon analyzes communication as a problem in information transmission. He uses the tools of systems analysis, flow charts and diagrams to transmit his message. His description of how a child "encodes" his messages is particularly astute. If a child is hungry, he has to communicate his hunger to someone who will do something about it; he does this by sending an encoded message. The particular code a child selects may vary. If he takes Gordon's lead and says "When's dinner ready?" the mother must then go through a process of "decoding" that message to get at the child's message that he is hungry. This process is represented by Gordon with the following diagram:

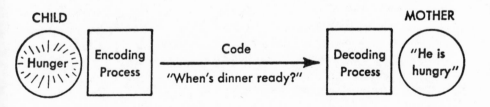

Gordon comments: "If the mother decodes accurately, she will understand that the child is hungry. But if Mother happens to decode the message to mean that the child is anxious to eat so he can go out and play before bedtime, she would be misunderstanding; the communication process has broken down."

Since the child nor the mother knows there has been a breakdown, (they cannot read one another's minds), the mother has to "check on the accuracy of her decoding," which she can do "by actually telling the child her thoughts — the result of her decoding process, 'You want a chance to play before bedtime.' Having heard his mother's 'feedback,' the child is able to tell his mother that she decoded incorrectly. 'No, I didn't mean that, Mother. I meant I'm real hungry and want dinner to be ready soon.'"

"What so often goes wrong in the communication process between two people," Gordon says, is that "there is a misunderstanding of the sender's message on the part of the receiver and neither is aware that the misunderstanding exists."

To improve communications, Gordon suggests that parents stop encoding their messages. When the father is tired, he suggests the father say, "I am very tired," rather than telling the child "You are a pest." If (as the late Eric Berne, a leading proponent of interactive psychology, suggests) raising children is largely a matter of "teaching them what games to play," then a little direct expression can go a long way towards remedying the problem. If the parent stops encoding, the child can.

Gordon deals with the question of "who owns the problem;" that is, when a problem arises, is the parent or the child responsible for solving it? Much of the conflict in the family arises, according to this book from the attempts of parents to usurp the problems of the child as their own. A child's performance in school is *his* problem. The role of the parent is to lend an ear and through the use of non-directive techniques similar to those we have examined in Ginott to let the child solve his own problem.

Later Gordon raises the question of authority; the "parent-child power struggle" has rarely been described more effectively. Rather than pretend, as many books suggest, that you can insulate the child from conflict and somehow miraculously resolve all confrontations by communication, Gordon takes a more balanced approach:

"Conflict in a family, openly expressed and accepted as a natural phenomenon, is far healthier for children than most parents think. In such families the child at least has the opportunity to experience conflict, learn how to cope with it, and be better prepared to deal with it in later life."

The traditional method of resolving conflict, where the parent simply lays down the law, or the reverse, where the child is permitted to get his own way all the time, are both described as equally ineffective. The first does not build responsibility in the child because the parent assumes the responsibility for the child's actions; the second frustrates the parent and does not provide a model of responsible adult behavior.

In Gordon's analysis, the root of these problems may be traced to the failure of parents to understand their relationship's to children; To illustrate his point he offers a diagram:

"If we were to try to represent parent and child by drawing a circle of each, it would be inaccurate to draw the circles like this:

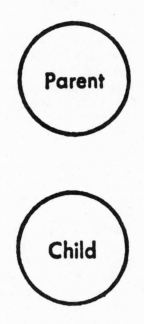

"As the child see it, the parent does not have equal 'size,' no matter what the age of the child. I am not referring to physical size (though a physical size differential is present until children reach adolescence), but rather to 'psycological size.' A more accurate representation of the parent-child relationship would look like this:

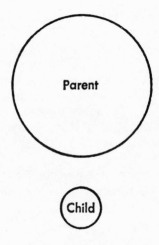

Given this natural authority or power advantage over the child, most of the problems in the home are traced to its abuses. It is almost impossible, Gordon argues, to use this power properly. The child, dealing with a giant on whom he depends, is either inflated with the notion that he can control this giant through various kinds of manipulation or resentful of the giant's influence in his life when the giant tries to train and discipline him. Instead of trying to exercise brute authority, Gordon offers parents a "no-lose" method in which a problem is analyzed objectively and a compromise solution is worked out. The essential ingredient of this compromise is that both (or all) parties have an input in its creation; as a result, all have an equal obligation to make it work out. The method of achieving this consensus begins with "identifying the conflict" and continues through finding possible solutions, choosing the best solutions, implementing the plan and finally evaluating how well it worked. It is a neat scheme, demanding an objective, professional, almost industrial attitude in parents.

Learning to deal with the child as a separate individual rather than treating him as an extension of his parents' ego, allowing him to handle his own problems, dealing with him as an equal on an adult-to-adult basis — all these represent steps toward maturity for both parent and child. The attitude implied by this approach — that child care is a job best handled in a rational, professional manner — while certainly not a new idea has some benefits. It presupposes that the adult is a good enough craftsman to treat the child well whatever his personal feelings may be at any moment.

In spite of P.E.T.'s humane virtues, a question arises. If child care becomes so systematic that it can be handled by a stranger as easily as by a parent, does the family have any meaning at all — aside from providing food, clothing, shelter and continuity (i.e. familiarity)? Even in P.E.T.'s scrupulous fairness there seems to be a certain lack of emotional reality about the family image presented. One gets the impression that Gordon is a sincere humane man who stresses that communication techniques should not be used without empathy between parent and child. An individual who truly had empathy, however, would hardly find it necessary to go through all this rigmarole to understand his or her children. Gordon's book, like Ginott's, seems most inclined to attract the parents who are incapable of intimacy and in whose hands it becomes merely a new list of techniques for avoiding dealing with the emotional needs of children.

Looking at the 1960s, one is struck by how much of the decade's energy and attention was focused on difficulties in communication. Not only child-care books but also much of the "generation gap" seems to have been regarded as a problem in communication. Yet, with all this emphasis on the problem, what we sense most in the period is how completely communications had broken down.

CHAPTER 15

The Confident Child

The first half of the 1970s witnessed wide interest in methods and theories of self-development and self-improvement, reflected in contemporary child-raising books assuming that the key to successful rearing is the child's self-esteem. Two books are particularly worth mentioning: *Your Child's Self-Esteem* (1970) by Dorothy C. Briggs and the very popular *How to Parent* by Dr. Fitzhugh Dodson, published the same year.

The jacket of the Briggs book, subtitled *The Key to His Life,* explains that the book contains a "new formula" that will keep the child away from dope and promiscuity, will solve problems of discipline, deal with anger, improve creativity, give the parent confidence and make the child happy. The child with improved self-esteem, the blurb promises, has "no choice" but to develop to his limits. Briggs in her introduction is almost as sweeping. With a solid sense of self-esteem, she says, "your youngster is slated for happiness in all areas of life."

Briggs's book may be described as a composite of two theories: one deals with the problem of self-esteem and is primarily an adaptation of the theories of Alfred Adler and Karen Horney; the second deals with discipline and parental power and is, as Briggs footnotes, "indebted to Thomas Gordon," and the P.E.T. schools.

Briefly stated, the theory of self-esteem as it applies to child development is that, first, we act in terms of who we think we are and, secondly, that who we think we are is largely a result of how we are treated. In its simplest terms this means that if a child is given love, he considers himself lovable and is then capable of confronting the world without insecurities about himself. He does not need to be put on the defensive. He does not develop neurotic behavior patterns to compensate for his own insecurities. When a child is denied love, on the other hand, his tendency is to defend himself against somebody finding out how "bad" or "unlovable" he is, or feels he is. If a person who feels this way is given love, the tendency is either to discount the giver ("You must be kidding or stupid to love me.") or to discount the statement ("If you *really* knew me, you'd know how bad I am.") or to become defensive ("You must think I'm pretty stupid to fall for a line like that."). Thus, a person who is not given a sense of being lovable early in life finds it almost impossible to accept love later on; adult life then becomes either a series of deliberate failures which prove to the subject that he is in fact unworthy, or else it becomes an endless striving after success in the attempt to prove self-worth. How then does a parent improve a child's self-esteem? Since we see ourselves in the mirror of other people's reactions to us, Briggs advises "polishing [the] parental mirrors":

> "Each of us sees our children to some degree through a haze of filters born of past experiences, personal needs, and cultural values. They all combine to form a network of expectations. And **these expectations become yardsticks by which we measure a child**.
>
> "Knowing *what* you expect and *why* is the first step towards polishing your parental mirror."

Among the things which distort the parental mirror are the "inexperience" of new parents, "borrowed standards" that offer unrealistic expectations of the child's behavior, "hang-over" wishes from our own childhoods, our current needs and "unfinished business" (i.e. unresolved conflicts from our own childhood). All these distort the image the child gets of himself from the parents' reflection of him. "Children rarely question our expectations," Briggs writes, "instead, they question their personal adequacy." Seeing themselves reflected inaccurately, they lose their true selves and take instead the parents' distorted image for the reality.

The first step in correcting this problem is that the parents adopt realistic expectations. As a necessary step towards confronting their own expectations openly and accurately, the author suggests taking an "expectation inventory" then examining each item on it:

> "Why do I have this expectation?
> "Where did it come from?
> "What's in it for me?

"Is it based on my needs or my child's?

"What purpose does it serve?

"Does it realistically fit this particular child at his age and with his temperament and background?"

An ambitious and possibly "painful" project, but, Briggs points out, "It is the forerunner of change, [and] your child's self-esteem is at stake."

"Weed out all the expectations that you've been following blindly but have no real meaning for you and your child. . . Hopefully, as more of us become aware of the importance of self-esteem, we will take active steps to strengthen our own self-respect. Our growth pays off, not only for us, but for countless generations to come as our children pass on their self-acceptance to their youngsters and they to theirs."

To improve self-image, Briggs proposes that parents "seek people who treat [them] with respect." She advises: "Get involved in activities that give you a feeling of competence and achievement," and, if necessary, "seek professional help."

"While you are working to improve your own self-attitudes, your children do not have to go wanting. Expose them to other adults and children who enjoy them as they are. Encourage those activities that bring them success. Positive mirrors they need, but if necessary their self-confirmation can come from sources other than you."

To build a better self-image in the child, what is necessary is a "climate of love" in the household.

"Every child needs periodic genuine encounters with his parents.

Genuine encounter is simply focused attention.

"It is attention with a special intensity born of direct, personal involvement. Vital contact means being intimately open to the particular, unique qualities of your child."

Briggs suggests some exercises to improve "focus" on the child, including concentration on the here-and-now and absorption in daily tasks such as "washing the dishes or the car."

In other chapters on love, Briggs covers such problems as trust and the security the child feels in being able to trust someone, "the safety of nonjudgment" (that the parents can accept the child as he is without judging him), "the safety of being cherished," "the safety of 'owning' feelings," "the safety of empathy" and the "safety of unique growing," which includes not only the right to advance at one's own pace but also the right to take one step backwards when it is necessary.

One advantage of using the child's self-esteem as a guide is that like Gesell's emphasis on objective standards of physical health, it offers the parent a relatively simple, fixed index of how well the child is doing in his psychological development. It lessens parental anxiety over the possibility that the child may become neurotic and concentrates instead on the positive aspects of building health into the child's personality.

The use of self-esteem as an index of mental health gives the child the right to make certain demands on his parents of a psychological nature. It gives the child the right to demand that his parents exercise some self-awareness and self-control in handling him. If that is done, the book suggests, it will be possible to pass down the family genes without passing down the family neuroses as well.

Parents are encouraged to learn how to express their love, both through learning how to avoid forcing their own expectations on the child and through attempting greater empathy. On the latter subject, Briggs says:

> "Empathy is being understood from your own point of view. . . . The empathetic person is with you not to agree or disagree, but rather to understand without judgment. . . .
>
> "Each of us normally communicates to others by two routes: *words* and *body language.* Ordinarily, our *words contain the facts,* while our *muscles and tones reveal our feelings towards those facts.* The total meaning of our messages is packaged together, and our hope is that others will understand our full message. In terms of being understood, however, **attitudes and feelings are more important than facts.**
>
> "When your child talks to you, you only demonstrate genuine understanding by reflecting back his *total meaning.* If Ted, for example, slumps into the family living room and says despondently, 'Well, I finished that term paper,' his words state that the project is complete. But his tone and posture reveal his feelings towards that fact; he's downhearted and discouraged.
>
> "If Ted's father only responds to his son's words, he reflects back only content by saying, 'Well, you finished the job.' Having his words parroted makes Ted feel heard to one level, but *certainly not fully understood in terms of what the project means to him. . . .*
>
> "If Ted's father hears his son's total message, however. . . he proves his understanding if he responds, 'Even though it's finished, you feel

downright discouraged.' Now he captures the full flavor of Ted's world and his son feels the warmth of human understanding.

"When you are empathetic, you do not try to change a child's feelings. You simply try to learn how he experiences his particular part of the elephant, as it were. You don't attempt to see *why* he feels as he does; you only try to capture all the nuances of his particular feelings at that moment. You come to see how he sees, to feel how he feels."

Empathy, she says, "bridges the gap of alienation" and helps to "overcome aloneness by establishing psychological intimacy."

Briggs does not shy away from negative feelings, such as anger and jealousy that naturally arise in every family. Throughout, she evidences a real concern, not simply to communicate a method, but to give an understanding of the reasoning behind the method. Briggs's concern for the value of love in the family is the closest modern tie to the erotic tradition in child care.

Dr. Fitzhugh Dodson's *How to Parent* is, overall, a humane intelligent book. Yet, like the Briggs book, the jacket emphasizes not the warmly progressive side of the book but the fact that it supposedly puts "discipline back in child-rearing." The back cover emphasizes that "discipline is not a four-letter word." Since the blurbs of two books in which discipline is a minor concern pitch discipline, publishers in the early seventies seem to have felt that sales would be best if a stand was taken against permissive child-care theory – probably in a reaction to the hippie culture of the sixties. Readers (primarily middle-class) did not want to devote time, money and energy to raising children who would reject their values. Yet child-care professionals, psychiatrists and pediatricians, were nearly unanimously against the return of the authoritarian family. As a compromise, the authors, when they deal with discipline, devote much energy to altering the *parents'* attitudes.

We can trace this change of focus from child care to parental re-education even in the titles of recent popular works, from the traditional *Baby and Child Care* through *Between Parent and Child* to *How to Parent*.

Dodson's book is based on the theory of personality developed by Erik H. Erikson. Erikson describes life as a progression through eight psychological stages, each of which precipitates a crisis as the personality seeks a new level of stability in terms of new needs and demands. The earliest stage is infancy. In infancy, the child learns "basic trust or mistrust." If his needs are satisfied, he learns to trust his environment which, at that age, is not separate from himself. If he learns, therefore, to trust himself, he will have a good foundation on which to build later social relationships. If he does not trust himself — that is, if his needs are not met — he will have difficulty trusting the world that paid no attention to his needs when he was a child and will, beyond whatever compensations he later adopts, have fundamental problems relating to people.

The second stage, early childhood, raises the crisis of "autonomy versus shame or doubt." It is represented in the struggle over toilet training at approximately two years old. If the child learns to control his own body processes, he will have a model of success on which he can later build other successes in manipulating his environment. The body is the first finite environment of the mind. It is from success or failure with his body that he will later derive an idea of his chances of success in handling the world. If a child's toilet training is "taken over" by the mother, through mechanical means for example, the child will in the future doubt his ability to control his environment. Much of the orneriness of age two — the "terrible twos" as they are called — comes from this attempt to explore the limits of control. In the adult, the neurotic need to control everything, excessive concern with neatness and form at the expense of content, can often be traced to problems that were poorly resolved at age two.

The next two ages — "play age" and "school age" — represent extensions of the learning process into various kinds of commitment, play versus work and individual efforts versus group efforts.

These are the essentials of the first part of Erikson's theory. The following is Dodson's treatment of this theory for parents:

"Your child's self-concept begins as soon as he is born.

"Think of the self-concept as a pair of glasses. With each of the four stages of development to age six, your child adds a new lens to his eyeglasses. The lens of each stage of development is superimposed over the lens of the preceding stage.

"Let's examine the first eyeglasses of infancy. . . .

"The most important thing your baby acquires during this stage. . . is *his basic outlook on life*. He is forming, from a baby's point of view, his philosophy of life, his basic feelings about what it means to be alive. He is developing a basic sense of trust and happiness about life, or one of distrust and unhappiness.

"Whether your infant will develop a sense of trust or distrust is determined by the environment you provide for him. . . . "

As part of this environment of trust, Dodson stresses the importance of fulfilling your baby's basic need to be fed when he is hungry, to have himself changed as he needs it. Many mothers, by rushing to keep the baby perpetually clean, "communicate their feelings of aversion" about the baby's waste products, "making the job of toilet training him later on more difficult."

Close contact, "physical cuddling," is essential and Dodson here mentions Harry Harlow whose studies with monkeys have shown just how necessary this aspect of maternal care is. Given a choice between a wire "mother" with a milk bottle, and a fur mother without milk, the baby monkeys choose the fur model, the one that reflects back their own warmth and gives them a sense of their own reality.

The need for variety and intellectual stimulation in the environment is also noted by Dodson. In an effort to protect the child from dirt, disease and noises that might scare him, the tendency was to move the child into an environment of sensory deprivation:

> "The children of middle-class parents are at a much higher level of cognitive and intellectual development at age three and four than the children of poor parents. Why? Because the children of middle-class parents receive greater sensory and intellectual stimulation, even as infants. They have access to a greater number of objects to play with. And their mothers make these objects available to them, respond to their use of the objects, and talk to them about such objects."

Dodson places considerable emphasis on the intellectual development of children. His appendix criticizes many of the books he recommends (including Spock) for neglecting this area. One wonders, though, how an earnest mother can be prevented from pushing her child too energetically. Dodson makes a point of telling mothers not to go to extremes: "Don't let playing with him become an obligation: keep it fun."

On the subject of discipline, Dodson offers a cross-section of all the modern theories on the subject. First he suggests the parent may try direct psychological conditioning using the techniques of "reinforcement psychology." Simply put, the child is to be rewarded for doing good things and to be ignored when he does bad things.

He covers the idea espoused by Gordon and Briggs that discipline is essentially a problem in self-regulation. The child is encouraged to develop a positive self-image:

> "How successful [your child] will be in school and in later life will depend on how strong and positive his self-concept is. Remember that our ultimate goal in discipline is to help him to become a self-regulating

person, and that the extent to which he will become self-regulating will depend upon the strength of his self-concept."

Building this positive self-concept requires the parent allowing the child a good deal of freedom which, as Dodson admits, "calls for patience" on the part of parents. Solid "emotional support" from the parents also "helps a child to overcome feelings of inadequacy and to build a strong self-concept."

A further technique Dodson proposes is that the parent allow the child to learn about the world through learning the "natural consequences" of his actions as much as possible. If the child gets burned, he will learn about fire. If the natural consequences are too extreme (such as playing ball in the middle of a highway), artificial consequences may be imposed. This artificial consequence (called the "logical" consequence by Rudolf Dreikurs who advocates this technique) is, in effect, the social consequences of the child's actions. Punishment, therefore, takes a social form − the child is isolated or deprived of something he wants. It is in its simplest terms negative feedback which should ideally be as closely related to the child's transgression as possible.

"If the child doesn't eat the food on his plate at breakfast. . . Mother does not get angry and threaten the child with punishment. Instead, she merely removes the food. . . . Before too long the child will probably want a snack. Mother can then say, 'I'm sorry you're hungry. We will have lunch at twelve o'clock,' . . . The hunger the child experiences is a natural consequence of not eating his breakfast."

This, Dodson adds, "promotes a far faster change in his actions than any amount of scolding or punishment."

If you have to spank a child, and sometimes that is a natural reaction, "what I advocate," Dodson says, "is the 'pow-wow" type of spanking: your 'pow' followed by his 'Wow!'"

"Spank your child only when you are furious at him and feel like letting him have it right there. . . . [Later] you can always say to your child, in your own way, 'Look, Mommy goofed. I lost my temper and I'm sorry I did.' Then you can go on from there. . . . It might be five minutes or five hours later. But if you feel you have blown your stack, *it's important to admit it to your child.* Above all, don't pretend to him that the sole reason you spanked him was for his benefit."

Under all the concern with the child's self-esteem and emotional health in the 1970s we can sense a deeper change. Earlier periods had emphasized the child's psychological and social adjustment in terms of the parents' or society's values. The new belief was that the child should be assisted to develop into a healthy adult on his own terms.

In a recent lecture, the psychologist Jeffrey Eisen summed up the contemporary position of parent and child in the following terms: "Children's energy to organize the world is awesome. The role of the adult in this process is. . . to offer the child the resources he will need to accomplish this task." In the most recent books, there is an emphasis on democracy, on adult-to-adult relationships, on equality between parent and child, as far as experience will permit.

CHAPTER 16

The Collective Child

With the severe and rapid changes that have taken place during the past two hundred years, there has been pressure to find new methods of social organization and child-care alternatives. One recurrent theme is the belief that family problems can be solved by either a return to or an advance to communal lifestyles in which children are no longer the sole responsibility of their parents.

Communal living takes many forms. The nuclear family with one child living in rural isolation (as occasionally happened in pioneering days) could be placed at one end of a spectrum. One can gradually move through levels of the enlarged family, the extended family (one containing grandparents or relatives living close by) to various kinds of nursery-school and day-care programs. The variety of urban communes (including everything from simple joint tenancy to economic pooling of resources and of talents) and of rural groupings is great. The spectrum's far end would be represented by tribal communities, where virtually every action is seen in the context of the social group.

Several principal forms of the collectivization movement include aspects of life in the Soviet Union and in Cuba. In the United States, experiments in this direction have only begun. Two valuable sources on Communist day care are Urie Bronfenbrenner's *Two Worlds of Childhood* (1970), which concerns methods in the USSR, and Marvin Leiner's *Children Are the Revolution* (1974), which covers Cuba.

Of the two systems, the Soviet strikes Americans as the more politically alien and culturally unfamiliar. Bronfenbrenner describes a society

229

where physical closeness between parent and child is common, where breast feeding is almost universal and where "even when not being fed, Soviet babies are still held much of the time." He points out that while the Russian child has the security that follows close physical contact, the system can be restrictive. The infant is given little opportunity for freedom of movement or initiative. "The mobility and initiative of the Soviet child are further limited by a concerted effort to protect him from discomfort, illness, and injury. There is much concern about keeping him warm. Drafts are regarded as extremely dangerous."

The general concern lest children misbehave or hurt themselves is carried over into another "distinctive feature" of Soviet child handling; "the readiness of other persons besides the child's mother to step into the maternal role." If a child transgresses, the child and his parents can be reprimanded for the child's behavior by strangers. In addition, "It is not uncommon, when sitting in a crowded public conveyance, to have a child placed on your lap by a parent or guardian. Strangers strike up acquaintances with young children as a matter of course. . . [and] older children of both sexes show a lively interest in the very young and are competent and comfortable in dealing with them. . . . "

In the Soviet Union, according to Bronfenbrenner, physical punishment is played down. A number of psychological punishments take its place and are even advocated in official Soviet guides on child care. The first method of obtaining obedience is the "method of persuasion," where the child's faults are explained to him. Secondly, the child may be encouraged and praised, but only if he is trying to be better than he is — to obey better, to "correct faults of character," to "become better organized." This Russian technique suggests a constant or close surveillance of the child to spot those moments when he is engaged in making self-improvements.

Finally, the child who has been raised with such warmth and closeness can be punished by the temporary withdrawal of love. "For example, a daughter not only disobeyed her mother by refusing to change her ridiculous hair-do but allowed herself to hurt her mother's feelings by a harsh word." This was punished by the mother's giving a "reproving glance" and then not speaking to the daughter "for several hours."

The emphasis on child self-improvement continues in the schools. The infant in the preschool center (*vasli*), is put in a group playpen with six to eight other children. For every four children there is an "upbringer" (that is, an adult attendant whose role is to interact with the children, play games with them and encourage them to learn).

"From the very beginning, considerable emphasis is given to the development of self-reliance, so that by eighteen months of age the children are expected to have completed bowel and bladder training and are already learning more complex skills such as dressing themselves. Physical activity outdoors is encouraged and it is usually followed by rest, with the windows open and the smallest children swaddled in thick quilts."

How this training is achieved so early is not clear, but partial training is possible by that age, so perhaps training failures are written off as "accidents."

Considerable emphasis is put on speech as a "vehicle for developing social behavior." More specifically, the development of speech permits the upbringer, or parent, to direct, instruct, manipulate and discipline the child as part of a group rather than individually. When two children in the book are seen fighting over a ball, the teacher is able to call them across the room with the words, "Children, come look. See how. . . [these other children] are swinging their teddy bear together. They are good comrades." Collective play is encouraged and solitary activities discouraged.

If this is one side of collective child care, the other side is group control of misbehavior. Bronfenbrenner describes a case where several youngsters have been reciting poetry in class, one after another.

"So far, there has not been a single lapse in memory. . . . It is now Larissa's turn. She walks primly to the front of the room, starts off bravely and finishes two stanzas. Suddenly silence. Larissa has forgotten. There is no prompting, either from the teacher or from friends. The silence continues.

"Then the teacher speaks, softly but firmly, 'Larissa, you have disappointed your mother, you have disappointed your father, and above all, you have disappointed your comrades who are sitting here before you. Go back to your place. They do not wish to hear anything more from you today.'"

Larissa returns to her seat in silence, crying.

Shaming, or the withdrawal of group approval, is a major method of achieving compliance in Soviet schools. It is fundamentally the procedure the mother used on the daughter with "the ridiculous hair-do," the withdrawal of love.

In other cases, the discipline combines shaming with deprivation. Bronfenbrenner tells of some children who go off swimming without permission. They are forced to make a public confession before the executive council of the school Pioneer organization and are "deprived of the privilege of attending the camporee." This is in addition to whatever punishment their parents may devise for them.

As a practical method of teaching children collective responsibility, group discipline appears to be effective. Bronfenbrenner comments on a series of tests comparing Soviet children to Western children:

> "Soviet children are much less willing to engage in antisocial behavior than their age-mates in three Western countries (the United States, England, and West Germany). In addition, the effect of the peer group was quite different in the Soviet Union and the United States. When told that their classmates would know of their actions, American children were even more inclined to take part in misconduct. Soviet youngsters showed just the opposite tendency. In fact, their classmates were about as effective as parents and teachers in decreasing misbehavior."

In a test comparing Soviet and Swiss children, where children were asked how they would handle misbehavior, similar contrasts appear. Given a choice of four alternatives (tell a grownup about it, tell other children, talk to the child himself or do nothing), Soviet children preferred to talk to the child himself in 75 percent of the cases, whereas only a third of the Swiss children chose this method. Swiss children preferred to rely on adult intervention (39 percent), but only 11 percent of the Soviet children felt that this was the best way to handle misbehavior.

Finally, Bronfenbrenner summarizes both the positive and negative sides of this method of upbringing:

> "It would seem that Soviet methods of upbringing, both within and outside the family, are accomplishing their desired objectives. The children appear to be obedient; they are also self-disciplined, at least at the level of the collective. But what about the individual? Is he capable of self-discipline when self-determination is required, particularly when the situation demands going it alone, perhaps in opposition to the group?
>
> "Some light is shed on this issue by a study. . . [of school children in England, Switzerland, the Soviet Union and the United States] . The results showed that Soviet youngsters placed a stronger emphasis than any other group on overt propriety, such as being clean, orderly and well-mannered, but gave less weight than the subjects from the other

countries to telling the truth and seeking intellectual understanding."

Cuba with a similar political philosophy but given a wholly different cultural background has developed the day-care center into a form that many an American mother would be glad to have available for her child. As described by Leiner in *Children Are the Revolution*, at its peak of diversity the Cuban day-care system was composed of two distinct kinds of schools: the *círculos,* more-or-less Russian derived day-care-schools, and the *jardines infantiles*, child-care centers modeled on the Finnish day nursery gardens. The educational emphasis of the two systems differed. The *círculos* emphasized a collectivized structural educational program and child care while the *jardines* emphasized "free play" and spontaneity, the mixing of age groups and a good deal of adult emotional support for the individual child.

The difference between Cuban and Soviet methods is evident even in the more restrictive *círculos.* The Cuban program offered an awesome pragmatism and clarity of purpose coupled with a willingness to examine some of the negative institutional effects of these schools:

"Even though day-care centers are open for children as young as forty-five days old, they do not encourage sleeping in. Boarding schools are available for children in the sixth year and beyond, but only during high school do. . . [they] become a significant feature of the educational program. The home is considered the place where young children learn to develop the Eriksonian sense of trust provided by devoted parent figures.

"But children raised in the traditional home environment often do not fare well. That loving, kind people are good for children is not to be questioned; that all mothers and fathers are loving and kind to their own children is not always true. Even those parents who claim that they know what is best for their children may be those who know least. . . . "

The aim of the *círculo* program was to compliment the home rather than replace it. As a result, the day-care centers, in theory at least, were not supposed to "exhibit any of the negative features of institutionalism."

Efforts were made to attract warm, loving *"asistentes"* (literally, assistants) to work in these centers, and from Leiner's description the idea met with some success. At one point, Leiner talks of the difficulty of encouraging independence in the children who have access to these warm, loving adults. Even in encouraging independence, as part of the program to encouraging children to relate to each other, the Cuban system stands in sharp contrast to the Soviet version. In the Soviet centers the children's relationship towards each other is essentially a replica of the way adults and teachers treat them. In the Cuban system, the emphasis is on encouragement. Shaming and other devices of the adult-child relationship are discouraged.

The *circulos* reject both thumb-sucking and pacificers. Hygenic arguments are presented against pacifiers though, in point of fact, studies have shown that the pacifier supports a far lower level of bacterial growth than the child's thumb. After a week at the schools, the pacifiers are taken away, and as for "little pillows and pieces of cloth brought from home, these too are gradually taken away from the children." Leiner writes, however, that "tough as the *círculo* leadership sounds in theory, in practice, many children do as they please."

Theory may meet defeat in other areas. Even with good plans and excellent intentions, institutional mishandling of children sometimes occurs in the *círculos*. In one case Leiner mentions, a child was left alone in a playpen with a large ball, too heavy to move or to play with. After a while, "with no other toy available, the baby finally gave up on the ball and sat staring off into space."

Perhaps the greatest difficulty of communist or socialist educational systems is their apparent need to select one right way to raise children, either educationally or politically superior. If a society is to be thus unified, the preference tends to be for the system that gives good paper results as opposed to one which may satisfy children's needs but is not as easily reduced to statistics. In the Cuban system, this trend is evidenced by the ending of the more liberal *jardines infantiles* system.

* * *

In the United States, day care has become a hot political issue with liberals arguing for its necessity both for children and for their mothers who, once the children are enrolled, may then be able to get productive or satisfying jobs. The conservatives argue that day-care weakens the family; they see it as a step towards socialism or communism. Yet day care seems to be an idea whose time has come, not only for the children of the poor but also from the standpoint of mothers who wish to be liberated from the role of babysitters. Emphasis in the United States has been on enriching children's environments rather than on collectivization, though at least one book, *The Day Care Book* (1974) by Vicki Breitbart, specifically sees day care as a way to compensate for the isolation of parent and child in the nuclear family:

"In this country, child care is supposed to be the family's job. This may have been possible in the past. Well into the 1900s, extended family groups that included grandparents, aunts, and cousins lived under the same roof or near enough for frequent visits. . . .

"Today, the extended family is a rarity. Relatives are either geographically separated or, with the change in values from one generation to the next, are psychologically distant from each other. The nuclear family − father, mother, and children − is now the rule. . . . The social, economic, and emotional needs once filled by family, kin, and community must now be met by this small social unit. . . . The task is enormous − it is almost impossible. Everyone feels the strain. . . .

"The answer is not to abolish the nuclear family. We all want certain things from it. But we have to find ways of separating and defining the family's different functions. . . .

"The existing alternatives for child care differ in the extent to which they challenge the isolation of the nuclear family and the roles of its members. . . . "

Day care is only one of the alternatives Breitbart mentions. Others include "communes, group marriages, [and] collectives" which range from living "in separate apartments in a large house" to living "communally in one unsubdivided house." In any such case, however, "a child can learn to relate − more than that, to love − other adults besides his or her parents. And if there is more than one child in the group, close relationships can develop between the children."

The majority of the new books on day care in America emphasize primarily the practical side of setting up and managing a day-care center. Breitbart's book is one of the few to suggest that day care and collective child care are more than a convenience or economic necessity for parents and more than an educational opportunity for children. She sees the system as the basis for radical change in the relationships between adult and child and among adults as well.

"It is not only the image of child care that is changing. People in communities throughout the country are changing the reality as well. They are struggling against the institutions that determine how, by whom, and for whom child care programs are run. They are creating their own child care alternatives that give children as much free space to grow in as possible; child care that provides an atmosphere in which each person can develop to be the person he or she wants to be. These new child care alternatives are the basis for building new communities based on cooperation rather than competition, on self-determination rather than exploitation, and on struggle for what can be, rather than adjustment to what is."

These are some of the more ambitious goals for day care or collective child care in America. Practical methods of managing groups of children are largely omitted from present books on the subject. The emphasis is on physical problems of running a center, real estate, salaries, insurance, government assistance and the like. Day care is seen as an extension of the kindergarten system; its purpose is primarily educational rather than to influence character development.

The need for new methods of child care is certainly present. The breakdown of the extended family, the isolation of the nuclear family and the loss of community ties in a mobile modern society are social ills; their cure requires a more basic level of communal involvement than exists at present. Modern mass communications, though largely dedicated to superficial amusements, have the potential of promoting greater social awareness and responsibility. Whether the challenge of our times to find appropriate child-care methods will be met with new and suitable techniques remains to be seen.

Conclusion

Modern birth-control methods have made it possible for parents to plan well in advance for children. Such advance planning assumes time to consult books as well as doctors, time to save money, to buy special clothes, furniture and even toys for the baby, time in short to learn the skills and joy of parenthood.

As the selections in this book reveal, most writers on child care lead parents to expect that if directions are followed, they will be able to raise the kind of child wanted. Parents have tried to create the ideal child through swaddling, cold baths, special diet, moral and religious training, scheduled feeding and a strict regimen, psychological conditioning, psychiatric analysis and even collective care.

The literature of child care vividly reflects changing attitudes of society and of parents toward their children. Attitudes change, but children don't. It is only recently that child-care specialists and parents have realized that children cannot be molded to conform to adult concepts and ambitions.

In a practical sense, it is my hope that this book will help guide parents and prospective parents through the maze of literature on child care and that reading *The Mechanical Baby* may provide enough perspective and understanding of this field to permit the reader to judge new books and to select the material best suited to the needs of his or her children. Readers may come to see, as the writer has, that the important thing is not to get the child you want but to care for and love the child you get.

Bibliography

This bibliography, although somewhat abbreviated, includes the material covered in the text as well as some of the more valuable backup resources for those who wish to pursue the subject. Certain listings are followed by an asterisk, indicating that a number of editions of the book, appearing over the years, are significantly different from one another and are worth examining. The edition date listed in the bibliography is the primary source from which material in this history was taken.

CHAPTERS 1, 2, 3

Aries, Phillipe. *Centuries of Childhood.* New York: Knopf, 1962.

Aristotle, *pseudo. Aristotle's Complete Masterpiece,* 26th Edition. London: [No publisher], 1755.*

Astruc, J. A. *A General and Compleat Treatise on All the Diseases Incident to Children.* London: John Nourse, 1746.

Avicenna. *The General Precepts of Avicenna's Canon of Medicine,* trans. Mazhar H. Shah. Karachi, Pakistan: Naveed Clinic, 1966.

Bracken, Henry. *The Midwife's Companion.* London: J. Clarke, 1737.

Brouzet, M. *An Essay on the Medicinal Education of Children.* London: Thomas Field, 1755.

Chrisman, Oscar. *The Historical Child.* Boston: Richard G. Badger, 1920.

Culpeper, Nicholas. *A Directory for Midwives.* London: C. Hitch, 1762.

Deruisseau, L. "Infant Hygiene in Older Medical Literature." *CIBA Symposium,* Volume 2 (1940), pp. 530-35.

Downman, Hugh. *Infancy or the Management of Children.* Exeter, G. B.: Trewman & Son, 1803.

Floyer, John. *An Essay to Prove Cold Bathing Both Safe and Useful.* London: Smith and Walford, 1702.

Gardner, Angustus K. *A History of The Art of Midwifery.* New York: Stringer and Townsend, 1852.

Guillemeau, Jacques. *The Happy Delivery of Women.* London: A. Hatfield, 1612.

Harris, Walter. *A Treatise on the Acute Diseases of Infants,* trans. John Martyn. London: Thomas Astley, 1742.*

Harvey, Williams. *The Works of William Harvey,* ed. Robert Willis. London: Sydenham Society, 1847.

McMath, James. *The Expert Midwife.* Edinburgh: George Mossman, 1694.

Mengert, William F. *The Origin of the Male Midwife.* New York: Paul B. Hoeber, 1932.

Pechey, John. *A General Treatise on the Diseases of Infants.* London: R. Wellington, 1697.

Phillips, Miles. *Percival Willoughby, Gent., A Man-Midwife in the 17th Century.* Altricham, G.B.: St. Ann's Press, 1952.

Portal, Paul. *The Compleat Practice of Men and Woman Midwives.* London: J. Johnson, 1763.

Rendle-Short, Jan. *Infant Management in the 18th Century.* New York Academy of Medicine, *Bulletin of the History of Medicine,* No. 34.

Roesslin, Eucharius. *The Byrth of Mankynde,* trans. Thomas Raynaldes. London: Thomas Adams, 1604.*

Ruhrah, John. *Pediatrics of the Past.* New York: Paul B. Hoeber, 1925.

St. Marthe, Schvole de. *Paedotrophia,* trans. H. W. Tytler. London: Nichols, 1797.*

Singer, Charles. *The Evolution of Anatomy.* London: Kegan Paul et al, 1925.

Smellie, William. *A Treatise on the Theory and Practice of Midwifery.* London: D. Wilson, 1752.

Snapper, I. "Midwifery Past and Present." *Bulletin of the New York Academy of Medicine,* Volume 39 (1963), No. 8.

Still, George F., *The History of Pediatrics.* London: H. Milford, 1931.

Sudhoff, Karl, *Erstlinge der Pädiatrischen Literatur.* Munich: Münchener Druke, 1925.

Quillet, Claude. *Callipaediae,* trans. Anonymous. London: John Morphew, 1710.*

Wurtz, Felix. *The Children's Book.* London: Gartrude Dawson, 1656.

CHAPTERS 4, 5, 6

Armstrong, George. *An Account of the Diseases Most Incident to Children.* London: T. Caddell, 1777.

Banks, John. *A Rebuke to Unfaithful Parents and a Rod for Stubborn Children.* London: T. Soule et al, 1709.

Bass, Benjamin. *Parents and Children.* Newport, R.I.: 1730. Early American Imprint Series, New York: Readex Microprint.

Baynard, Edward. *Health, A Poem.* Boston: 1724. Early American Imprint Series, New York: Readex Microprint.

Buchan, William. *Domestic Medicine.* Philadelphia: J. Dunlap, 1772.*

Cable, Mary. *The Little Darlings.* New York: Scribner's, 1975.

Cadogan, William. *An Essay on the Nursing and the Management of Children.* London: John Knapton, 1757.

Comstock, Cyrus. *Essays on the Duty of Parents and Children.* Hartford, Connecticut: Cooke, Gleeson, 1810.

Dewees, William P. *A Treatise on the Physical and Medical Treatment of Children.* Philadelphia: Carey and Lea, 1825.*

Dutch West India Company, *Letter, April 16, 1663.* Museum of the City of New York, New York.

Edwards, Jonathan. *Original Sin,* ed. Clyde A. Holbrook. New Haven, Connecticut: Yale University Press, 1970.

Faust, C.B. *The Catechism of Health.* Edinburgh: William Creech, 1797.

Griffith, Mrs. [Elizabeth]. *Essays Addressed to Married Women.* London: T. Cadell, 1782.

Hamilton, Alexander, MD. *A Treatise on the Management of Female Complaints and of Children in Early Infancy.* Worcester, Massachusetts: I. Thomas, 1793.

Hitchcock, Enos. *Memoirs of the Bloomsgrove Family.* Boston: Thomas and Andrews, 1790.

Hoare, Mrs. Louisa. *Hints for the Improvement of Early Education and Nursery Discipline.* Salem, Massachusetts: J.R. Buffum, 1820.

Langer, William L. "Checks on Population Growth 1750-1850." *Scientific American,* Volume 226, No. 2 (February 1972), pp. 92-99.

Levison, Abraham. *Pioneers of Pediatrics.* New York: Froben, 1936.

Locke, John. *Some Thoughts Concerning Education,* ed. F.W. Garforth. Woodbury, New York: Barron's Educational Series, 1964.

Mather, Cotton. *Elizabeth in her Holy Retirement.* Boston: 1710. Early American Imprint Series, New York: Readex Microprint.

——. *A Child of Light Singing in the Valley of Darkness.* Boston: 1726. Early American Imprint Series, New York: Readex Microprint.

Mather, Increase. *Prayer for the Rising Generation.* Boston: 1678. Early American Imprint Series, New York: Readex Microprint.

Moss, William. *Essay on the Nursing and Management of Children.* London: Johnson, 1781.

Nelson, James. *Essay on the Government of Children.* Dublin: William Williamson, 1763.

Oliver, John. *A Present for Teeming American Women.* Boston, 1674. Early American Imprint Series, New York: Readex Microprint.

Phillips, Samuel. *Advice to a Child.* Boston: 1729. Early American Imprint Series, New York: Readex Microprint.

Robinson, John. *New Essays.* Boston: Doctrinal Tract and Book Society, 1851.

Rousseau, Jean-Jacques. *Emile. Oeuvres Complètes.* Paris: Gallimard, 1959.

Struve, C. A. *A Familiar Treatise on the Physical Education of Children,* trans. A. F. M. Willich. London: Murray and Highley, 1701.

Tissot, S.A.D. *Advice to the People in General with Regard to their Health,* trans. J. Kirkpatrick. London: Becket and DeHoudt, 1771.

Trench, Melesina. *Thoughts on Education by A Parent.* Southampton, G.B.: T. Baker, 181-.

Tyerman, Daniel. *The Importance of Domestic Discipline.* Newport, Isle of Wight, G.B.: R. Tilling, 1807.

Underwood, Michael. *A Treatise on the Diseases of Children.* Philadelphia: T. Dobson, 1793.*

Williard, Samuel. *The Child's Portion.* Boston: 1687. Early American Imprint Series, New York: Readex Microprint.

Wishy, Bernard. *The Child and the Republic.* Philadelphia: University of Pennsylvania Press, 1968.

Worcester, Thomas. *Two Sermons.* Concord, Massachusetts: G. Hough, 1804.

CHAPTER 7

Abbott, Jacob. *Gentle Measures in the Management and Training of the Young.* New York: Harper, 1871.

Abbott, John S. C. *The Mother at Home.* Boston: Crocker and Brewster, 1833.

Ackerly, G. *On The Management of Children in Sickness and Health.* New York: Bancroft and Holley, 1836.

Alcott, William A. *The Moral Philosophy of Courtship and Marriage.* Boston: John P. Jewett, 1854.

Aldrich, Auretta Roy. *Children, their Models and Critics.* New York: Harper, 1893.

An American Matron. *The Maternal Physician.* New York: Isaac Riley, 1811.

A Physician. *Remarks on the Employment of Females as Practitioners in Midwifery.* Boston: Cummings and Hilliard, 1820.

Babyhood, A Monthly Magazine, December 1884-1902.

Baker, T. Herbert. *On the Hygenic Management of Infants and Children.* London: J. Churchill, 1859.

Barnes, Earl. *Discipline in the Family and School.* Chicago: Illinois Society for Child Study, 189-.

Barwell, Mrs. [Lousia Mary] .*Infant Treatment,* adopted by Valentine Mott. New York: James Mowatt, 1844.

Beecher, Catherine. *Letters to Persons Engaged in Domestic Service.* New York: Leavitt and Trow, 1842.

——. *The Evils Suffered by American Women and American Children.* New York: Harper, 1846.

——. *The American Woman's Home.* New York: J.B. Ford, 1869.

Blake, Mary. *Twenty-Six Hours a Day.* Boston: Lothrop, 1883.

Booth, William. *Training of Children.* London: Salvation Army, 1888.

Boston Board of Health. *Rules for Management of Infants and Children.* Boston: Rockwell and Churchill, 1876.

Carus, Paul. *A Few Hints on the Treatment of Children.* Chicago: Monist, 1899.

Chavasse, Pye Henry. *Advice to a Wife* [and] *Advice to a Mother,* New York: George Routledge, 1873.

Child, Mrs. Lydia Maria. *The Mother's Book.* Boston: Carter and Hendee, 1831.

Clarke, John. *Commentaries on Some of the Most Important Diseases of Children.* London: Longman, 1815.

Combe, Andrew. *Treatise on the Physiological and Moral Management of Infancy.* Philadelphia: Carey and Hart, 1840.

Darwall, John. *Plain Instruction for the Management of Infants.* London: Whittaker, Treacher and Arnot, 1830.

Dewar, John. *What Ails the Baby?* New York: Brentano, 1890.

Donné, Al. *Mothers and Infants, Nurses and Nursing.* Boston: Phillips, Sampson, 1859.

Dwight, Theodore. *The Father's Book.* Springfield, Massachusetts: Merriam, 1834.

Flint, Joseph Henshaw. *Dissertation on Prophylactic.* Northampton G.B.: T. W. Shepard, 1826.

Getchell, F. H. *The Maternal Management of Infancy.* Philadelphia: Lippincott, 1868.

Griffith, J. P. Crozer. *The Care of the Baby.* Philadelphia: W. B. Saunders, 1898.*

Grinnell, Elizabeth. *How John and I Brought Up the Child.* Philadelphia: American Sunday School Union, 1894.

Harland, Marion. *Eve's Daughers.* New York: Anderson and Allen, 1882.

——. *Common Sense in the Nursery.* New York: Scribner's, 1885.

Hartmann, Jacob. *The Modern Baby or the Art of Nursing and Raising Children.* New York: E. H. Bliss, 1881.

Hayes, Mrs. Harriet E. editor. *The Home Nurse and Nursery.* New York: Union, 1888.

Hellier, John Benjamin. *Infancy and Infant Rearing.* London: C. Griffin, 1895.

Herrick, Mrs. Christine Terhune. *Cradle and Nursery.* New York: Harper, 1889.

Hersey, John. *Advice to Christian Parents.* Baltimore: Armstrong, 18—.

Hopkins, Eliza. *On the Early Training of Girls and Boys.* New York: B. M. Hammett, 1884.

Hoare, Louisa. *Hints.* New York: Collins, 1826.

Ireland, W. M. *Advice to Mothers on the Management of Infants and Young Children.* New York: B. Young, 1820.

Jacobi, Abraham. *Infant Hygiene.* Gerhardt, 1877.

Jex-Blake, Sophia. *The Care of Infants.* London: Macmillan, 1884.

Keeting, John M. *The Mother's Guide in the Management and Feeding of Infants.* Philadelphia: Henry C. Lea's Son, 1881.

——. *Maternity, Infancy and Childhood.* Philadelphia: Lippincott, 1887.

Keasberg, Edwina L. *The Culture of the Cradle.* New York: J. Pott, 1886.

Kelley, Samuel W. *About Children.* Cleveland: Medical Gazette Publishing, 1897.

Kissam, Richard Sharpe. *The Nurse's Manual and Young Mother's Guide.* Hartford: Cooke, 1834.

Lefavre, Caroline W. *Mother's Help and Child's Friend.* New York: Brentano, 1890.

Martineau, Harriet. *Household Education.* Philadelphia: Lea and Blanchard, 1849.

Metropolitan Working Class's Association. *The Rearing and Training of Children.* London: J. Churchill, 1847.

Montgomery, Fanny. *Early Infuences.* London: Rivingtons, 1883.

Mosher, Martha B. *Child Culture in the Home.* London: S. Low, Marston, 1898.

Murray, Nicholas [pseudo. Kirwan]. *The Happy Home.* New York: Harper, 1858.

Napheys, George H. *The Physical Life of Women.* Philadelphia: George Maclean, 1869.

——. *The Transmission of Life.* Philadelphia: J. G. Fergus, 1871.

Parton, Sara Payson [pseudo. Fanny Fern]. *Fresh Leaves.* New York: Mason Bros., 1853.

Preyer, Wilhelm. *The Mind of the Child.* New York: D. Appleton, 1893.

Ryle, John. *How Should a Child Be Trained?* New York: Protestant Episcopal Society, 1859.

Scovil, Elizabeth R. *A Baby's Requirements.* Philadelphia, H. Altemus, 1892.

Searle, Thomas. *A Companion for the Seasons of Maternal Solicitude.* New York: Moore and Payne, 1834.

Sedgwick, Catherine M. *Home.* Boston: J. Monroe.

Shinn, Millicent Washburn. *Notes on the Development of a Child.* University of California Studies Vol. 1. Berkeley, California: 1893, 1909.

Stevens, John. *An Important Address to Wives and Mothers of the Dangers and Immorality of Man-Midwifery.* London: O. Hodgson, 1830.

Trumbull, Henry Clay. *Hints on Child Training.* Philadelphia: J. D. Wattles, 1896.

Tuthill, Mrs. L. C. *Joy and Care, A Friendly Book For Young Mothers.* New York: Scribner's, 1855.

Uffelmann, Julius. A. C. *Manual of Domestic Hygiene.* New York: Putnam's, 1891.

Verdi, Tullio Suzzara. *Maternity, A Popular Treatise for Young Wives and Mothers.* New York: J. B. Ford, 1870.

Walker, Jerome. *How We Raised Our Baby.* New York: Derby, 1877.

Warren, Eliza. *How I Managed My Children from Infancy to Marriage.* Boston: Loring, 1865.

White, Rhoda Elizabeth. *From Infancy to Motherhood.* London: S. Low, Marston, 1882.

Wilderspin, S. *Early Discipline Illustrated.* London: 1840.

Winterburn, Florence. *Nursery Ethics.* New York: Merriam, 1895.

CHAPTER 8

Abbot, Ernest Hamlin. *On the Training of Parents.* Boston: Houghton, Mifflin, 1908.

Allen, Annie Winsor. *Maxims of Home Discipline.* Philadelphia: American Institute of Child Life, 1907.

Allen, Mary Wood. *Making the Best of our Children.* Chicago: A. C. McClurg, 1909.

A Mother (A University Woman). *The Baby: A Mother's Book.* London: T. C. & E. C. Jack, 1912.

American Motherhood. Numbers 1-47. Cooperstown, New York: A. H. Crist, 1912.

Arizona State Board. *Baby Welfare.* Phoenix: 1915.

Bainbridge, William S. *The Growing Years.* Buffalo, New York: H. H. Otis, 1906.

· Beery, Ray Coppock. *Practical Child Training.* New York: Parents' Association, 1917.

Betts, George. *Fathers and Mothers.* Indianapolis: Bobbs-Merrill, 1915.

———. *The Roots of Disposition.* New York: Abingdon, 1915.

Birney, Alice. *Childhood.* New York: Frederick A. Stoakes, 1905.

Blackham, Robert J. *The Care of Children.* London: Scientific Press, 1913.

Bradford, Thomas L. *Autobiography of a Baby.* Philadelphia: David McKay, 1912.

Bradish, Prudence. *Mother-Love in Action.* New York: Harper. 1919.

Bradley, F. S. *The Care of the Baby.* New York: Russell Sage Foundation, 1913.

Brewster, Theresa M. *The Economics of Babyhood.* London: Scientific Press, 191-.

Brown, Daniel Rollins. *The Baby.* Boston: Whitcomb and Barrows, 1908.

Burgess, Mildred M. *The Care of Infants and Young Children in Health.* London: H. K. Lewis, 1910.

Burrell, Caroline F. *The Mother's Book.* New York: University Society, 1919.

Campbell, Helen. *Practical Motherhood.* London: Longmans, Green, 1910.

The Care of Babies. John Carle, 190-. [Pamphlet.]

Carrick, Manton. *Care of the Baby.* Austin, Texas: State Board of Health, 191-.*

Cautley, Edmund. *The Natural and Artificial Methods of Feeding Infants and Young Children.* London: J. & A. Churchill, 1897.

Chance, Mrs. Burton. *Self-training for Mothers.* Philadelphia: Lippincott, 1914.

Chapin, Henry Dwight. *The Theory and Practice of Infant Feeding.* New York: William Wood, 1902.

Cheadle, W. B. *Artifical Feeding of Infants.* London: Smith, Elder, 1902.*

Chenery, Susan. *As the Twig is Bent.* Boston: Houghton, Mifflin, 1901.

Clock, Ralph O. *Our Baby.* New York: Appleton, 1912.

Conroy, Joseph P. *Talks to Parents.* Cincinatti: Benziger, 1919.

Cooke, Joseph B. *The Baby Before and After Arrival.* Philadelphia: Lippincott, 1916.

Coolidge, Emelyn L. *The Mother's Manual.* New York: A. S. Barnes, 1904.

Cradock, Mrs. H. C. *The Care of Babies.* London: G. Bell, 1908.

Croy, Mae Savell. *1000 Things a Mother Should Know.* London: Putnam's, 1917.

Dampier, Catherine. *The Upbringing of Daughters.* London: Longmans, Green, 1917.

Dawson, George E. *The Right of the Child to Be Well-Born.* New York: Funk & Wagnalls, 1912.

Dennett, Roger Herbert. *The Healthy Baby.* New York: Macmillan, 1912.*

Dickerson, May Bliss. *Children Well and Happy.* Boston: LeRoy Phillips, 1918.

Drake, Mrs. Emma Frances. *What a Young Wife Ought to Know.* Philadelphia: Vir, 1901.

Drummond, William B. *The Child: His Nature and Nurture.* London: Dent, 1901.

Eghian, Setrak G. *The Mother's Nursery Guide.* New York: Putnam's, 1907.

Eldred, Mrs. Myrtle and Helen C. LeCron. *For the Young Mother.* Chicago: Reilly & Lee, 1921.

Fischer, Louis. *The Health Care of the Baby.* New York: Funk & Wagnalls, 1906.

Fisher, Dorothy C. *Mothers and Children.* New York: Holt, 1914.*

——. *Self-Reliance.* Indianapolis: Bobbs-Merrill, 1916.

Fitz, Rachel. *Problems of Babyhood.* New York: Holt, 1906.

Forbush, William Byron. *The Boy Problem.* Boston: Pilgrim Press, 1902.

——. *The Coming Generation.* New York: Appleton, 1912.

——. *The Education of the Baby.* Philadelphia: American Institute of Child Life, 1913.

——. *The Government of Children.* Cincinatti: Abingdon, 1913.

——. *Child Study and Child Training.* New York: Scribner's, 1915.

——. *The Character Training of Children.* New York: Funk & Wagnalls, 1919.

Fox, Selina F. *Mother and Baby.* London: J. & A. Churchill, 1912.

Frayser, Mary E. *The Care and Feeding of Children.* Rock Hill, South Carolina: Record Printing, 1914.

Gavit, Lucy. *Mother-Love in Action.* New York: Harper, 1919.

Gilman, Charlotte. *Concerning Children.* Boston: Small and Maynard, 1900.

Gray, Thomas N. *Common Sense and the Baby.* New York: Bewick, 1907.

Gruenberg, Sidonie. *Sons and Daughters.* New York: Holt, 1916.

Griffith, John. *Percentage Feeding.* Philadelphia: *Philadelphia Medical Journal,* 1900.

Harrison, Elizabeth. *Misunderstood Children.* Chicago: Central Publishing, 1910.

——. *When Children Err.* Chicago: National College Kindergarten, 1916.

Hart, Edith V. *Baby's Physical Culture.* New York: Rand McNally, 1913.

Herb, Ferdinand. *The Care-Feeding of the Baby.* Superior, Wisconsin: R & S Publishing, 1907.

Hewitt, Emma. *How to Train Children.* Philadelphia: G. W. Jacobs, 1908.

Hirshberg, Leonard K. *What you Ought to Know about your Baby*. New York: Butterick, 1910.

Hodgson, Helen S. *Mrs. Blossom on Babies*. London: Scientific Press, 1909.

Holt, Luther Emmett. *The Care and Feeding of Children*. New York: Appleton, 1903.*

Hunter, Eleanor A. *Children and the Home*. New York: American Tract Society, 1904.

Indiana State Board of Health. *The Indiana Mother's Baby Book*. Indianapolis: 1914.

Jacoby, George W. *Child Training as an Exact Science*. New York: Funk & Wagnalls, 1914.

Judson, Charles F. and J. Claxton Gittings. *The Artificial Feeding of Infants*. Philadelphia: Lippincott, 1902.

Kellogg, John Harvey. *Hygiene of Infancy*. Battle Creek, Michigan: Good Health Publishing, 1916.

Kerley, Charles Gilmore. *What Every Young Mother Should Know about Her Infants and Young Children*. New York: P. B. Hoeme, 1915.

Kerr, Le Grand. *The Care and Training of Children*. New York: Funk & Wagnalls, 1910.

Key, Ellen. *The Century of the Child*. New York: Putnam's, 1909.

Kilmer, Theron Wendell. *The Practical Care of the Baby and Young Child*. Philadelphia: F. A. Davis, 1903.

Kimball, Mrs. May Bliss. *Children Well and Happy*. Boston: L. Phillips, 1918.

Kinne, Helen and Anna M. Cooley. *The Home and the Family*. New York: Macmillan, 1919.

Lamb, Edith M. *What the Baby Needs*. Baltimore: Lord Baltimore, 1906.

Los Angeles Education Board. *Syllabus of Hygiene*. School Publication 8, 1917.

Lowry, Edith B. *Your Baby*. Chicago: Forbes, 1915.

Lyman, George D. *Care and Feeding of the Infant*. San Francisco: P. Elder, 1915.

M—, Mrs. B. G. *How one Real Mother Lives with her Children*. Philadelphia: American Institute of Child Life Monograph 621, 1913.

MacCarthy, Francis Hamilton. *Hygiene for Mother and Child*. New York: Harper, 1910.

McCracken, Elizabeth. *The American Child*. Boston: Houghton, Mifflin, 1913.

McFarland, John T. *Preservation versus the Rescue of the Child*. New York: Eaton and Mains, 1906.

MacMillan, J. *Infant Health*. London: H. Frowde, 1915.

Meigs, Arthur V. *Feeding in Early Infancy.* Philadelphia: W. B. Saunders, 1896.

Miller, Millicent Wells. *Helps for Young Mothers.* Philadelphia: G. W. Jacobs, 1908.

Mixell, Harold Rudsman. "A Short History of Infant Feeding." New York Archieves of Pediatrics, April 1916.

Nestle, Henri. *A History of Infant Feeding from Elizabethan Times.* New York: The Nestlé Company, 1912.

Newton, Anne B. *Mother and Baby.* Boston: Lothrop, Lee, 1912.

Noyes, Anne. B. *How I Kept My Baby Well.* Baltimore: Warwick and York: 1913.

Nurse Margaret's Book on Babies. London: C. A. Pearson, 1917.

Paget, Stephen. *The New Parent's Assistant.* London: Smith, Elder, 1914.

Patch, Kate. *The Sensitive Child.* New York: Moffat, Yard, 1910.

Pritchard, Eric. *The Physiological Feeding of Infants.* Chicago: W. T. Kenner, 1904.

Ramsey, Walter R. *Infancy and Childhood.* New York: Dutton, 1916.

Read, Mary L. *The Mothercraft Manual.* Boston: Little, Brown, 1916.

Richardson, Anna Steese. *Better Babies and their Care.* New York: F. A. Stokes, 1914.

——. *Making Motherhood Easy.* Philadelphia: Smith, Kline and French, 1915.

Rotch, Thomas Morgan. "A Historical Sketch of the Development of Percentage Feeding." *New York Medical Journal*, March 23, 1907.

Routh, C. H. F., *Infant Feeding and its Influence on Life.* London: Churchill, 1860.

Rowe, Stuart H. *The Physical Nature of the Child and How to Study It.* New York: Macmillan, 1900.

St. John, Edward. *Child Nature and Child Nurture.* Boston: Pilgrim, 1911.

Scott, Miriam. *How to Know your Child.* Boston: Little, Brown, 1915.

Scurfield, Harold. *Infant and Young Child Welfare.* London: Cassell, 1919.

Smith, E. D. *Maternity and Child Welfare.* London: P. S. King, 1915.

Smith, Hugh. *The Female Monitor, Letters to Married Women.* London: G. Kearsley, 1767.

Smith, Richard Mason. *The Baby's First Two Years.* Boston: Houghton, Mifflin, 1915.*

Spiller, Gustav. *The Training of the Child.* New York: Dodge, 1912.

Story, Alfred T. *How to Make a Man.* London: L. N. Fowler, 1907.

Tucker, Blanche. *Notes on the Care of Babies.* London: Longmans, Green, 1907.

Twedell, Francis. *A Mother's Guide.* New York: J. T. Dogherty, 1911.

Tyler, John Mason. *Growth and Education.* Boston: Houghton, Mifflin, 1907.

U.S. Bureau of Publications. *Training Little Children.* Washington, D.C.: U.S. Government Printing Office, 1919.

Visanska, Samuel. *Better Babies.* Atlanta: Foote and Davis, 1917.

Warner, Francis. *The Nervous System of the Child.* London: Macmillian, 1906.

Washburn, Marion F. *The Mother's Yearbook.* New York: Macmillan, 1908.

West, Mrs. Max. *Infant Care.* Washington, D.C.: U.S. Department of Labor, Children's Bureau, 1914.*

Wheeler, Marianne. *The Baby: His Care and Training.* New York: Harper, 1901.

——. *Plain Hints for Busy Mothers.* New York: E. B. Treat, 1903.

Willson, W. P. *The Child that Does Not Stumble.* Boston: R. G. Badger, 1917.

Wood, Alice. "The History of Artificial Feeding of Infants." *Journal of the American Dietetic Association,* Volume 31, No. 5 (May 1955).

CHAPTER 9

Adler, Felix. *The Punishment of Children.* Cincinatti: Abingdon, 1920.

Arlitt, Ada Hart. *The Child from 1 to 6.* New York: McGraw-Hill, 1930.

Asquith, Cynthia. *The Child at Home.* New York: Scribner's, 1923. New York.

The Baby in the House of Health. New York: American Child Health Association, 1926.

Baker, Sarah Josephine. *Talks with Mothers.* New York Milk Committee, 1913.

——. *Healthy Babies.* Boston: Little, Brown, 1923.

Beggs, S. T. *The Hygiene of Infancy.* London: J. Bale, 1926.

Bell, Albert J. *Feeding, Diet and the General Care of Children.* New York: Putnam's, 1923.*

Blatz, William E. and Helen Bott. *Parents and the Pre-School Child.* New York: Morrow, 1929.

——. *The Management of Young Children.* New York: Morrow, 1930.

Bocker, Dorothy. *Mother's Manual.* New York: Brentano, 1925.

Bolt, Richard A. *The Baby's Health.* New York: Funk & Wagnalls, 1924.

Brown, Alan. *The Normal Child its Care and Feeding.* New York: Century, 1923.

Buhler, Charlotte. *The First Year of Life.* New York: John Day, 1930.

Bundesen, Herman N. *Our Babies.* Chicago: 1928.

Cabot, Ella. *Seven Ages of Childhood.* Boston: Houghton, Mifflin, 1921.

Chaloner, Len. *Modern Babies and Nurseries.* London: H. Milford, 1929.

Chapin, Henry Dwight. *Heredity and Child Culture.* New York: Dutton, 1922.

Cleveland, Elizabeth. *Training the Toddler.* Philadelphia: Lippincott, 1925.

Eliot, Martha M. *Infant Care.* Washington, D.C.: U.S. Department of Labor. Children's Bureau, 1929.

Fenton, Jessie M. *A Practical Psychology of Babyhood.* Boston: Houghton, Mifflin, 1925.

Galland, W. H. *Maternity and Child Care.* Chicago: Drake, 1920.

Goodspeed, Helen C. and Emma Johnson. *The Care and Training of Children.* Philadelphia: Lippincott, 1929.

Groves, Ernest. *Wholesome Parenthood.* Boston: Houghton, Mifflin, 1929.

King, Frederick Truby. *The Expectant Mother.* London: Macmillan, 1924.

Lovell, Philip M. *The Health of the Child.* Los Angeles: Times-Mirror, 1926.

MacDougal, William and John B. Watson. *The Battle of Behaviorism.* New York: Norton, 1929.

McFadden, Bernard A. *How to Raise Your Baby.* New York: McFadden, 1926.

Morse, John Lovett, et al. *The Infant and Young Child.* Philadelphia: W. B. Saunders, 1923.

Morton, Claire. *The Perfect Baby.* New York: Vanguard, 1929.

Mother's Own Book. New York: Parents Publishing Association, 1928.

Moxcey, Mary Eliza. *Parents and their Children.* New York: Methodist Book Company, 1922.

O'Shea, Michael. *Everyday Problems in Child Training.* Chicago: F. J. Drake, 1920.

——. *Newer Ways with Children.* New York: Greenberg, 1929.

Patri, Angelo. *Child Training.* New York: Appleton, 1922.

Pierson, Clara, *Living with our Children.* New York: Dutton, 1923.

Pyle, William H. *Training Children: Principle and Practice.* New York: Century, 1929.

Richardson, Frank H. *Parenthood and the New Psychology.* New York: Putnam's, 1926.

Sachs, B. *The Normal Child and How to Keep it Normal.* New York: Paul B. Hoeber, 1926.

Scharlich, Mary. *Health and Sickness in the Nursery.* London: Williams and Norgate, 1926.

——. *Maternity and Infancy.* London: Williams and Norgate, 1926.

Shaw, Henry L. K. *The Happy Child.* New York: Dodd, Mead, 1925.

Schultz, Gladys and Beulah Schenk. *The House that Runs Itself.* New York: John Day, 1929.

Thom, Douglas A. *Everyday Problems of the Everyday Child.* New York: Appleton, 1927.

Thomas, William I. *The Child in America.* New York: Knopf, 1928.

Thompson, Ruth Williams. *Training my Babes.* Boston: Richard G. Badger, 1929.

Walsh, James Joseph. *Safeguarding Children's Nerves.* Philadelphia: Lippincott, 1924.

Waters, R. *Auto-Suggestion for Mothers.* New York: G. Doran, 1924.

Watson, John B. *Psychology from the Standpoint of a Behaviorist.* Philadelphia: Lippincott, 1919.

——. *Behaviorism.* New York: Norton, 1925.

——. *Psychological Care of Infant and Child.* New York: Norton, 1928.

Wexberg, Erwin. *Your Nervous Child.* New York: Albert and Charles Boni, 1927.

Wheelock, Lucy. *Talks to Mothers.* Boston: Houghton, Mifflin, 1922.

Whitaker, Mary. *Mothercraft.* Cleveland: Judson, 1926.

Whitcomb, Emeline S. *Typical Child Care.* Washington, D.C.: U.S. Government Printing Office, 1927.

Wilson, Owen H. *The Care and Feeding of Southern Babies.* Nashville: Baird-Ward, 1920.

CHAPTER 10

Adams, Grace. *Psychology: Science or Superstition?* New York: Covici, Friede, 1931.

——. *Your Child is Normal.* New York: Covici, Friede, 1934.

Adler, Alfred. *Guiding the Child,* trans: B. Ginzburg. New York: Greenberg, 1930.

Aldrich, C. Anderson and Mary M. Aldrich. *Babies are Human Beings.* New York: Macmillan, 1938.

Allen, Arthur B. *The Psychology of Punishment.* London: Allman, 1936.

Alschuler, Rose H. *Two to Six.* New York: Morrow, 1933.

Anderson, Harold H. *Children in the Family.* New York: Appleton-Century, 1937.

Anderson, John E. *Happy Childhood.* New York: Appleton-Century, 1933.

Bartlett, Frederic H. *Infants and Children: Their Feeding and Growth.* New York: Farrar and Rinehart, 1932.*

Braithwaite, E. Wrigley. *Parent and Child.* London: T. Nelson, 1939.

Budden, Charles W. *100 Popular Fallacies.* London: J. Bale, 1932.

Buhler, Charlotte. *The First Year of Life.* New York: John Day, 1930.

Cowan, Edwina. *Bringing up Your Child.* New York: Duffield, 1930.

Crawford, Nelson A. *The Healthy-Minded Child.* New York: Coward, McCann, 1930.

Dafoe, Allen Roy. *Dr. Dafoe's Guide Book for Mothers.* Toronto: Smithers and Bonellie, 1936.

——. *How to Raise Your Baby.* New York: Bartholomew House, 1942.

DeKok, Winifred. *New Babes for Old.* London: Gollancz, 1932.

Deering, Ivah E. *The Creative Home.* New York: Richard Smith, 1930.

Dunham, Ethel C. and Marian M. Crane. *Infant Care.* Washington, D.C.: U.S. Department of Labor, Children's Bureau, 1938.

Dwyer, Hugh. *Your Child in Health or Sickness.* New York: Knopf, 1936.

Eggleston, Margaret. *Faith or Fear in Child Training.* New York: Round Table, 1934.

Fisher, Dorothy C. and Sidonie M. Gruenberg. *Our Children.* New York: Viking, 1932.

Gesell, Arnold. *The Mental Growth of the Pre-School Child.* New York: Macmillan, 1925.

——. *Infancy and Human Growth.* New York: Macmillan, 1928.

——. *The Guidance of Mental Growth in Infant and Child.* New York: Macmillan, 1930.

——. *The Atlas of Infant Behavior.* New Haven: Yale University, 1934.

——. H. Thompson and C. Amatruda. *Infant Behavior, its Genesis and Growth.* New York: McGraw-Hill, 1934.

——. *The Psychology of Early Growth.* New York: Macmillan, 1938.

Gesell, Arnold and Ilg. *Child Development.* New York: Macmillan, 1949.

Glover, Katherine. *Children of the New Day.* New York: Appleton-Century, 1934.

Gruenberg, Sidone M. *We, the Parents.* New York: Harper, 1939.

Housden, Leslie George. *The Art of Mothercraft.* London: Carnegie House, 1939.

Howden, Richard. *Child Upbringing.* New York: Oxford, 1933.

Kenyon, Josephine. *Healthy Babies are Happy Babies.* Boston: Little, Brown, 1934.*

Kugelmass, I. N. *Growing Superior Children.* New York: Appleton-Century, 1935.

Langdon, Grace. *Home Guidance for Young Children.* New York: John Day, 1938.

Law, Mary E. *Baby Care.* Philadelphia: Lippincott, 1938.

Levy, John and Ruth Morrow. *The Happy Family.* New York: Knopf, 1938.

Libby, Violet K. *How to Care for the Baby.* Washington, D.C.: Plymouth, 1933.

Lowenburg, Harry. *Care of Infants and Children.* New York: Whittlesey House, 1938.

Mannin, Ethel E. *Common Sense and the Child.* Philadelphia: Lippincott, 1932.

Monash, Louis. *Know your Child.* New York: Whittlesey House, 1931.

Moss, Sallie Rust. *Give Your Child a Chance.* Nashville, Tennessee: Broadman, 1938.

Myers, Garry C. *The Modern Parent.* New York: Greenberg, 1930.

——. *Building Personality in Children.* New York: Greenberg, 1931.

New York City Health Department. *Care of the Baby.* New York: 1932.

Reilly, Mrs. John S. *Common Sense for Mothers.* New York: Funk & Wagnalls, 1935.

Richards, Mrs. Noel and Amy D. Baker. *Healthy Babies.* London: Casell, 1935.

Saltzman, Eleanor. *Learning to be Good Parents.* Boston: Manthorne and Burack, 1937.

Schick, Bela. *Child Care Today.* Garden City, New York: Garden City, 1932.

Strang, Ruth. *Introduction to Child Study.* New York: Macmillan, 1930.*

Steen, Robert E. *Infants in Health and Sickness.* London: H. Milford, 1937.

Smith, R. M. and Douglas A. Thom. *Health, Physical, Mental, and Emotional.* New York: Houghton, Mifflin, 1936.

Tenney, Horace K. *Let's Talk about your Baby.* Minneapolis: University of Minneapolis, 1934.

Tisdall, Frederick F. *Home Care of the Infant.* New York: Morrow, 1931.

Van Blarcom, Carolyn C. *Getting Ready to be a Mother.* New York: Macmillan, 1937.*

Wilson, Frank T. *Guiding our Children.* New York: House of Field, 1939.

Zabriski, Louis. *Mother and Baby Care in Pictures.* Philadelphia: Lippincott, 1935.

CHAPTERS 11, 12

Abrams, Irving R. *Junior Speaks Up.* New York: Macmillan, 1948.

Applebaur, Stella. *Baby: A Mother's Manual.* Chicago: Ziff-Davis, 1946.

Baruch, Dorothy. *You, Your Children and War.* New York: Appleton-Century, 1942.

——. *New Ways in Discipline.* New York: McGraw-Hill, 1949.

Batten Lindsey W. *The Single-Handed Mother.* London: Allen & Unwin, 1945.

Bauer, W. W. *Stop Annoying Your Children.* New York: Bobbs-Merrill, 1947.

Blanchette, Alice B. *Lessons in Personality Development.* Austin, Texas: Steck, 1942.

Blatz, William E. *Understanding the Young Child.* Bickley, Kent, G. B.: University of London, 1944.

Bloom, Lynn Z. *Dr. Spock.* New York: Bobbs-Merrill, 1972.

Bowley, Agatha H. *The Natural Development of the Child.* Edinburgh: Livingstone, 1942.

——. *The Problems of Family Life.* Edinburgh: Livingstone, 1946.

——. *Modern Child Psychology.* London: Hutchinson's University Library, 1948.

Bradbury, Dorothy E. and Edna P. Amidon. *Learning to Care for Children.* New York: Appleton-Century, 1943.

Bundesen, Herman N. *The Baby Manual.* New York: Simon & Schuster, 1944.*

Buxbaum, Edith. *Your Child Makes Sense.* New York: International Universities, 1949.

Chadwick, Mary. *The Toddler in the Home.* London: Allen & Unwin, 1940.

Chaloner, Len. *What about a Family?* London: Pearson, 1944.

Couture, Ernest. *The Canadian Mother and Child.* Ottawa: National Health and Welfare, 1947.*

Dallavaux, John. *How to Raise a Brat.* Rutland, Vermont: Tuttle, 1946.

Dixon, C. Madeleine. *Keep them Human.* New York: John Day, 1942.

Edge, Patricia. *Training the Toddler.* London: Faver & Faber, 1944.

Evans, Eva Knox. *Children and You.* New York: Putnam's, 1943.

Garland, Joseph. *The Youngest of the Family.* Cambridge, Massachusetts: Harvard, 1943.

Garrison, Charlotte and Emma Sheehy. *At Home with Children.* New York: Holt, 1943.

Gesell, Arnold and Frances Ilg. *Infant and Child in the Culture of Today.* New York: Harper & Row, 1943.

Glemser, Louise Cripps. *Your First Baby.* New York: A. S. Barnes, 1943.

Gruenberg, Sidonie M. *Then and Now.* [Reprint] *Women's Day Magazine,* 1945.

Halpern, Louis J. *How to Raise a Healthy Baby.* New York: Prentice-Hall, 1940.

Hardcastle, Mildred J. *For the New Mother.* Philadelphia: J. C. Winston, 1948.

Hudson, Dorothy B. *Your Baby Looks to You.* London: Century, 1948.

Hurlock, Elizabeth. *Modern Ways with Children.* New York: McGraw-Hill, 1943.

———. *Child Growth and Development.* New York: McGraw-Hill, 1949.*

Isaacs, Susan. *Troubles of Children and Parents.* New York: Vanguard, 1948.

Jenkins, Gladys G., et al. *These Are Your Children.* Chicago: Scott, Foresman, 1949.

Jersild, Arthur T. *Joys and Problems of Child Rearing.* New York: Columbia, 1949.

Kanner, Leo. *In Defense of Mothers.* New York: Dodd, Mead, 1941.

Meek, Lois Hayden. *Your Child's Development and Growth Told in Pictures.* Philadelphia: Lippincott, 1940.

Middlemore, M. P. *The Nursing Couple.* London: H. Hamilton, 1941.

Moodie, William. *The Doctor and the Difficult Child.* New York: Commonwealth Fund, 1940.

New York City Health Department. *New York City's Baby Book.* New York: Health Department, 1947.

Ribble, Margaret A. *The Rights of Infants.* New York: Columbia, 1945.

Ross, Isie Younger. *The Happy Mother and Child.* London: Warne, 1940.

Sauer, Louis. *From Infancy through Childhood.* New York: Harper, 1942.

Spock, Benjamin. *The Common Sense Book of Baby and Child Care.* New York: Duell, Sloan, 1946.*

Strain, Frances Bruce. *Your Child, His Family and Friends.* New York: Appleton-Century, 1943.

Valentine, Charles W. *The Difficult Child.* London: Methuen, 1940.

Washburn, Ruth W. *Children are the Reasons.* New York: Appleton-Century, 1942.

Whipple, Dorothy V. and Marian Crane. *Infant Care.* Washington, D.C.: U.S. Department of Labor, Children's Bureau, 1942.

Whipple, Dorothy V. *Our American Babies.* New York: M. Barrows, 1944.

Wolf, Anna. *Parents' Manual* New York: Simon & Schuster, 1941.

CHAPTER 13

Beasley, Cristine. *Democracy in the Home.* New York: Association Press, 1954.

Berenberg, Samuel R. *The Modern Book of Infant and Child Care.* New York: Bartholomew, 1957.

Carrier, Blanche. *Integrity for Tomorrow's Adults.* New York: Crowell, 1959.

Clifford, Edward. *Discipline in the Home.* Minneapolis: University of Minneapolis, 1957.

Cutts, Norma and Nicholas Moseley. Better Home Discipline. New York: Appleton, 1952.

Davis, Adele. *Let's have Healthy Children.* New York: Harcourt Brace, 1959.

Edwards, Ruth. *How to Enjoy your Baby.* New York: Citadel, 1954.

English, O. S. and Constance Foster. *Fathers are Parents Too.* New York: Putnam's, 1951.

Erikson, Erik. *Childhood and Society.* New York: Norton, 1950.

Faegre, Marion E. *Infant Care.* Washington, D.C.: U.S. Department of Labor, Children's Bureau, 1951.

——. et al. *Child Care and Training.* Minneapolis: University of Minnesota, 1958.*

Fraiberg, Selma H. *The Magic Years.* New York: Scribner's, 1959.

Fromme, Allan. *The Parent's Handbook.* New York: Simon & Schuster, 1956.

Illg, Frances L. and Louise Bates Ames. *Child Behavior.* New York: Harper 1955.

——. *Parents Ask.* New York: Harper, 1962.

Gilmer, B. Von Haller. *How to Help Your Child Develop Successfully.* Englewood Cliffs, New Jersey: Prentice Hall, 1955.

Gruenberg, Sidonie M. *The New Encyclopedia of Child Care and Guidance.* New York: Doubleday, 1954.

Holt, L. Emmett, Jr. *Good Housekeeping Book of Baby and Child Care.* New York: Appleton, 1954.

Jones, Eve. *Natural Child Rearing.* Glencoe, Illinois: Free Press of Glencoe, 1959.

Katz, Barney *How to Be a Better Parent.* New York: Ronald Press, 1953.

Langdon, Grace and Irving Stout. *Bringing Up Children.* New York: John Day, 1952.

Owen, Catherine M. *Parenthood.* London: Heinemann, 1950.

Palisades Pre-School. *The Challenge of Children.* New York: Morrow, 1957.

Parke, Cummings. *I'm Telling You Kids for the Last Time.* New York: H. Schuman, 1951.

Ritter, Paul *The Free Family.* London: Gollancz, 1959.

Sara, Dorothy and Lucille Gidseg, eds. *The New American Baby Book.* New York: Books, Inc., 1954.

Schwartz, Berthold and Bartholomew Ruggieri. *Parent-Child Tensions.* Philadelphia: Lippincott, 1957.

———. *You CAN Raise Decent Children*. New Rochelle, New York: Arlington, 1971.

Smith, Elinor G. *The Complete Book of Absolutely Perfect Baby and Child Care*. New York: Harcourt Brace, 1957.

Stewart, Maxwell S., ed. *The Growing Family*. New York: Harper, 1955.

Thomas, Ruth. *Habit Training*. London: Family Health Publications, 1954.

U.S. Book of Baby and Child Care. New York: Eaton, 1951.

Wallace, William H. S. *Infant and Child Care*. London: Cassell, 1951.

Winnicott, Donald W. *The Child and the Family*. London: Tavistock, 1957.

Wold, Anna and Suzanne Szasz. *Helping Your Child's Emotional Growth*. New York: Doubleday, 1954.

Younger, Joan. *The Stork and You*. Philadelphia; Westminister, 1952.

CHAPTER 14

Auerbach, Aline. *Parents Learn Through Discussion*. New York: Wiley, 1968.

Bahr, Edith-Jane. *Everybody Wins, Nobody Loses*. New York: McKay, 1968.

Bernhardt, Karl S. *Discipline and Child Guidance*. New York: McGraw-Hill, 1969.

Bel Geddes, Joan. *Small World*. New York: Macmillan, 1964.

Bettelheim, Bruno. *The Children of the Dream*. New York: Macmillan, 1969.

Brazelton, T. Berry. *Infants and Mothers*. New York: Delacorte, 1969.

———. *Toddlers and Parents*. New York: Delacorte, 1974.

Claxon, Philander P. *Some Rights of Children and Youth*. New York: Exposition Press, 1962.

Crow, Lester and Alice Crow. *Being a Good Parent*. Boston: Christopher Publishing, 1966.

Donovan, Frank. *Raising Your Child*. New York: Crowell, 1968.

Dreikurs, Rudolf and Vicki Soltz. *Children: The Challenge*. New York: Duell, Sloan, 1964.

Dreikurs, Rudolf and Loren Grey. *A Parent's Guide to Child Discipline*. New York: Hawthorn, 1968, 1970.

Fass, Jerome. *A Primer for Parents*. New York: Trident, 1968.

Feathergill, Eve. *How to be a Successful Mother*. New York: Morrow, 1965.

France, Beulah. *How to Raise a Happy, Healthy Baby*. Larchmont, New York: Argonaut, 1964.

Gersh, Marvin. *How to Raise Children at Home in Your Spare Time.* New York: Stein & Day, 1966.

Ginott, Haim. *Between Parent and Child.* New York: Macmillan, 1965.

Goodman, David. *What's Best for your Child – And You.* New York: Association Press, 1966.

Goodrich, Jr., Frederick W. *Infant Care: The U.S. Government Guide.* Englewood Cliffs, New Jersey: Prentice-Hall, 1968.

Gordon, Thomas. *P.E.T. Parent Effectiveness Training.* New York: Wyden, 1970.

Fass, Jerome. *A Primer for Parents.* New York: Trident, 1968.

Hellyer, David Tirrell. *Your Child and You.* New York: Delacorte, 1966.

Hesse, Emily. *How to Raise a Superkid.* New York: Macmillan, 1968.

Holmes, Carl A. *Letter to Tricia.* Los Angeles: Sherbourne Press, 1966.

Homan, William. *Child Sense.* New York: Basic, 1969.

Hymes, Jerome. *The Child Under Six.* Englewood Cliffs, New Jersey: Prentice-Hall, 1963.

Illingworth, Ronald and Cynthia Illingworth. *Babies and Young Children.* London: Churchill, 1964.

Jones, G. Curtis. *Parents Deserve to Know.* New York: Macmillan, 1960.

Jones, Molly Mason. *Guiding Your Child from Two to Five.* New York: Harcourt, 1967.

Klein, Ted. *The Father's Book.* New York: Morrow, 1968.

Kraft, Ivor. *When Teenagers Take Care of Children.* Philadelphia: Macrae Smith, 1965.

Langford, Louise M. and Helene Rand. *Guidance of the Young Child.* New York: Wiley, 1960.

LeShan, Eda. *How to Survive Parenthood.* New York: Random House, 1965.

Neill, A. S. *Summerhill.* New York: Hart, 1960.

Newson, John and Elizabeth Newson. *Infant Care in an Urban Community.* London: Allen & Unwin, 1963.

——. *Four Years Old in an Urban Community.* London: Allen & Unwin, 1968.

O'Connor, Grace. *Helping Your Children.* Austin, Texas: Steck-Vaughn, 1966.

Piers, Maria W. *Growing up with Children.* Chicago: Quadrangle 1966.

Pitcairn, Lenore. *Parents of the Future.* London: Cambridge University Press, 1968.

Potts, Willis John. *Your Wonderful Baby.* New York: Rand McNally, 1966.

Pruden, Bonnie. *How to Keep Your Child Fit from Birth to Six.* New York: Harper & Row, 1969.

Richardson, Frank Howard. *A Christian Doctor talks with Young Parents.* Washington, D.C.: Herald Publishing Association, 1962.

Sackett, Walter Wallace. *Bringing up Babies.* New York: Harper & Row, 1962.

Salk, Lee. *How to Raise a Human Being.* New York: Random House, 1969.

——. *What Every Child Would Like His Parents to Know.* New York: McKay, 1972.

——. *Preparing for Parenthood.* New York: McKay, 1974.

Saltman, J., ed. *Your New Baby and You.* New York: Grosset & Dunlap, 1966.

Shepard, Kenneth S. *Care of the Well Baby.* Philadelphia: Lippincott, 1960.

Silver, Henry K. *Healthy Babies, Happy Parents.* New York: McGraw-Hill, 1960.

Spock, Benjamin. *Problems of Parents.* Boston: Houghton, Mifflin, 1962.

Sproul, Dorothy N. *Your Child: Step by Step Towards Maturity.* New York: Doubleday, 1963.

Trese, Leo J. *Parent and Child.* New York: Sheed & Ward, 1962.

CHAPTER 15, 16

Breitbart, Vicki. *The Day Care Book.* New York: Knopf, 1974.

Briggs, Dorothy C. *Your Child's Self-Esteem.* New York: Doubleday, 1970.

Bronfenbrenner, Urie. *Two Worlds of Childhood.* New York: Russel Sage Foundation, 1970.

Caplan, Frank., ed. *The First Twelve Months of Life.* New York: Grosset & Dunlap, 1972.

Church, Joseph. *Understanding your Child from Birth to Three.* New York: Random House, 1973.

Corsini, Raymond J. and Genevieve Painter. *The Practical Parent.* New York: Harper & Row, 1975.

Dobson, James. *Dare to Discipline.* Wheaton, Illinois: Tyndale House, 1970.

Dodson, Fitzhugh. *How to Parent.* Los Angeles: Nash, 1970.

Evans, E. Belle, et al. *Day Care.* Boston: Beacon, 1971.

Evans, E. Belle and George E. Saia. *Day Care for Infants.* Boston: Beacon, 1972.

Faber, Adele and Elaine Mazlish. *Liberated Parents, Liberated Children.* New York: Gosset & Dunlap, 1974.

Fein, Greta G. and Alison Clarke-Stewart. *Day Care in Context.* New York: Wiley, 1973.

Gilbert, Sara D. *What's a Father For?* New York: Parents Magazine Press, 1975.

Harlow, Nora. *Sharing the Children.* New York: Harper & Row, 1975.

Hoover, Mary B. *The Responsive Parent.* New York: Parents' Magazine Press, 1972.

Keyserling, Mary D. *Windows on Day Care.* New York: National Council of Jewish Women, 1972.

LeShan, Eda. *On How do your Children Grow.* New York: McKay, 1972.

Leiner, Marvin. *Children Are the Revolution.* New York: Viking, 1974.

Makarenko, A. S. *The Collective Family: A Handbook for Parents.* New York: Doubleday, 1967.

Milinaire, Caterine. *Birth.* New York: Harmony, 1974.

Moyer, K. E. *You and Your Child.* Chicago: Nelson Hall, 1974.

Olshaker, Bennett. *The Child as a Work of Art.* New York: Dutton, 1975.

Pomeranz Virginia and Dodi Schultz. *The First Five Years.* New York: Doubleday, 1973.

Sidel, Ruth. *Women and Child Care in China.* New York: Hill & Wang, 1972.

Skinner, B. F. *Walden Two.* New York: Macmillan, 1948.

Smith, Lendon H. *New Wives Tales.* Englewood Cliffs, New Jersey: Prentice-Hall, 1974.

Spock, Benjamin. *Raising Children in a Difficult Time.* New York: Norton, 1974.

Turtle, William J. *Dr. Turtle's Babies.* New York: Popular Library, 1973.

Weiner, Joan and Joyce Glick. *A Motherhood Book.* New York: Macmillan, 1974.

Index

263